Understanding Scotland

From the reviews of the first edition:

'It will be a benchmark for all future arguments about Scotland, both in its subject area and in the wider common culture'
Tom Nairn author of 'After Britain' and 'Faces of Nationalism'

'The balance of theory, data and analysis is just right. . . . Anyone with an interest in the changing social and political contours of late twentieth century Europe should read this book'
Gordon Marshall, Chief Executive, ESRC

Understanding Scotland has been recognised since publication as the key text on the sociology of Scotland. This wholly revised edition provides the first sustained study of post-devolution Scottish society. It contains new material on

- the establishment of the Scottish Parliament in 1999
- social and political data from the 1997 general election
- the new cultural iconography of Scotland
- Scotland as a European society

For anyone wishing to understand Scottish society in particular or the general issues involved in nation-building, McCrone's clear-headed, cogently argued account of the main issues will be essential reading.

David McCrone is Professor of Sociology, and Convenor of the Unit for the Study of Government in Scotland, at Edinburgh University.

International Library of Sociology
Founded by Karl Mannheim
Editor: John Urry
Lancaster University

Understanding Scotland

The Sociology of a Nation
Second edition

David McCrone

London and New York

First edition published 1992 and reprinted in 1992, 1993 and 1996
by Routledge
2 Park Square, Milton Park, Abingdon, Oxon, OX14 4RN

Second edition published 2001

Simultaneously published in the USA and Canada
by Routledge
270 Madison Ave, New York NY 10016

Transferred to Digital Printing 2006

Routledge is an imprint of the Taylor & Francis Group

© 1992, 2001 David McCrone

Typeset in Bembo by BC Typesetting, Bristol

British Library Cataloguing in Publication Data
A catalogue record for this book is available from the British Library

Library of Congress Cataloging in Publication Data
McCrone, David.
    Understanding Scotland : the sociology of a nation/
    David McCrone. – 2nd ed.
        p.   cm. – (International library of sociology)
    Includes bibliographical references and index.
    ISBN 0–415–25163–X – ISBN 0–415–25164–8 (pbk.)
    1. Scotland – Social conditions. 2. Nationalism – Scotland.
    3. Regionalism – Great Britain. I. Title. II. Series.

HN398.S3 M38 2001
306′.09411 – dc21   00-051738

ISBN 0–415–25163–X (hbk)
ISBN 0–415–25164–8 (pbk)

Contents

Tables

Acknowledgements

I am indebted to a number of friends and colleagues who helped, often unwittingly, in the writing of this book, especially Lindsay Paterson who read through the whole draft when he had much better things to do. His comments have made this a better book. I have also benefited over the years from the fellowship of Frank Bechhofer, Alice Brown, Anthony Cohen and Neil MacCormick. Knowledge is always socially produced.

Scotland has been an interesting and challenging place in the past decade or so, and many readers of the first edition have made helpful comments and suggestions, which, if I have not taken them all on board, have made me think. Books are transient things, and that is how it should be.

The book is dedicated to my wife, Mary, who has had to live with two editions, well beyond the call of duty. None of this would have happened without her.

Introduction

Scotland in the twenty-first century: how are we to understand it socio-logically? Should we even try? It might seem that we would be better focusing on the broad social, economic and cultural processes which shape the modern world as a whole, and that there is little to be said that is different about a small, north-west European nation to make the effort worthwhile. Do we not, after all, live in a 'global' world in which individual societies, especially small ones which are part of bigger states, seem to be unimportant players? That would be to misunderstand the modern world. Globalisation does not create bland, uniform homogeneity. How territories react to these broad social forces is very different, and the local and the global are but two sides of the same coin. Further, we are frequently more likely to spot social change in small societies before we do so in bigger ones, just as we notice the turn of the tide by observing small boats rather than large ships.

It is almost ten years since the first edition of this book was published. What has changed? First of all, and significantly, the title has altered. It is no longer the sociology of a 'stateless nation'. Recovering its parliament, albeit a devolved one, after almost 300 years of union means that Scotland is no longer stateless. To be sure, it never was, for it had retained and developed considerable institu-tional autonomy within the British Union such that it was always semi-detached in what was constitutionally a unitary state. Scotland was – and remains – of course, stateless in the sense that it is not formally independent, but one of the features of the past decade has been that few would lay odds against that possibility in the next. Whether or not the United Kingdom of Great Britain and Northern Ireland will survive even in its present devolved form remains to be seen. The people of these islands, the English not least, but at last, have entered a debate about who they are and how they wish to be governed. This is an argument as much about the new Europe as anything which is happening within the British archipelago. The UK has long had a constitutional contradiction at its heart: it is manifestly a multinational state, but its system of governance has been unitary, and nowhere has been more anomalous than Scotland, with its considerable apparatus of self-government.

What has this to do with sociology, as opposed to politics? This is to make a false dichotomy, for political change in Scotland has largely been driven by social and cultural pressure. If anything, the political system was inordinately slow in coming to terms with demands for constitutional change, and it took sustained pressure from civil society on Scotland's political classes throughout the 1980s and 1990s to bring about a parliament. Further, it would be a brave politician to assume that devolution is the final, settled will of the Scottish people.

The decade since the first edition was published has been an intensely political one, and that is properly reflected in this book. There is, however, no longer the same need to show that 'Scotland' exists as a unit for sociological analysis. The lazy assumption that 'societies' were nothing more than 'nation-states' is no longer tenable. Indeed, even the term 'nation-state' is no longer tenable, if by that we mean that all states are in some real sociological sense cultural units, or 'nations'. We now recognise that there are very few genuine nation-states in which political and cultural boundaries intersect, and that the world is a much messier – and more interesting – place because of that. We are living through a period of major political and social re-formation such that the old view that the world resembled a large jigsaw puzzle of sovereign nation-states is hopelessly dated.

We do not know what the political and social world of the twenty-first century will look like, but we do know that the past will be a fairly poor predictor of the future. There is a growing interest in how territories – hitherto stateless nations – such as Scotland, Wales, Catalunya, the Basque Country, Quebec, Flanders and so on make the adjustments in this global world. One senses that they are more optimistic about their future than the conventional states which they are currently part of, namely the UK, Spain, Canada, and Belgium. Lying behind this is a feeling that the old notion of sovereignty as a zero-sum game – all or nothing – no longer makes sense. A new process whereby political authority is layered and shared seems more meaningful. The debate which ensues concerns how levels of governance interact in the interests of the nation.

In Scotland, this debate has been intense throughout the 1990s. It has been framed by fundamental political and social changes which make a new edition all the more pressing. Since the previous edition of this book was written, the politics of Thatcherism have ended, a Labour government, styling itself 'New' to distance itself from its past, has been elected with a massive majority at Westminster; Scotland has regained a parliament; and the process of Europeanisation has been both broadened and deepened. In sociological terms, we no longer need to work so hard at justifying Scotland as a unit for social and political analysis. Hence, there is no longer a chapter on whether or not Scotland is 'different'. That debate, in so far as it related Scotland to the rest of the UK, is over. The past decade has also seen a considerable increase in writing about Scotland, and the UK. What is striking about that literature is how eclectic it is: history, politics, sociology and culture are woven into each other, and that is how it should be. Addressing the big questions demands it.

Asking what kind of society this is, and where it is going, is a quest for all disciplines and perspectives. No one has all the answers.

Neither does this book. Ten years on, the sociology of Scotland cannot be captured in one volume. This book tackles the ways in which Scotland's social structure and its culture interact with each other. It seeks to relate broad social change to how people make sense of that; in other words, the debate about how Scotland's culture and its politics are shaped by and help in turn to shape social processes. It tries to relate social and economic development to systems of political and cultural meaning. In that sense it is not a 'postmodern' book. 'Scotland' is not simply what you want it to mean. It is a complex theatre of memory in which different ways of 'being Scottish' are interpellated and handed down, constructed and mobilised by social and political forces which seek to naturalise them. There is a complex interaction of social process and cultural meaning.

There are two major changes in this edition. The opening chapter is a sociological history of Scotland in the twentieth century. Its purpose is to tell a story by focusing on the dominant motifs of that century: consecutively, the market, the state and the nation. The point is not that these followed each other, but that, as in a piece of music, they are interconnected themes. Chapter 1 sets the scene for a discussion of the relevant concepts and theories which follow, especially in Chapter 2. The other change from the previous edition is that there is now a sustained discussion of national identity (Chapter 7). Identity is not a 'thing' which can be treated as real or unreal, but a social space in which matters of structure and culture come together. What it means to be 'Scottish' is far less important for the answers than for the terms in which the debate occurs. Identity politics, then, becomes a sphere in which history, society and culture interact. It is a debate about different versions of being Scottish, which seek to mobilise process and iconography. The reader will also find much of the material recast in other chapters. That there is no longer a chapter entitled 'Who runs Scotland?' does not imply that this is no longer an important question. It seems more sensible to locate it in the context of Scotland's development (Chapter 3), and power and politics (Chapter 5). These chapters which analyse economic, social and political processes set the context for the discussion of social opportunity and social mobility in Chapter 4. The final three chapters focus on culture, identity and nationalism.

There is, of course, more than one way of understanding Scotland in sociological terms. It would be possible to have chapters dealing with social institutions: the family, gender, education, deviance, media and so on. Another approach would be to write a sociography of Scotland describing in some statistical detail what society looks like with regard to, for example, demography and social inequality. Given the relatively healthy state of sociology in Scotland compared with a decade ago, there is room for more than one approach. There are now a number of sociologists in Scotland involved in social research, and undoubtedly the greater focus on policy which a parliament brings will be beneficial in research terms. There is also much greater interest in these islands in comparative research, and funding bodies like the Economic and Social Research Council and The Leverhulme Trust have invested considerable sums in empirical work. What is especially heartening is that there is now a new generation of sociologists who will take the sociology of Scotland on to a higher analytic plane. If this book does anything to encourage them, and their students, then it will have achieved its purpose. For this author, and his generation, the comment made by Tom Burns, the first professor of sociology at Edinburgh, that the business of sociology is to conduct a critical debate with society about its social institutions (Burns, 1966), has been a guiding motif. In the new Scotland, it continues to be so.

1 The making of modern Scotland

The purpose of this chapter is twofold. First, it sets the scene for the book as a whole by telling the sociological story of Scotland in the twentieth century. Second, it highlights the key processes which have driven social change in the country, and around which much of the sociological debate about Scotland has taken shape. The rest of the book will then outline these debates to provide a sociology of the country. First, however, let us tell Scotland's story in socio-logical terms.[1]

Where does Scotland stand at the end of the twentieth and beginning of the twenty-first century? How much of it would be recognisable to Scots of a hundred years ago? Answers to these questions depend very much on what we choose to highlight as similarities and differences. Supposing the Scots of 1900 were able to project themselves forward to the beginning of the twenty-first century, how much would be familiar to them? They would prob-ably be struck by how similar Scotland was to other West European societies of the present day. Compared to other Europeans, we live in similar houses, drive similar cars and eat similar food. We are educated in much the same way, work at the same kind of jobs, and produce the same kind of products, even for the same companies. We have roughly the same number of children as they do, and we spend our money on similar products and cultural pursuits. We inhabit the same electronic world, and have reduced geographical distance to negligible proportions when it comes to communicating with each other. We visit each other's countries, and while we enjoy the different ways of doing things that we find there, we are able to operate within them quite quickly and happily because so much is familiar to us. Given that the similarities seem to outweigh the differences, we might be hard pushed to spot meaningful differences between Scotland and other countries. Are we simply indulging in what Sigmund Freud called the narcissism of minor difference, our ability to enhance the cultural significance of small differences because that is all we are left with these days?

1 This chapter tells the story of Scotland in the twentieth century as simply as possible, and hence references are kept to a minimum. At the end of the chapter there are some sugges-tions, should the reader wish to follow up further reading.

Let us for a moment adopt the perspective of our 1900 predecessors. They would be struck by the fact that so much that was familiar to them had disappeared: the fact that work no longer seemed the exclusive preserve of men in dungarees and bunnets (flat caps), working in mass, noisy factories and yards; that people no longer lived in densely packed tenements which clustered round these workplaces, close to the city centres: that it seemed so much harder to place people in social class terms by how they dressed and how they spoke. At the end of the twentieth century, in contrast, the majority of the labour force is female, albeit working part-time. While the revolution which took place in the nineteenth century to create industrial Scotland was probably more profound, social change in the twentieth century transformed the lives of Scots.

Certainly, the pace of social and economic change altered the twentieth century in quite remarkable ways. Two world wars, the growing power of the state, the extension of the democratic franchise, growing and extensive affluence, albeit with pockets of abiding poverty, the move to the suburbs driven by the car, were factors quite unknown to the Scots of 1900. One thing they would have recognised, however, was that their compatriots were living in a society structured overwhelmingly by the power of private capital. We might debate whether this is a post-industrial rather than an industrial world, but no one could surely deny that it remains a thoroughly capitalist one.

The images of Scotland continue to resonate the past. It is in many ways a rural, a pre-industrial history which we reach for when we try to explain what makes Scotland 'different'. The 'Scotland' of our imaginations remains not only rural but largely Highland, replete with tartanry and clans. Ordinary Scotland does not figure much in tourist iconography. All societies, of course, have a tendency to reach for the culturally and historically exotic when trying to justify what makes theirs essentially different, but Scotland is more problematic than most. Put simply, it is not a state, and the conventional wisdom is that in modern times sovereign, independent states are the political actors of our age. There is, of course, no denying that Scotland has a degree of statehood (a devolved parliament, a governing bureaucracy), but it is still best described as a stateless nation, an imagined community with considerable institutional autonomy, and, at least as yet, no sovereign parliament. There is no doubting, however, that Scotland is a modern society because it has been transformed by the major global processes of industrialism and capitalism from the late eighteenth century onwards. These shared processes, however, have not reduced the modern world to uniformity, even though the motors of change – economic, social, cultural – may be the same. Each society is equipped with a set of cultural perspectives with which to make sense of these common changes. That is why our time-travellers from 1900 would still recognise Scotland as a familiar place. Its institutions and cultural systems provide the signposts, the means for understanding just how the common processes impact on place.

Let us follow our time-traveller through twentieth-century Scotland so that we can better comprehend what has brought us to the present. Our journey takes us past three key dates, 1900, 1950 and 2000: stopping-off points which enable us to highlight the key determining features of that changing century. Our purpose is not to describe the minutiae of events in those years but to use them as motifs which enable us to capture what was central at these times. Why these dates, and why these motifs? The first, 1900, may be characterised as dominated by 'capital', by unalloyed market power. This was an age of empire as well as capital, but it was one on which the sun was beginning to set even though it seemed at the time never stronger. Our second date – 1950 – is not simply and conveniently mid-century, but captures a new set of processes, essentially political ones, in which the unrestrained market was thought to have caused more problems than it had solved: hence the motif of 'state', for this describes the ways in which the political system intervened in market forces to allocate jobs, housing, education, and other life-chances for its people. Finally, by the year 2000, we encounter a new motif – let us call it 'nation' – which comes to play an increasing role in debates about Scotland. By 'nation' we mean that social life in Scotland is framed by cultural factors rather than simply economic (capital) and political (state) ones. The debate comes to be structured around Scotland's constitutional position in the modern world, in a word, by 'nationalism'. We do not mean here that before this point Scotland was not a 'nation'. Indeed, it never ceased to be one, even when it more or less willingly gave up its statehood for a share in the economic and political gains of wider British union in 1707. What we encounter at the start of the new century is a reconfiguring of Scotland around its sense of being a nation, a way of explaining why it is the way it is, as well as a route-map for its future.

Characterising periods in this way is, of course, crude, for it is not as if one motif had replaced the others. Perhaps it is better to think of it like a piece of music in which new themes emerge, while previous ones do not disappear, but become secondary, and interwoven with the existing ones, subtly changing their meaning. Each motif or theme helps to capture the mood of the times, even though the processes they symbolise were actually interacting with each other in a complex and continuing way. At each of our time-points, let us focus on the key aspects and institutions which matter. These are the key issues: how economic resources are owned and allocated; the class system, and the cultural systems which go with it; the education system, and how it gives access to society's goods; and how political power operates at the different levels of society. We need to focus too on aspects of Scotland's demography and social structure, and how these change; on internal divisions such as region, urban–rural differences, religion; and on the cultural means available to people to make sense of the world around them. Finally, we must explain who the Scots think they are, and what competing or complementary identities they have. We cannot of course hope to capture all the intricacies of a changing Scotland, but this introductory chapter tries to provide a route-map to the key features so that we can gauge just how the twentieth century differed from the one before it. Our task too is to explain why Scotland at the start of the twenty-first century has reached such an important conjuncture in its history, when no one can predict with any degree of accuracy where the restoration of even a devolved parliament is going to lead. Let us begin our journey.

The world of capital: Scotland 1900

What did Scotland look like at the start of the twentieth century? The Scottish population stood at 4.5 million in 1901, and at 4.76 million in 1911. By the final decade of the century it was just over 5 million, and that is where it is projected to stay well into the twenty-first century. In this respect Scotland is unusual, for there is no other European country which has such low levels of population growth. While the population of Great Britain grew by 38 per cent between 1911 and 1991, Scotland's had a relatively stagnant growth rate of a mere 7 per cent. Indeed, Scotland's 1991 population fell in real terms, for it was actually 1.5 per cent lower than 1971, in contrast to Wales which grew by 5.5 per cent in that period, and England, by 3.9 per cent. In comparison with other countries in the European Union, this was a most unusual situation. Not a single national state has lost population in this period, and only Denmark and Belgium have growth rates lower than England and Wales, and nowhere has a lower population growth rate than Scotland.

How are we to explain this? The population of any country is the outcome of the changing and differential rates of births, deaths and migration patterns. Scotland entered the twentieth century with a high but falling birth rate and a lower and falling death rate, so that the first decades of the century revealed a fairly typical pattern of a demographic transition from high fertility and high mortality, to low fertility and low mortality.

Scotland, like England, experienced a decline in infant mortality from 1900, although it was gradual and erratic. Girls had a better life expectancy than boys, so that those born between 1910 and 1912 could expect to live until age 53, compared with 50 for boys. Mothers too benefited from falling mortality rates. The chance of a woman dying in childbirth was one in 4000 by the 1970s, literally a hundred times better than it had been at the beginning of the century, a remarkable turnaround in the public health of the country. Childhood diseases like measles, scarlatina, whooping-cough, diphtheria and croup accounted for as much as one-third of deaths between the ages of 1 and 4 before the Great War. These too had been virtually eradicated by the 1990s.

Fertility rather than mortality and migration are in the main responsible for much demographic change throughout twentieth-century Europe. Scottish marital fertility was for a considerable time higher than in England, while fewer women married. In the early part of the century, most Scottish men married at age 28, and women two years younger. Up until the Second World War and beyond, fewer women in Scotland compared with England were married. Indeed, these low levels of nuptiality in the early decades of the century put Scotland well below all other countries, with the exception of Ireland and Iceland. Levels of marriage were especially low in rural areas, but above all in the crofting counties.

The reasons for this are complex but they seem to have had much to do with arrangements in rural Scotland for hiring and housing agricultural labour, as well as rules for Poor Relief. In lowland Scotland, rural housing was only provided with the job, so that failure to get a 'fee' to work meant moving to a farm where one was available. The Poor Law in Scotland also discouraged the risk of marrying improvidently, as the able-bodied received only transitory payments. By the late nineteenth century, delayed marriage or permanent celibacy was a characteristic of the crofting counties, largely because people had problems establishing and maintaining new families in the social and economic conditions which prevailed. These peculiar conditions of the turn-of-the-century local economy which had the effect of depressing marriage patterns did not alter until well into the twentieth century when Scotland became in essence an urban rather than a rural society.

What about families? The twentieth century saw a dramatic fall in family size. In 1911 it was not uncommon for established families to have six or more children. Family size at this time was also class-specific, for manual labourers had almost twice the number of children as middle-class professionals. The lower the social class you belonged to, the more children you had. Only in the second half of the century did these social class differences come to narrow significantly. The control of family size in Scotland, as elsewhere, was the result of a complex of factors including birth control technology and lengthening child dependency, especially for the middle classes. Not only did family size fall as the century progressed, but child-bearing was concentrated into shorter periods of time.

Family size was also shaped by the housing available. In 1911, over half of all Scottish households lived in houses (in Scotland the term 'house' includes flats) with two rooms or fewer (compared with only 7 per cent in England). More than one in ten Scots lived in houses with only one room. This state of affairs took a considerable time to change, so that even as late as 1951 over a quarter of Scotland's urban population still lived in two-roomed accommodation. 'Overcrowding' remained a fact of everyday life in Scotland for much of the twentieth century.

In the industrial cities like Glasgow and Dundee, the 'single-end' was a matter of moral and social outrage for Victorian and Edwardian reformers, the best known of whom was James Burn Russell, who, as Glasgow's Medical Officer of Health, wrote a best-selling pamphlet in 1905, 'Life in one room', based on his lecture series. The aim was to shock the Victorian middle classes into action on the grounds that one room permitted all sorts of unwarranted intimacies, none more so than the rituals of death. He wrote:

> The beloved dead is laid on the bed, and all the usual rounds of domestic duties, including the taking of meals, has to be done with ever that still, pale

form before their view. Night comes on and the household must go to rest, so the sad burden is now transferred from the bed and laid on the table, or it may be the coal-bunker lid. In the morning, to admit of the table being used for breakfast, or let coals be got for the fire, the body has to be lifted on to the bed again, and so on for the customary three days, the broken-hearted relatives feeling it to be a sacrilege thus to hustle about the mortal remains of a much loved one.

(Russell, 1905: n.p.)

In these desperate circumstances, it fell to women to keep the household economy going. Working-class women had the burden and responsibility of maintaining and sustaining the family in these conditions, in which there were few of the labour-saving devices to which we have grown so accustomed such as washing machines, vacuum cleaners, or the household gadgetry of today. More significantly, women of the 1900s had the responsibility of negotiating with the landlord, both on their own behalf and on that of their sons and daughters looking for accommodation of their own.

The typical working-class family was chronically in debt. At the turn of the century, most found it impossible to survive from week to week on the money coming into the house, a reflection not only of the level of wages but of the nature of casual work. Family budgets had to take past and future debts into account, and thrift and savings were essential for the social security of the family as it negotiated its way through unemployment and illness. Most tenants required a 'character' or reference from the previous landlord before a new one took the family on. In Scotland at the turn of the century, the law underpinned the landlord's position in a quite remarkable way. The so-called 'right of hypothec' allowed the landlord the right to sequester the tenant's furniture and tools in case they went into rent arrears. To escape the dreadful and cramped conditions of intimate life, men spent much of their leisure time on the street corners or in the pubs. Women, meanwhile, given the drudgery of working-class life, had no option but to stay at home.

House-capitalists were people of modest means, but were not so untypical of business generally in Scotland at the end of the nineteenth century. The housing market was supported by small owners with small amounts of capital, marshalled by local house factors and lawyers. It did not interest major employers of labour. Large entrepreneurs did not normally provide housing for their workers unless labour was specialised and/or scarce, as in the case of coal-mining or locomotive-building.

Life in Scottish towns and cities was atrocious. In desperation, authorities were forced to intervene in the housing market, and the cities in particular led the way in slum clearance by way of improvement acts. They also developed the tradition of civic enterprise, known as 'municipal socialism'. Glasgow could boast of the Loch Katrine water scheme in 1859, the dredging of the Clyde in 1869 and 1893, the municipalisation of gas and public lighting, the pioneering of tramways, public baths and municipal wash-houses – the steamies, which became the subject of nostalgia later in the century. By 1902, Glasgow Corporation owned 2488 houses, 78 lodging houses, 372 shops, 86 warehouses and workshops, 12 halls, 2 churches, and a bakehouse (Allan, 1965: 608).

This was an all-too-familiar world to our time-travellers of 1900. They would easily recognise the reliance on this complex mix of local private and public services in the political economy of Scotland's towns and cities. This of course was to be utterly transformed by the 'nationalising' and politicising of these services: in other words, the rise of the state, both national and local, and the challenge to business at both levels.

The most obvious state institution was the school. The 1872 Education Act and its aftermath had created the main features of the education system which were to last well into the twentieth century. Above all, the Act made education compulsory, laying down that 15 was the minimum school-leaving age, and tightening up considerably on exemptions whereby pupils could leave to enter the labour market as early as age 12. Scotland had entered the modern age with a relatively literate population, at least in the sense that people could sign their names. As many as 65 per cent of men could do so by the mid-eighteenth century (Houston, 1985). This was, of course, a limited skill, and by 1900 schooling for most meant primary education, with modest extensions, unless one was unusually gifted academically so as to be allowed into secondary education.

The legacy of the nineteenth century had bequeathed to Scotland a universal elementary system of education, enshrined in the 1872 Education Act. The subsequent 1918 Act was, if anything, even more revolutionary in its purpose, for it asserted the principle of free secondary education for all in schools of a common type. It also brought Catholic schools into the formal state system, but allowed them to retain influence over parts of the curriculum and the appointment of teachers. The system of higher education was to remain virtually unchanged, apart from admitting women, until the mid-twentieth century, and the proportion of the relevant age group at university did not rise until the 1950s. Teaching as a profession was highly gender segregated such that women dominated the primary schools, and men the secondary system. Teacher training was the main form of higher education open to women, who had to suffer the 'marriage bar' whereby they had to leave teaching if and when they got married, a ban which was not lifted until after 1945.

In spite of its highly segregated system in terms of both social class and gender, Scotland's education system was a keystone of its economic development. Robert Anderson has observed: 'In responding to the problems created by the industrial revolution, Scotland was given a good start by its tradition of national education and by a cultural disposition with religious, political and social roots, to value educational achievement' (1999: 223).

The power of capital

With the exception of small landlords, Scottish capitalism in the early days of the twentieth century was self-confident and buoyant. Above all, it was local, not so much in its operations as in its ownership. Central to the structure of Scottish business were the railway companies, and their interconnections with coal, steel and engineering. Nor was this simply a west of Scotland phenomenon, for regional clusters were also significant. In Dundee, for example, the juteocracy (local owners of the jute industry) of the Cox, Baxter and Fleming families ruled. In Edinburgh, business clustered on the banks and the North British railway, while the Glasgow segment focused on Tennants' companies, the Caledonian railway and the Clydesdale Bank. The banks and the financial system were central to these clusters of business interests. Nor were the landed gentry excluded. The Marquess of Linlithgow was a director of the Bank of Scotland and Standard Life; the Duke of Buccleuch, of the Royal Bank, Standard Life and Scottish Equitable; the Earl of Mansfield, of the National Bank and Scottish Equitable; and the Marquess of Tweeddale, of the Commercial Bank, Edinburgh Life and Scottish Widows.

Scottish business at the beginning of the twentieth century was a complex network of interlocking ownerships and directorates within Scottish dynasties. It was fairly secure from external takeover, even from England. Nevertheless, by the outbreak of the Great War, its dependence on family control and family capital meant that it could not compete with the managerial and technological revolutions taking place in Germany and the United States. The expansion of the banks and finance houses further into Scottish business could not disguise the fact that they were ill equipped to compete in a twentieth-century world in which imperial markets were being challenged. Scotland was undoubtedly well adapted to take advantage of Britain's highly advantageous structural position in the world economy which was at that time shaped around Britain's own commercial interests, but that was its ultimate weakness rather than its strength. As these interests atrophied, so Scottish capital found it difficult to adapt to what was to become a post-imperial world economy. Not until the 1930s was it recognised that radical surgery had to be carried out to open up new markets and methods of production, and that, ultimately, was to be the role of the state.

The dominance of local capital in Scotland at the beginning of the twentieth century was firmly reflected in politics. At the municipal level, power lay in the hands of small-scale local capital, mainly small shopkeepers and local landlords. The 'Independent' label kept alive the view that local government was in essence 'non-political', an enterprise in which individuals were elected on their merits rather than political affiliation. Above all, what was revealed was resistance to the 'nationalising' of local politics, expressed in the view that running the town was a matter strictly for local businessmen with proven experience.

At the national level, party preference was almost evenly split between Liberals and Conservatives (including their Liberal-Unionist allies). At the 1900 'Khaki' election Liberals were still able to win 50 per cent of the popular vote, but ended up with two fewer seats than the Tories, who won 36 seats on their 49 per cent vote share. In hindsight, this election was to mark the beginning of the end of the Liberals as they failed to win half of Scotland's seats for the first time since 1832. The Liberal Party broke its back over the issue of Irish Home Rule, when a significant minority of pro-Union liberals sided with the Conservatives.

Here we see the power and importance of politics and religion in early twentieth-century Scotland. It was a society which saw itself as 'unionist', taking pride in empire, firmly imperialist, as well as Protestant in ethos and religious practice. 'The Bible: Basis of Empire Greatness' was the self-confident banner of the Bible Society at the Empire Exhibition of 1938. Being a Protestant, a Unionist and proud of empire confirmed an identity which treated Scottish and British as complements of each other.

The beginning of the twentieth century also saw continuing migration from Ireland, both north and south. The arrival of the Irish exacerbated pressure among a developing urban proletariat already facing the social dislocations of rapid modernisation, and Catholic Irish labour was, on occasion, used by employers to depress local wage levels. These Catholic Irish were often seen as more than simply economic rivals: many viewed them as a root cause of many social evils. Integration would have been difficult enough, given the differences in speech, custom and religion which divided them from their new neighbours. Crucially, however, a sizeable minority of Irish arrivals were Ulster Protestants who brought their virulent anti-Catholicism with them.

These divisions were to prove significant for at least half a century in Scottish politics, with Catholics showing a solid propensity to vote Labour after 1921, while the Conservatives drew disproportionately on Protestant support, both native and immigrant. Only in the second half of the twentieth century did this link between religion and politics begin to fragment. This Scotland framed by Protestantism, Unionism and Imperialism was not short of internal divisions. Apart from the religious divide between Catholics and Protestants, and between the social classes, especially the working class and their bourgeois masters, Scotland inherited significant regional divisions, none more so than the Highland/Lowland one. Migration from north to south continued to erode the Gaeltacht, while according to the 1901 census, over 5 per cent of Scots (almost a quarter of a million) continued to speak Gaelic. Indeed, by this time, there were probably more Gaels in the southern cities, notably Glasgow, where localities (such as Maryhill) and occupations (the police) became important redoubts of the Gael.

How best, then, to sum up Scotland at the beginning of the twentieth century? It was already a modern, mature industrial society built around imperial market opportunities. It was one in which most people – as many as three out of four – belonged to the manual working class, with a much smaller but significantly more powerful middle class. This class ruled over different aspects of its society and politics, leaving the provision of mass housing to its *petite bourgeoisie*, while self-confidently running its developing system of capitalism. The motif of the market ruled in housing as in much else, and it took the threat of social unrest in the second decade of the century before it was eroded by state action – rent controls, followed by direct state housing in the 1920s.

In short, Scotland in 1900 was firmly framed by empire, Protestantism and capital. Scotland was a supremely modern and industrial country, in which Glasgow proudly proclaimed itself the second city of the empire, and Scots were as strong supporters of imperial endeavours as anyone, notably in southern Africa where the war with the Boer settlers was taking place. Pride and recruitment in the Scottish regiments were buoyant. The year 1900 was to prove the beginning of the end for both empire, and Scottish commitment to Union in its historic form, although it was to take virtually the whole century for this to happen.

The power of the state: Scotland 1950

If our Victorian predecessors would have felt comfortable in Scotland in 1900, what would they have made of mid-century Scotland? They would have found it an altogether stranger place. The old locality-based systems of power were rapidly eroding in favour of central state power. While the world of empire was coming to an end, the impact of two world wars had helped to re-forge a sense of Britishness among the Scots which was different from that older, imperialist sense to which they had become accustomed. By mid-century, Scots were, if anything, confirmed in their Britishness. Above all, Scotland in 1950 was part of an integrated all-British welfare state. If 'capital' was the defining motif of Scotland in 1900, then 'state' defines its mid-century counterpart.

Why should mid-century Scots have felt so confidently British? Mass wars have the capacity to mobilise. The impact of the First World War on the population was unprecedented. In the UK, nearly five million men – some 22 per cent of the total male population – were recruited into the armed forces. Most of these were volunteers, some two-thirds, with the rest joining as conscripts after 1916. As the social historian John Stevenson (1984) points out: 'In retrospect, one of the most striking features of the Great War was the readiness, indeed the enthusiasm, with which hundreds of thousands of British males, drawn from every walk of life and every geographical area, volunteered to fight for "King and Country".'

The phrase 'King and Country' is the key. Imperialism and patriotism were virtually indistinguishable. Britain, in other words, was still an imperial state – with colonies and dominions which came to embody its identity. Why should war have such an impact? Almost a quarter of the male population had experience of military service, well over half of those of military age. But war was more important than that. In short, it created the modern British state: warfare and welfare went together.

The extension of demands on the state had, of course, pre-dated the war, but it provided the catalyst for radical change, both with regard to the mobilisation of manpower and the organisation of production. Translating this into practical changes, it meant greater state involvement in the economy, especially labour relations, housing and unemployment relief; a major extension of taxation; greater control of industry by managerially controlled corporations; the transfer of land to tenant farmers; and, above all, the integration of the working class into the democratic process.

The other dimension of British national identity, alongside war and democracy, was social class. Labour was the mechanism for enfranchising the manual working class, and it derived enormous benefit from this association until the final quarter of the twentieth century when the working class fell in size from around 60 per cent to around 40 per cent of the workforce largely as a result of de-industrialisation and economic restructuring.

The Labour Party's role in mid-twentieth-century Britain was to deliver the manual working class into the democratic process, and to fix its politics into the British–national dimension of class. In comparison with those in continental Europe where religious –'confessional' – politics was much more common, British politics was essentially about social class. In Scotland, for example, the century began with Labour making no showing at all in 1900, the year of its founding. By 1906 it took a mere 2 per cent of the vote, and two seats, in contrast to 65 per cent for the Liberals and 38 per cent for the Unionists. Labour's major breakthrough in Scotland came in the 1918 election when the party won 23 per cent of the vote against 33 per cent for the Tories with the Liberals already split between pro-coalition (19 per cent) and non-coalition forces (15 per cent). Labour held its share thereafter, never dropping below 33 per cent (in 1931) and winning 48 per cent (and 37 seats) in 1945.

There was no room for explicitly 'nationalist' politics in mid-century Scotland, largely because the two main repertoires of Scottish politics squeezed it out. On the one hand, the Conservative Party was able to mobilise the powerful nexus linking Unionism and Protestantism welded together by a strong sense of British national/imperial identity. This version of Scottishness sat quite easily with Conservative rhetoric about being British. It was fostered too by a powerful strand of militarism which continued to run through Scottish society. Over half a million Scots enlisted in the army, over 40 per cent of all men between the ages of 15 and 49. One of the key and abiding icons of Scottishness was the Scottish soldier. Here was a figure which confirmed that being Scottish and British were not at all at odds. The Scottish regiments were recruiting sergeants for British imperial and world wars, and helped to make Scottish and British national identities complementary. On the other hand, Labour politics made the Scottish (and the Welsh) working class safe for the British Union. 'National' politics were deemed to be British, not Scottish or Welsh. Both Conservative and Labour ideologies were, in fact, thoroughly Scottish, but both in their different ways were complements of being British.

Another – alternative – version of national politics was, however, slowly emerging. The inter-war period saw the first stirrings of modern nationalism in Scotland and Wales. Saunders Lewis founded Plaid Cymru (the Welsh Party) in 1925, and the Scottish National Party (SNP) was formed in 1934, an amalgam of the National Party of Scotland and the Scottish Party. While the SNP did not make an electoral impact until the late 1960s (it won just 30,000 votes in the eight seats it contested in 1945), it had begun its long political march. Ireland, Scotland and Wales were flexing their national muscles as the British empire lost its force. What these fledgling political movements showed was that the British imperium was beginning to lose its power – first, in the white Dominions, then in the Celtic countries, most noticeably in Ireland. The later threats from Scotland and Wales to secede from the United Kingdom undoubtedly have their roots in this period.

Shaping a new Scotland

How had Scotland changed socially between 1900 and 1950? By the mid-twentieth century Scotland had made the demographic transition to a low birth rate, low death rate society. There were birth surges in 1921 and 1947 at the end of the wars, but Scots had adopted birth limitation, so that, combined with falling levels of child and young adult mortality, there were only marginally more children than middle-aged adults by mid-century. The national death rate had bottomed out by this time, and falling death rates in the population at large were balanced by greater longevity. There were, however, still significant class differentials in terms of mortality rates. In the 1950s and 1960s, working-class men and women in social class 5 had a mortality rate six times that of people in social class 1. Post-war babies in social class 5 were three times more likely to die in the first year of life than their class 1 counterparts.

Fertility and mortality trends in Scotland mainly followed those in the rest of Great Britain. Where Scotland did differ was that far more people emigrated. This is the key to understanding why its population has been so static, compared with other Western European countries. Scotland in the 1920s saw the highest rates of emigration, so that the small increase in improving birth over death rates was reversed by net emigration which totalled almost 400,000 in the decade, an enormous proportion in a country of only five million people. The rates of emigration slackened in the following decade, only to increase once more during the 1950s and 1960s when Scotland had a net loss of almost half-a-million people. Scotland had long had a history of emigration which continued in the inter-war period when many Scots emigrated to Australia, New Zealand and Canada, thereby continuing patterns laid down in the previous century. There was no counter in-migration to Scotland such as occurred in England from new Commonwealth countries after the Second World War. Scotland, however, saw no major net incoming of population since the Irish arrived in the nineteenth century. This helped to reinforce the sense that Scotland was manifestly a society of emigrants, not immigrants.

The post-war period did see a substantial redistribution of population within Scotland. Glasgow, whose population stood at over one million as late as 1961, tried to solve its overcrowding problems by exporting significant numbers to new towns via its overspill policies, first in East Kilbride, then in Cumbernauld. Only later did it discover that those who went were disproportionately the younger and more skilled, and that it was retaining within the city's boundaries a disproportionately ageing and unskilled workforce. Scotland was one of the most urbanised societies in the world by the early twentieth century. By 1911, 30 per cent of Scots lived in one of the four main cities, rising to 38 per cent by 1951, before falling back to 28 per cent in 1991.

The cities were slow to introduce council housing because it both undermined the market principle and threatened the livelihoods of the property men, the landlords and house factors, who sat on many local councils. The 1915 Rent Restrictions Act, as we have seen, sounded the death-knell of the small landlord, but he took a long time dying. The solution to the housing question was tackled by the solid Victorian 'deserving' principle. Those who could afford it and were judged morally able to look after good property (defined as 'General Purposes' housing) were allocated the best-quality council houses, while 'slum clearance' housing was confined to those on lower incomes, uncertain jobs, and implied moral inferiority. 'Ordinary' housing went to those whom the housing visitor judged 'clean and decent', while those who failed this inscrutable test were given 'Rehousing' homes. The sociologist Sean Damer has captured how this moral code worked. The stigma was conveyed by the nicknames Wine Alley, The Jungle and The Promised Land. He comments:

> Tenants distance themselves from the reputation of their scheme by differentiating themselves from the deviants. They tend to displace their fears and fantasies to the point in the scheme furthest from them. The animals are always in another zoo; the witch is always at the far end of the village.
>
> (Damer, 1974: 238)

The perceptions of those in authority that certain schemes were full of criminals, vandals, junkies and prostitutes were in turn internalised by the tenants themselves as social stigmata. They also came to believe the moral tales being told about them. In practice, of course, these tales could not possibly be true, for if they were, there would be more criminals than people like themselves in the schemes. The moral codes of deserving and undeserving operated effectively to discriminate and allocate scarce resources.

By mid-century, Scotland had undergone the 'occupational transition' common to all modern industrial societies. It had shifted from an economy dependent on manufacturing to one based on services. Primary industry – agriculture, quarrying and mining – employed only one in ten workers compared with double that at the beginning of the century. Further significant falls were in store. These were trends which Scotland shared with the rest of the UK as well as other modern industrial societies. They involved the expansion of white-collar work, especially in the number of professional employees, people like teachers and clerical workers. By mid-century, Scotland was still a working-class society, for over half of Scots were in manual work, a figure that was to drop significantly in later years. Women's employment also reflected wider trends. In Scotland, however, the economic activity rate for married women until well after 1945 was only two-thirds that of the rest of Britain, and it was not until the late 1970s that Scotland caught up. Just as more women were working, so certain occupations such as clerical work which had hitherto been a male preserve shifted to being overwhelmingly female. The percentage of clerks who were female rose from about half in 1961 to three-quarters by 1981.

The transformation of Scottish business was also taking place. Even before the war, it was recognised that Scotland's economy needed to be restructured and diversified. In the inter-war period, the civil service was reorganised, Scotland was designated a separate area for industrial development, and the Scottish Economic Committee was created. This set off a dynamic in Scottish business which, with the aid of the state, was to have far-reaching effects. The old dynastic families may have retained control of traditional industry, but foreign and English capital came to play a much greater role in Scotland's economic affairs in the second half of the century.

Many of these initiatives had grown out of the activities of a much more proactive Scottish Office under the leadership of Tom Johnston, who was Secretary of State for Scotland during the Second World War, and who, with Churchill's connivance, built it up into a formidable apparatus of economic development. The Second World War had given a belated boost to traditional economic interests, but the fortunes of Scotland's traditional capitalists – the Colvilles, Tennants and Beardmores – were slipping away with new competition. The post-war period saw the decline of this capitalist class. The dominant nexus in Scottish heavy industry of the 1930s, the Colville–Lithgow–Nimmo complex based on coal, iron and steel, disappeared with nationalisation, and the links between financial companies and banks became more pronounced as the defining element of Scottish business.

By the mid-1950s, the 'managerial revolution' which had transformed American and English business had largely passed Scotland by, as did the establishment of the new automotive and white goods industries. This crisis came to a head in the 1960s which forced on the traditionally dominant dynastic families a major crisis of confidence. In this vacuum, the government through the Scottish Office induced external capital to play a much greater role in Scotland. From the 1950s, new industries were set up, guided by state directive: the steel strip mill at Ravenscraig, the Rootes Car Company at Linwood, and new timber and aluminium plants in the Highlands. All were to fail in the cold market climate of the final quarter of the century.

Along with its economy, Scotland's politics were also being transformed. Only Labour and the Unionists mattered at mid-century, and between them they took nine out of every ten votes in Scotland, just as south of the border. Two-party – all-British – politics ruled. Further, there was virtually no difference between Scotland and England in terms of support for the parties. Labour had an identical share of the vote north and south of the border, with the Tories in 1950 actually taking a marginally higher share of the vote in Scotland than they did in England (44.8 per cent to 43.8 per cent), and they were the only party to win a majority of the vote in 1955. Seen from the vantage point of the end of the century, when they lost every seat they contested in the 1997 election, this seems an almost incredible situation. How are we to explain it?

In large part, the success of the Conservatives in mid-twentieth-century Scotland reflected their capacity to capture substantial sectors of the working-class vote. While they did not operate directly in local politics, they were able to wield influence through the diverse 'non-political' labels such as Moderate and Progressive in the major cities. These were loose coalitions of anti-Labour support designed, as they saw it, to keep 'politics' out of local government.

The Scottish Unionist Party, as the Conservatives were called until 1965, also relied on capturing a disproportionate share of the Protestant working-class vote. In the 1920s and 1930s, both Edinburgh and Glasgow saw militant Protestantism become a significant force in local politics. In Edinburgh, Protestant Action operated an informal electoral pact from the 1930s until the late 1950s with the self-styled 'Progressives' – basically an anti-Labour coalition. Religion was a significant force in mid-century Scottish politics, with the Conservatives able to carry a disproportionate number of Protestants. As late as the 1960s, working-class members of the Church of Scotland in Dundee were over six times more likely to vote Tory than Labour. This association was mirrored by Catholic support for Labour. Conservatives were also happy to play a Scottish card in the post-war period while in opposition, complaining that Labour's centralising agenda at a UK level was eroding the autonomy of Scotland.

Religion continued to matter, and not only in politics. The Church of Scotland saw a significant growth in members between the early 1940s and mid-1950s when it reached an all-time high. This peak was not sustained however, and by the early 1960s membership had fallen to its lowest level since the twentieth century began, and was to keep falling. Church membership was reasonably buoyant for much of the century, but church attendance showed a substantial decline much earlier. Between the mid-nineteenth century and the final quarter or so of the twentieth, attendance at Presbyterian churches fell by four-fifths, and as a result it ceased to be a mass church. Catholic attendance was sustained for much of the century however, so that the Catholic share of total church adherents rose from about one-seventh in 1914 to more than one-fifth by 1970. In part, this was a reflection of the major investment which Catholics put into building churches in the new peripheral housing schemes, and in maintaining and extending Catholic schools in these areas. The opportunities for that had been created by the 1918 Education Act, which had guaranteed Catholics influence over aspects of the curriculum and the appointment of teachers. Scottish schools generally saw only incremental growth between the 1930s and the 1960s, and the 1945 Education Act confirmed the distinction between what became 'senior' and 'junior' secondary schools. Nevertheless, by the late 1950s over 40 per cent of secondary pupils were in senior secondary schools. After the war, central government and local authorities had embarked on a programme of primary school-building and reforming its curriculum, but it was not until the 1960s that higher education expanded such that only 5 per cent of the relevant age group entered university.

How, then, had Scotland transformed itself in the first half of the twentieth century? It was still a society in which workers were largely men, in many ways a turnaround from the war years when women took over many men's jobs. However, Scotland, like almost all other Western European countries, reverted back to a strict gender division of labour in which child-rearing and home-making were seen as primary female roles, and women's place became once more the home. This of course was both a reflection as well as a cause of the baby-boom in the late 1940s and 1950s. Smaller family sizes, the fact that children survived infancy more successfully, and that there was a lengthening period of childhood and adolescence brought about by education put greater focus on the family. A major programme of house-building sought to ensure that every nuclear family had its own domestic space, and helped to generate home-centredness – later to be called 'privatism' – which became the norm, or at least the ideal.

The world after 1945 brought greater affluence and greater mobility, both geographical and social. New processes were grafted on to older belief-systems. The notion that Scots had a particular commitment to 'getting on', notably through the medium of education, had its modern origins in a late nineteenth-century fiction which celebrated the virtues of small-town and rural Scotland. This Scottish myth of social advancement had its educational manifestation in the 'lad o' pairts', a talented youth (almost always male) who had the talent but not the financial means to improve himself. The image of small-town, conservative Scotland which the lad o' pairts exemplified belonged in strict historical terms to the late nineteenth and early twentieth centuries. The social opportunity which was being celebrated drew on a meritocratic ideal rather than an egalitarian one. Its key point was that everyone should have the opportunity to take advantage of education, rather than that there should be equality of outcome. Its justification was that those who failed were judged not to have the ability and/or the commitment to take advantage of what was offered them. The 'Scottish myth' was sustained by post-war evidence that Scotland had similar patterns of educational achievement as the meritocratic United States, which had its own social myth, the American

Dream. The implicit point of comparison was with England, which was believed to have a much more socially restricted educational system.

The 1950s were the high point of 'Britishness' in Scotland, as well as being a turning point. While it was true that Scottish schools and universities retained important social and rhetorical differences from England, the creation of the Welfare State had forged a new and significant meaning of Britishness. This was reflected in the unprecedented similarity in voting behaviour north and south of the border in the 1950s, and in the shared view that the state was a vehicle for transforming the economy, something desperately needed in Scotland. Despite the success of the Scottish Covenant in 1948 calling for Home Rule which was signed by two million people, the time was not right for a politically explicit nationalism in Scotland. The Welfare State might have had a distinct Scottish dimension, but it was an all-British solution to the problem of social and economic reform.

The compromises reached in the inter-war years to strengthen the Scottish Office as the vehicle for transforming the Scottish economy helped to deliver an unprecedented level of prosperity to Scotland. While there were important differences within the United Kingdom (Scotland's unemployment rate was twice that of the UK, and out-migration to well-paid jobs in England was running strongly), there was little political pressure to detach Scotland from the British state. Two world wars in less than half a century, coupled with a new UK-wide welfare system, welded the Scots firmly into the British state. It was to be another 25 years before this contract began to lose its power, and an explicit Scottish political nationalism emerged. This was to be the running motif of the final quarter of the century.

Rediscovering the nation: Scotland 2000

Let us recap our argument. We have selected three time-points in Scotland's complex story in the twentieth century because they help us to see more easily the processes which are impacting on the country. Certainly, the pace of social change in the late twentieth century has been bewildering, and most of the old certainties have slipped away. The nature of work and the social relations around it have been transformed. Employing people – overwhelmingly men – to make things in mass factories is no longer the norm. Women are no longer confined to the home. If at the turn of the century the claims of the family took precedence over those of individuals, by the end of the century the positions were reversed. Individualism ruled. Personal satisfaction and happiness took priority, and in a rapidly changing world which changes dramatically over people's lifetimes, new ways of meeting the individual's needs emerge.

The Scots of 1900 would probably be quite shocked at what had become of the classical family. Families of six children or more were becoming exceptional by the Great War, and were rare by mid-century. Not only had the family shrunk dramatically in size – Scotland had the lowest birth rate in the whole of the UK in the 1990s – but new household types had become the norm. Less than a quarter of households now comprise the 'classical' family of two parents and dependent children. Almost one-third of Scottish households now contain only one person, and just over a quarter consist of couples with no children.

By the 1990s, Scotland had, like other comparable countries, the lowest birth and death rates it had ever seen. The late 1990s also saw the lowest number of marriages this century. Emigration too had diminished, but the lack of inward migration, coupled with low fertility rates, meant that the Scottish population was barely reproducing itself. In 1901 there had been 165 live births for every 100 deaths, and in 1951 the ratio was 138 to 100. By the 1990s, however, more people were dying than were being born.

The old killer diseases and epidemics which had been so familiar – the communicable infectious diseases caused by viruses and bacteria – had been all but eradicated. By the 1990s, people were dying mainly of cancers and ischaemic heart disease, and these alone were each responsible for around a quarter of all adult deaths in Scotland. Considerable class differentials remained, so that the death rate in eastern Glasgow in 1991, even allowing for age and sex differences, was 77 per cent above middle-class Bearsden and Milngavie, and even considerably higher than in the Western Isles.

What seems to have brought about this dramatic improvement in health was less the discovery of new medical techniques and treatments, and more the impact of rising living standards during much of the second half of the twentieth century. Only after 1945 did families expect all their children to survive into adulthood, and the death of a child became even more of a tragedy because it was so uncommon. Men in the 1990s could now expect to live until age 73, and women to age 78.

While people were living longer, they were far less likely to remain with the same marriage partner. Marriages in the late 1970s had around five times more chance of ending in divorce than those of the early 1950s. By 1997, Scotland recorded the lowest annual number of marriages for over a century. Well over half of divorced people in Scotland, however, remarried within a year of divorce, and by 1997, over a quarter of everyone marrying had been married before. High divorce rates coupled with lower rates of marriages were compounded by increasing rates of cohabitation.

A concomitant of this trend was a rising level of illegitimate births, especially among cohabiting couples. By the late 1990s, four out of every ten live births were to unmarried parents. In the early part of the century, illegitimacy had been a feature of rural areas like the north-east, where cohabitation and births frequently preceded marriage as a response to prevailing economic and social conditions. By the late twentieth century, on the other hand, illegitimacy was mainly a feature of city life; 40 per cent of all births to unmarried parents took place in Scotland's four city areas.

The cities and towns of Scotland were themselves transformed. Gone were the inner-city slums of 'single-ends', without baths or inside toilets. The private landlord had been swept away in the process, and by mid-century had been replaced by the state as urban landlord. By the 1980s, huge swathes of Scotland's housing was municipally owned, and in some areas in the major cities it was virtually 100 per cent. This represented the high tide of municipal ownership, for the Conservative government of 1979 set about selling off council houses, and restricting the building of new ones. By the 1990s, over one-third of all council houses in Scotland had been sold. The year 1980 saw private housing completions overtake those in the public sector for the first time since 1920, and council housing fell as a form of tenure to less than one-third by the mid-1990s (still double the proportion in England).

A visitor from 1900 would have found it very difficult to tell people's class simply by life-style. This is the result of an emerging diversity of consumption habits and behaviours in the population generally, rather than the end of class as a key determinant of people's life-chances. In other words, differences within classes rather than between them have become more important. People's life-styles as well as their ages frequently cross-cut matters of economic class so that reading off a person's social position becomes a much more complex and hazardous process than it ever was in 1900 and 1950. The essence of class – how people are connected into the system of production, consumption and exchange – has not disappeared, but class has undoubtedly changed its shape and form. Compared with the rest of the UK, Scotland has marginally fewer rich and more poor people, though the territorial similarities are much greater than the differences.

The overall shape of the social class structure in modern Scotland is now quite different than it was even in mid-century. The traditional working class of manual workers is now barely 40 per cent of the labour force, while professional and administrative workers – the 'service' class – is over 30 per cent. Around a quarter of workers are in 'intermediate' non-manual occupations, largely clerical, and comprise mainly women. By the late twentieth century, there were far more people working in health and social work (around one in eight), while only one in fifty work in agriculture, forestry or fishing.

The transformation of the Scottish economy – and with it, society – began perforce in the 1930s with the failure of much of traditional industry. In the inter-war period, the designation of Scotland as an area in need of economic diversification saw the creation of the Scottish Economic Committee. While the old dynastic families retained control of traditional industry, foreign and English capital began to play a much greater role in Scottish economic affairs. The post-war period saw the 'decline of the Scottish capitalist class, from the self-made local businessman, to the dynasties of the Clyde' (Fry, 1987: 193).

The transformation of the Scottish economy aided and abetted by the state in the form of the Scottish Office helped to foster a pattern of policy networks (Moore and Booth, 1989: 29) in which the values and culture of decision-making elites were promoted by 'a close-knit community where high level of individual contact is possible' (ibid.). Central to this policy network were bodies such as the CBI in Scotland, the Scottish Trades Union Congress, the

Scottish Council (Development and Industry), and the Scottish Development Agency, later called Scottish Enterprise. This level of consensus, or 'meso-corporatism' helped to produce a post-war economy which would have been unrecognisable to our time-traveller.

Scotland, in other words, is now a 'middle-class' society, in terms of what people do for a living. It is also a much more open society, with considerable amounts of upward social mobility. Since 1945, each generation has been able to count on being in better-paid occupations than those of its parents. Occupational mobility between generations is now commonplace, with a substantial proportion of the 'service class' drawn from manual working-class backgrounds. This has made for a much more socially diverse upper stratum, a feature which Scotland shares with other advanced industrial societies, and aided by the sheer expansion in middle-class jobs in the second half of the twentieth century. The manual working class, on the other hand, in part because it is diminishing in size, is much more homogeneous and self-recruiting – and working class in its social origins. The changing shape of Scotland's class structure, with many more middle-class jobs than before, helps to explain why there is considerable upward mobility into the top social classes, but very little downward mobility into the working class. Indeed, Scotland is a more open society in the late 1990s than it ever was, even in the 1970s.

The key reason for this social mobility was the expansion in educational opportunity. The abolition of selection for different types of secondary school had been much easier to effect in Scotland than in England, in part because 'comprehensive' schools had long been a feature of its towns in particular. It was, however, the expansion of higher education which was most marked. By the early 1960s under 10 per cent of the school-age group were in universities or colleges, compared with 25 per cent in the late 1970s, and almost double that by the end of the century. Lindsay Paterson has commented: 'with nearly forty per cent of young people entering higher education, it could be argued that Scotland is closer now than it has ever been to opening its universities to the mass of the people' (1996: 244). While it is true that social-class differentials remain in terms of access to higher education, the expansion of the system seems to have led to a narrowing of these differentials by the 1990s as a result of rising family aspirations in particular.

Social opportunity, however, remains by no means evenly distributed. The chances of middle-class children remaining in their class of origin are disproportionately high. Middle-class families confer on their children considerable cultural capital, most obviously in terms of educational skills and qualifications, which almost guarantees that they will do at least as well in financial and occupational terms as their parents. Access to 'top jobs' continues to be considerably class-skewed, and for women especially the barriers are great. The 'glass ceiling' (the real but opaque barriers to women's mobility) as well as the 'double shift' (the fact that many women with families have domestic as well as employment responsibilities to handle in their lives) help to explain why women in modern Scotland do less well than their male counterparts.

Scotland, to be sure, is little different in these respects from any other advanced industrial society, including England. We should not be surprised at these similarities. Early industrialisation in Britain as a whole, as well as the demise of the peasantry, have shaped occupational structures in a very similar way. While it is true that Scotland has a slightly smaller middle class and a slightly larger manual working class compared with England, the processes of social mobility which have created these structures are very similar on both sides of the Tweed.

What, however, of social differences in Scotland? What, for example, of religious sectarianism, which so marked this country's politics and social life for much of the century? We can safely conclude that by the 1990s Scotland had survived the worst period of economic hardship since the 1930s without a return to the heightened ethno–religious tensions of that decade. Today it is difficult to talk in any meaningful sense of a 'Catholic community' or a 'Protestant community' in present-day Scotland: individuals of all faiths and none now work together, drink together and, most significantly, marry each other. The continuing rivalry between Rangers and Celtic football clubs in what is, essentially, the national pastime of urban males has masked the decline of sectarianism elsewhere in Scottish society. The songs of Glasgow's football terraces represent less than the noise might suggest, for they are, to a great extent, nostalgic echoes of another time and another place. The Rangers–Celtic 'Old Firm' are perhaps the only popular symbols of sectarian division, football elsewhere in Scotland having shed most, or all, of its religious connotations, and the quasi-masonic organisations of both Protestant and Catholic now seem to be placed firmly at the margins of Scottish life. For the majority of Scots, political sectarianism is an irrelevance which belongs firmly in the past. We can see this in the voting behaviours of different religious groups. By mid-century the Conservatives were beginning to lose their hold on Protestant Scots. Processes of secular change and in particular the impact of the Welfare State had loosened working-class attachments to traditional political associations. These processes speeded up as the century progressed. The secularisation of Scotland can be gauged from the fact that whereas in the 1950s eight out of every ten marriages took place in church, by the 1990s there were almost as many civil as religious marriages.

Just as religion has been losing its force as a key emblem of identity and political behaviour, so nationalism has grown in importance. From the 1960s, the Scottish frame of reference figured more centrally as the key dimension in politics. The discovery and exploitation of North Sea oil opened up the political possibility of an alternative, and explicitly Scottish, future. It was no accident that the discovery of oil and the rise of the SNP coincided. From the 1970s, the Scottish National Party was in the right place at the right time, and provided a political alternative in the final quarter of the century when the British settlement began to fail.

At the height of its electoral success in the mid-1970s, the SNP took votes across all social classes, but especially among skilled manual and routine non-manual workers. The 'classless' appeal of the SNP allowed it to present itself as an alternative to the traditional class-based parties. Although the party did well among all social classes in Scotland, its particular appeal in the 1970s was to those who were socially and geographically mobile. The lack of a class connotation for the SNP was perhaps the key appeal to those people who came from working-class origins but no longer did manual jobs. Such people were susceptible to a kind of political perspective which was different from the one with which they had grown up.

There was a shift to a more 'privatised' life-style, in which television provided an appropriate frame of political and social reference. No longer did people take their political values from family-of-origin or peer group, but from the new images and life-styles which the new media offered. Increased affluence coupled with greater family-centredness as people moved away socially and geographically from traditional communities was not unique to Scotland, for these social changes were happening in the rest of the UK and beyond. The rise of the SNP, however, gave these processes a particularly political resonance in Scotland. The party captured the generation who were beginning to vote in the 1970s and 1980s, and who, in England, gravitated to the Conservatives or the Liberals. To say this is not to imply that they had similar political views, for the Scottish frame of reference had generated a new way of doing politics.

The end of the long boom in the early 1970s, coupled with the transformation of Scotland's economy from one dependent on heavy industry founded on imperial markets to a post-industrial economy driven by foreign capital and global markets, ushered in a new economic era. As a by-product of these forces, many of the traditional repositories of labour solidarity were swept away. These were the occupational communities built around single industries like coal-mining, the 'Little Moscows' of Fife and Ayrshire. A new genre of literature grew up as a panegyric to a declining way of working-class life. The novelist William McIlvanney, for example, invented 'Graithnock', an industrial town 'under siege from farmland' – a thinly disguised Kilmarnock. The image is one of communitarianism, 'where so little was owned, sharing became a precautionary reflex'. Even the sectarian rivalries of West of Scotland life are reduced to ritual conflict – 'the whole thing had the quality of a communal action, and had been conducted without rancour'. McIlvanney's novel describes Graithnock in 1914, and by the contemporary period (1985) its decline is obvious: 'When the money went, Graithnock turned funny but not so you would laugh.' The town becomes the past, somewhere to retreat to from the big city (Glasgow), and Graithnock is made to represent 'decaying industrialism', 'an aridity surrounded by the green world, a desert in an oasis'. That description resonated across much of post-industrial central Scotland.

By the late 1970s, the crisis of Labourism, and its challenge by political nationalism, led to an abortive and half-hearted attempt by the government of the day to introduce a measure of Home Rule in the form of 'devolution'. This was too late, even too little, and was caught up in the incoming

Thatcherite revolution which sought to sweep away state dependency and impose the iron rule of markets. This curious amalgam of 'free market, strong state' had a particular impact on Scotland. On the one hand, the Scottish Office which had been founded in the 1880s and which had turned itself a hundred years later into a Scottish semi-state was in the front line of the New Right onslaught. In a country which had turned against the Conservatives as early as the mid-1950s, the attack on the state seemed as much an attack on Scotland itself. By the 1990s, only a quarter of Scots were voting Conservative, and by 1997 no Tory MPs whatsoever remained north of the border.

Alongside the decline of the Conservatives went a changing relationship between social class and politics. In the 1997 election, the professional middle classes were more likely to vote Labour than Conservative. Manual workers still voted Labour, though the party's main challenger for the working-class vote was the SNP. In terms of how people defined themselves, however, Scotland still thought of itself as a working-class society. People in Scotland who had been born into working-class families and who had moved into middle-class jobs were much more likely than their counterparts in England to describe themselves as working class. Further, nationality seems for most people to take precedence over social class in determining identity, thereby confirming the importance of the Scottish national dimension.

In the final quarter of the twentieth century, a social-political agenda had emerged in Scotland which was frequently at odds with that of its southern neighbour. By the end of the 1990s people in Scotland saw themselves as more socialist, liberal and less British-national than people in England. Simply put, Scotland had evolved a different agenda, and one which seemed to be growing more different as the decades passed. Defining oneself as a Scot is a way of expressing certain political values. National identity and political values are connected, so that to say that one is Scottish is to say that one has left-of-centre values; and to say that one is British is to assert distinctly more right-of-centre views, largely the opposite of the meaning in England.

By the end of the century, Scotland was renegotiating its place in the Union, or even considering whether the 'marriage of convenience' which had been negotiated in 1707 should hold at all. True, Scots had gained considerable economic and political influence within the imperial framework, but that had long gone. The ideological support systems of unionism, imperialism and Protestantism no longer functioned to bind Scots to the United Kingdom. Scotland's economy too had been transformed and reoriented towards Europe and a post-imperial world. A new Union – a European one – provided an alternative political structure, especially one in which sub-state power-sharing, or 'subsidiarity', appeared to work well in countries like Germany, Spain and even France. The new variable geometry of territorial power involving the European Union, the UK state and Scotland was becoming more significant, reflected in the fact that, like the Welsh, Scots saw in Europe a new Union to augment or even replace the older British one. There were few of the English anxieties concerning the loss of political sovereignty in a country which had to trade off its independent parliament in return for a considerable measure of economic and political benefit. The long march from British imperial integration had virtually ended.

Conclusion

What are we to make of this modern Scotland? Looking back over the century it seems apt to invoke L. P. Hartley's comment: 'The past is a foreign country: they do things differently there.' Scotland 1900 and Scotland 2000 are, to all intents and purposes, foreign countries. Consider the fictional words spoken by Lewis Grassic Gibbon's minister at the Kinraddie memorial to the dead of the Great War at the end of his novel *Sunset Song*: 'A new generation comes up that will know them not, except as a memory in a song, they with the things that seemed good to them with loves and desires that grow dim and alien in the days to be.' The Revd Mr Colquhoun was referring to the 'old Scotland that perished then', the 'last of the peasants, the last of the old Scots folk'. The peasants, of course, have gone, driven to the wall by economic and technological change of the twentieth century, but so too are the old certainties of working-class and bourgeois life.

So what has Scotland become? In essence, it is a northern European country which has outgrown its junior partner role in British imperialism. Empire no more. Possibly Britain no more. While few Scots (as yet) claim to be European (around one in ten), being British is a secondary identity to being Scottish. Feeling British is now mainly a descriptor of those of pensionable age, who remember the Second War and the creation of the Welfare State. Feeling British is becoming a matter of memory, of history, rather than of the future. The young by and large do not feel British, except in so far as it says so on their passports. Being British has become a matter of speaking, not a matter of feeling.

If Britishness is eroding, then is Scottishness a substitute? There are those who will point out that Scotland is a divided country: they point to region (north/south, east/west, Highland/Lowland), to religion, to gender, to class, and to race. Scotland remains a country of 'city-states' with distinctive identities and cultures – Aberdeen, Dundee, Edinburgh and Glasgow – and while they are no longer as demographically dominant as they once were, the cities wield considerable economic and cultural pull, and most of the Scottish population lives in their hinterlands. Like the United States, but unlike England, Scotland's main daily newspapers are city rather than nationally based. Over the course of the century, the fortunes (and populations) of Glasgow and Dundee have waned, and those of Edinburgh and Aberdeen have grown. Glasgow, erstwhile second city of empire, was twice the size of the capital city in 1900. By the 1990s, it was barely a third bigger, and on present trends will be the same size as Edinburgh by the second decade of the twenty-first century. All the cities, however, have lost populations to smaller towns and even to rural areas, where the phenomenon of counter-urbanisation has been strongest. The island of Skye, for example, has seen one the biggest proportional increases in population in Scotland in the past two decades of the century, as people – from Scotland and beyond – sought out a better way of life.

Scotland at the end of the twentieth century remained a society which exported its people, but in nothing like the numbers of the 1920s, 1950s and 1960s. Scottish emigration counted as one of the largest outflows of population in the Western world before the Great War, and the Commonwealth countries continued to attract many thereafter. The lack of substantial in-migration in the second half of the century resulted in Scotland's population falling as a proportion of that of the UK. Only one person in a hundred living in Scotland in the 1990s belonged to an ethnic minority, compared with one in four in London. Around 10 per cent of the Scottish population was born elsewhere, of which the largest number – 7 per cent – came from England. The claim from some quarters that Scotland was becoming 'anglicised' foundered on the evidence that English incomers were much more likely to 'go native', and to end up sharing the political and social habits of native Scots. As the century drew to a close, debates about whether or not Scots were racist in their treatment of either the English or non-English in-migrants were given a new context by the changing political and constitutional position in Scotland.

Scotland in the new millennium: how are we to sum it up? It is a society transformed by the twentieth century in economic, social and cultural terms. Its history left it the legacy of an open economy which started the century as the maker of ships and engineering for the world. By the century's end, it was providing world markets with a disproportionate share of its new technologies, notably silicon chips, but unlike ships, it was not inventing them. Scotland remained a society shaped by class, but one in which it was easier than it had ever been to cross class barriers by means of education. Scotland's masculinist cultures of work, politics and leisure were on the defensive. Workers were now mainly women. Girls were outperforming boys in the classroom. A Scottish parliament had a much higher proportion of women Members of the Scottish Parliament (MSPs) – 37 per cent – than had seemed possible even a few years before. The last redoubts of male leisure culture were under attack from a far less masculinist world and a more privatised family life. Scotland entered the new millennium as a relatively affluent European society, semi-detached from the UK, and better able to sit with other European nations.

In this chapter, we have told the story of Scotland in the twentieth century. The task in subsequent chapters is to put this narrative into a sociological framework by connecting it to the concepts and theories which the discipline makes available. Let us start with the building blocks of sociology, and try to place Scotland within them.

Further reading

For general historical accounts of Scotland in the twentieth century, see the collection edited by T. M. Devine and R. J. Finlay, *Scotland in the Twentieth Century* (1996); and Volume III of *People and Society in Scotland, 1914–1990*, edited by A. Dickson and J. H. Treble (1992). This volume is especially valuable for the chapters by Michael Anderson on population, and Andrew McPherson on education. Lindsay Paterson's chapter on education in Devine and Finlay (op. cit.) is also particularly useful. T. C. Smout's *A Century of the Scottish People, 1830–1950* (1987) remains an outstanding social history of this period. T. M. Devine's *The Scottish Nation, 1700–2000* (1999) is useful on the first period of the twentieth century. C. H. Lee's *Scotland and the United Kingdom: The Economy and the Union in the Twentieth Century* (1995) provides a survey of the economic transition of Scotland. J. Scott and M. Hughes' *The Anatomy of Scottish Capital* (1980) charts the key changes in patterns of business ownership in Scotland in the twentieth century. The Scottish Executive's *Scottish Household Survey* provides invaluable information on contemporary social trends (details are available on http://www.scotland.gov.uk/shs).

For analyses of political change in Scotland, see A. Brown *et al.*, *Politics and Society in Scotland* (1998), A. Brown *et al.*, *The Scottish Electorate* (1999), and L. Paterson *et al.*, *New Scotland, New Politics?* (forthcoming). Lindsay Paterson's *A Diverse Assembly* (1998b) provides the key documents on the debate about a Scottish parliament since 1968.

2   What is Scotland?

As far as the discipline of sociology is concerned, Scotland is largely invisible. The two dominant modes for understanding Scotland have been the historical and the cultural, both focusing on Scotland as 'past'. Much historical work saw Scotland as 'over', because it had lost its formal political independence in 1707, although it had retained its key civil institutions of law, religion and education. The other mode of studying Scotland – the cultural – focused on language, literature and folklore, and formed the basis of another academic speciality. One problem with this division of the intellectual map was that culture has seemed cut off from political, economic and social developments in contemporary Scotland.

The neglect of Scotland by sociology is especially odd because there is a strong case for arguing that the discipline was largely invented here, given that the Scottish Enlightenment founded its knowledge upon sociological assumptions about humankind. Enlightenment thinkers such as Adam Ferguson and Adam Smith wrote histories of 'civil society' based upon their analysis of social structures and social institutions. People, said Ferguson in his famous essay on civil society, are in essence social creatures who derive happiness, ease and a sense of identity as well as security and sustenance from society. While this 'science of man' took in more than the social sciences currently defined, such a science was predicated upon a sociological vision of human nature. Adam Ferguson anticipated the negative effects of the division of labour later identified by Karl Marx. He analysed different forms of society as they were affected by different social structural factors. Histories of the discipline, however, seem to have written out his contribution in favour of the French writer Auguste Comte, who is normally credited with founding sociology in 1838. Ferguson's sociological ideas were themselves subsumed in the minds of later generations into the dominant, and more optimistic, school of classical economy associated with Adam Smith and the Scottish Enlightenment, and social ideas were lost in the welter of a more individualistic and economistic theory of society.

Scotland does not fit the mainstream orthodoxies of modern sociology, for it is not a 'society' in the conventional sense. To put it simply, Scotland is not a state. As Norbert Elias observed: 'Many twentieth century sociologists when speaking of "society" no longer have in mind, as did their predecessors, a "bourgeois society" or a "human society" beyond the state, but increasingly the somewhat diluted image of a nation-state' (1978: 241). Hence, sociologists talk of 'British society', 'American society' and so on, for these are meaningful abstractions which short-circuit the analytical problem of what, in sociological rather than political terms, a society actually is. This essentially modern view of society is somewhat at odds with an older meaning. The historic task of sociology was to analyse 'society', to understand how social systems operate and lay down rules and procedures for people within them. This is much closer to the way the term was used by writers such as Adam Ferguson. Upper-case 'Society' in this sense operates at a higher level of abstraction than the nation-state – which one might call lower-case 'society'. The specificities of actual or 'real' societies can thus be ignored in favour of broad similarities between them. Hence, as Elias comments, sociologists have talked about 'human society', or 'industrial society' or 'capitalist society' and so on. In this perspective, the common features of societies are deemed to have much more theoretical or predictive importance than their specific features.

In practice, however, the distinction between upper-case 'Society' and lower-case 'society' is hard to maintain. In the early 1980s, the French sociologist Alain Touraine commented:

> The abstract idea of society cannot be separated from the concrete reality of a national society, since this idea is defined as a network of institutions, controls and education. This necessarily refers us back to a government, to a territory, to a political collectivity. The idea of society was and still is the ideology of nations in the making.
>
> (Touraine, 1981: 5; my translation)

Other sociologists have suggested that 'society' is far too problematic a term and should be jettisoned. Michael Mann goes as far as to say: 'It may seem an odd position for a sociologist to adopt; but if I could, I would abolish the concept "society" altogether' (1986: 2). Using the term 'society', he says, generates two problems. On the one hand, as we have seen, most accounts simply equate polities or states with 'societies'. As a result, Mann comments: 'the enormous covert influence of the nation-state of the late nineteenth and early twentieth centuries on the human sciences means that a nation-state model dominates sociology and history alike' (ibid.). On the other hand, the term 'society' implies a unitary social system, but, he says, 'we can never find a single bounded society in geographical or social space' (ibid.: 1). In other words, even nation-states are not 'bounded totalities'.

How then are we to treat 'society'? Mann argues that society should be treated not so much as a unitary concept implying internal homogeneity, rather as a 'loose confederation', as 'overlapping networks of social interaction'. Hence, a society is a unit within whose boundaries social interaction is relatively dense and stable, and while interactions will take place across these boundaries, those taking place within it are the most significant and consistent. Let us ask ourselves, then, what society we live in. We may inhabit different levels such as 'Western society' or 'capitalist society', as well as 'British society', 'French society' and so on, which represent the state species of the former. To do so is to imply that the so-called 'national' level (a problematic term as we shall see later) is the real, or most important, interaction network. That, however, may well not be the end of the matter. What if the sub-state level proved to be more important than the state level? What too if social, economic and cultural networks were operating above the state level, even drawing power away from it? To be more explicit and relevant to our purposes in this book, what if the significant level of social boundedness was Scotland rather than the United Kingdom? Further, what might the impact be of more power gravitating to the supra-state level as well, in this case the European Union? What if 'British society' has been hollowed out in sociological terms so that other levels of society, sub- and supra-state, have become more important?

What is happening in the United Kingdom may well be a particular version of a wider process. The conventional nation-state, as a self-contained and bounded social system, has been losing its *raison d'être* in the modern world. In political terms, the argument goes, the nation-state is too small to solve the major problems, and yet too large to be sensitive to smaller ones (McGrew, 1992: 87). The nation-state is under pressure to cede decision-making power upwards to supranational bodies such as the European Union and the International Monetary Fund, as well as downwards to regional or national units seeking greater control over their own affairs. Such political pressures are connected with economic and cultural forces most commonly described as 'globalisation'. The ability of national politicians to manipulate the levers of economic power in the interests of the 'national' economy begin to fail as transnational corporations and supranational organisations assert their considerable and growing influence. In military terms, too, the capacity of the nation-state to control its own means of destruction and defence – its *raison d'état* – is eroding in a nuclear world. Similarly, a simple association of the nation-state with a national culture – the essence of nationalism – has loosened considerably under multicultural and multi-ethnic pressures. In short, in economic, political and cultural terms, the capacity of the nation-state to control its own affairs, to operate in sociological terms as a self-contained society, has begun to seem less sure.

The easy equivalence of state and society seems increasingly redundant. This presents sociology with considerable difficulties. Sociologists can still speak of 'society' in the abstract, as reflecting the broad, common patterns in all or most human societies, especially so since the collapse of communism in central and eastern Europe has removed 'socialist society', at least for the present. To some, of course, this redundancy is long overdue. Michael Mann's view is that 'societies are much messier than our theories of them' (1986: 4). On reflection, much of Western post-war sociology was ethnocentric, based on the imputed characteristics common to all societies described as 'developed'.

What the United States did today, for example, the rest of the (developed) world would do tomorrow. Where the south of England led, the rest of Britain would follow. This washing out of specificities, of what made societies different rather than similar, was not simply a reflection of post-war socio-political realities, but quite fundamental to the sociological project. As Gianfranco Poggi pointed out: 'The notion of society as normally used in sociological argument reflects historically distinctive circumstances associated with the advent of modernity' (1990: 182).

Modernisation and modernity have been quite fundamental to sociology. The discipline's founding fathers, notably the trinity of Marx, Weber and Durkheim, had set out to explain how societies became 'modern', whether in capitalist, bureaucratic or industrial forms respectively. In Krishan Kumar's words, 'all lived, wrote and theorised under the overwhelming impression that "a terrible beauty was born"' (1978: 54). In essence, sociology came into existence to make sense of the 'great transformation' to modern industrial society. Modernisation represented the process by which 'traditional' societies achieved modernity. Hence, in economic terms, improved technology, the growth of commerce and an increasing division of labour in industry were matched by urbanisation, the extension of literacy and the decline of traditional authority. In essence, industrialism and modernity were treated as the same thing. 'To become modern was to go through the process of industrialisation, which is to say, to arrive at something like the state of society envisaged in the sociologist's image of industrialism' (ibid.: 111).

These economic processes of modernisation were matched by political changes, notably the extension of the franchise and the binding of the population to the allegiance of the state. Processes of industrialisation and democratisation went together as part of a larger movement towards the 'nationalisation' of society. Virtually all individuals living within the borders of the state were identified with a national political order, usually because they had rights as citizens. In its classical form, the nation-state claimed the notion of sovereignty, namely that it had supreme authority over the territory which it did not share with another power. The population was bound to the nation-state by means of the ideology of nationalism through which people developed an emotive identity with this sovereign community. Classical sociology saw nationalism, albeit implicitly, as the ideological cement which held complex industrial societies together, as the new secular religion of the modern state. In this scheme of things, modern society was industrial, a vast productive enterprise, whose political expression was the nation-state which provided citizenship rights for the population and demanded its national allegiance in return. By the mid-twentieth century, sociologists were struck by the sameness of the industrialisation process, by the similarities between those societies deemed to be industrial and modern. As Kumar pointed out: 'It appeared that the Western model of industrialism in its 20th century form was in the process of vanquishing all other competing models, and increasingly standing out as the common feature of the whole globe' (1978: 181).

By the late 1960s the general and particular versions of modernisation theories of social change were being challenged. The notions that all societies were undergoing convergence and that differences between capitalist and socialist countries no longer mattered came under attack. Some writers had begun to argue that the notion of 'industrial' society was being superseded by a 'post-industrial' one in which knowledge had become the new capital, post-scarcity had overcome want, and service industry had come to replace manufacturing as the key form of production. While some critics argued that post-industrialism was a very unspecified term, and seemed to involve simply adding another stage to the industrialising process, it was clear that old certainties were falling away, and that new questions were being asked. Post-industrial theorising was valuable 'more for re-opening certain questions to do with social change than for supplying much help in answering them' (Kumar, 1978: 239).

'Modernisation' also became a questionable concept. It was thoroughly and implicitly ethnocentric, based on developments in the West, but it was plain that by the 1970s it did not lead to automatic economic growth, particularly in the Third World countries seeking to catch up with the developed West. As an already industrialised society, Scotland seemed to offer little to this perspective. Nevertheless, by the 1970s, a burgeoning sociology of development had lent a new perspective on Scotland. Some argued that abiding economic inequalities between England and Scotland might well be explained by obstacles placed in the way of 'development' by economic and political structures, notably the concentration of economic resources in the south-east of England and the United States, and the absence of political autonomy north of the border. These new perspectives in the 1970s appeared to offer a way out of the traditional sociological blindness about Scotland, and to fuse a concern with the 'branch-plant' syndrome whereby much of Scottish industry was controlled furth of its boundaries with the resurgence of political nationalism in the late 1960s and early 1970s.

By the 1980s, much of the debate about the sociology of Scotland focused upon the extent of similarities and differences with the rest of the UK. This was a debate not simply about how to interpret the welter of statistics on industrial, occupational and social change in general, but more fundamentally about which sociological model best fitted Scotland. It was a debate which ran across the traditional boundaries between sociology and history, a relationship which had always been close, in the search for appropriate data and models to fit them. Above all, it served to confront sociology with the 'problem' of Scotland. Students in particular wanted to understand Scotland sociologically, and there was a feeling that the old models had failed. Much of the conventional wisdom had produced an 'us-too' sociology of Scotland, one which focused on its similarities with other countries, notably England. Instead, there was a new 'not-us' sociology, stressing the differences rather than the similarities. Scotland was 'different', critics claimed, because it followed a different trajectory of economic and social development; that was why the 'colonial' metaphor was so powerful in the 1970s and 1980s. Whatever the truth or otherwise of such claims, Scotland was beginning to appear on the sociological map.

By the1990s, the classical paradigms of sociology associated with modernity were further undermined. The critique of post-industrialism may have beaten off one assault, but the fundamental weakness remained, only to be attacked again under the label of late- or post-modernity. If the modernity thesis had stressed scientific rationality, post-modernity emphasised the erratic and unpredictable nature of much social behaviour. Modernity had associated itself with industrialism and organised capitalism; post-modernity focused on consumerism and 'disorganised' capitalism. Modernity had aligned the national economy, polity and culture in such a way that citizenship and allegiance to the sovereign state provided clear and unambiguous identity. Post-modernity, on the other hand, pointed up the limited nature of state sovereignty in an increasingly interdependent world, and highlighted the competing identities on offer. The plethora of new social movements with their limited and often shifting aims contrasted with the predictability of class-based movements associated with modernity. The broadening of politics beyond the narrowly material were but symptoms of major shifts in late twentieth-century societies. Economic and social changes, it was argued, were leading to a radical redefinition of politics. Social movements, as Alberto Melucci (1989) described them, no longer operated as characters, to use a theatrical metaphor, but as forms of symbolic challenge, with the consequence that traditional labels like Right and Left became increasingly vacuous.

Critics like Melucci were arguing that a new trans-societal order was emerging in which traditional nation-states were losing their purpose:

> The decline of the nation-state is not due to socialism (the myth of the abolition of the state), but because nation-states are losing their authority: from above, a global, multinational political and economic interdependence moves the centre of decision-making elsewhere; from below, the multiplication of autonomous centres of decision-making gives 'civil societies' a power they never had during the development of modern states.
> (Melucci, 1989: 86–7)

The multiplication of contacts and the constant flow of messages was steadily destroying the homogeneity of individual cultures, and the media and mass tourism were eroding specific traditional cultural practices. On the other hand, ethnicity did not wither, but revived as a source of identity to meet new emergent needs. It was well placed to do this because it had dual significance. Ethnic or national movements exposed problems relating to the structure of complex societies, while they were also rooted in history. Melucci commented:

> Unless we link their appearance with the transformations of complex societies, they become simple historical by-products of the process of

nation-building or incidental events in the narrative of international relations. If on the other hand we ignore their origins in 'national questions' and in their conflict with the states, we risk reducing them to mere cultural appeals in the name of diversity'.

(Ibid.: 91)

This new sociological agenda in the 1990s with its emphasis on post-modern diversity brought a new dimension to the study of Scotland. The resurgence of nationalism in Scotland and elsewhere came to be seen not as in direct contradiction to increasing globalisation of economic, political and cultural power, but as part of that process itself. While ethno-nationalisms are plainly rooted in the past, they also highlight continuing societal transformation and discontinuity. These are general processes at work in the contemporary world, but they forefront Scotland in a novel and interesting way. In other words, far from the survival of Scotland as a nation, and the assertion of nationalism being a leftover from an earlier age, these were central concerns of the age. The fact that Scotland was a nation without a state in the conventional sense did not relegate it to being an odd anomaly. Rather, Scotland became a prime example of those fissiparous tendencies threatening to remake the world political and social order, an order in which the correspondence between states, societies and nations was far less clear-cut. In other words, it could be argued that Scotland stands at the forefront of sociological concerns at the start of the twenty-first century. Instead of being an awkward and ill-fitting case, it moved to the centre of the discipline's post-modern dilemma concerning the autonomy and boundedness of societies.

How then are we to understand Scotland? At first glance, this may seem like a non-problem, because at a common-sense level Scotland plainly exists. It is a territory, a place on a map with a long historical pedigree, even with an ancient border which distinguishes it from its southern neighbour, England. To treat Scotland as in any way problematic might seem to many to be academic play-acting. Yet, as we have seen, Scotland as a meaningful sociological category is problematic. Put simply, if only nation-states are societies, and if sociology is the science of society, can we have a sociology of Scotland?

The challenge for the sociologist in analysing Scotland lies in assessing its claim to be a society in a meaningful sense. 'Scotland' exists at different levels of meaning, not all of them of central interest to the sociologist, but each with some sociological content. At its most basic, Scotland refers to a geographical place, a territory on a map, a collection of rocks, earth and water, defined by its topography, its climate and natural resources. Lest we dismiss this level as unimportant to a sociological account, let us remind ourselves of the ways these elements are central to our image of Scotland. Scotland as land of mountain and flood is captured in literature and mobilised by the tourist industry in its representations of Scotland. Above all, it is a powerful landscape of the mind, which carries potent resonances for cultural as well as political action.

Scotland as country

Deciding whether or not Scotland is a society is bound up with other notions of what Scotland is. For example, in the search for relevant terms, many who would hesitate to call it a society or even a nation might be quite content to refer to it as a 'country' This seems a neutral enough term referring to place or territory. 'Country', however, carries its own set of meanings. Raymond Williams pointed out that:

> 'country' can mean both a nation and part of a land; the 'country' can be the whole society as well as its rural area. In the long history of human settlements, this connection between the land from which directly or indirectly we all get our living and the achievements of human society has been deeply known.
>
> (Williams, 1973: 1)

'Country', in other words, has come to stand for the essential values and images of place, hence the fusion of land and nation.

The historian Simon Schama has argued that national identity would lose much its 'ferocious enchantment' without the mystique of a particular landscape tradition: that is, 'its topography mapped, elaborated, and enriched as a homeland' (1996: 15). This process may involve taking liberties with landscape. Schama reminds us that the engravings by the eighteenth-century artist Paul Sandby of a view in Strathtay in Scotland showed a marked increase in the elevation of the mountains between 1747 and 1780 to conform to expectations of what mountains should be like. Imagining the nation implies that it has a picture, and Schama argues that landscapes are culture before they are nature, that they are constructs of the imagination projected on to wood and water and rock. German culture was seen as rooted in its native soil, and such a vision drove Herder, the romantic nationalist, to view the essence of the nation as organically rooted in the topography, customs and communities of the local native tradition (ibid.: 102). Schama observes that in England the mythic memory of 'greenwood freedom' was prime material for nineteenth-century novels, including Walter Scott's *Ivanhoe* in which Anglo-Saxon rural liberties were contrasted with Norman tyranny. He comments: 'The forest as the opposite of court, town and village – the sylvan remnant of arcady, or what Shakespeare called the "golden world" – was an idea that would lodge tenaciously in the poetic and pious imagination' (ibid.: 142).

Just as the idealised England is essentially a rural idyll, a place, where country and Country come together, so the 'real' Scotland (and Wales and Ireland for that matter) is in essence rural: 'Welsh Wales', and the Gaeltachd in Scotland and in Ireland are deemed to be the heartland of the nation, and are promoted as such by the tourist industry. Central to identity is the sense of place: in other words, *where* is Scotland? Scottish culture has adopted, or had thrust upon it, a 'Gaelic vision'. Malcolm Chapman (1978) has shown how, as Scotland was becoming industrialised in the late eighteenth century, and its lowlands became much like other urbanised and industrialised regions, so the symbols, myths and tartans of the Highlands were appropriated by lowland Scots, notably Sir Walter Scott, in a bid for some distinct culture. The irony was that the part of Scotland which had been reviled as barbarian, backward and savage found itself extolled as the 'real' Scotland – land of tartan, kilts and heather.

Scotland as 'country', then, is a landscape of the mind, a place essentially of the imagination. This has made Scotland much easier to market by the tourist industry, as a 'land out of time', as an 'enchanted fortress in a disenchanted world' (Rojek, 1993: 181). The point is that tourist Scotland is an imaginary place. There is little point in visiting a country that looks like the one back home. Scotland has a major feature to play as 'country', its association with wilderness. 'Wilderness', as a version of 'nature', is the antithesis of 'culture'. We know, of course, that much of this conception of wilderness was actually fabricated, that it is a social construction of the late eighteenth century. Recall the representation of the Highland landscape by Paul Sandby. His second engraving, thirty years after the first, has higher mountains, more rugged terrain, and a man in a kilt is added to compound authenticity. What was taken to be a barren and desolate landscape of mid-century becomes a romantic and tragic icon of the late eighteenth century. The representation of the Highlands of Scotland as a people-less place, in spite of the lonely kilted figure, is the direct outcome of social forces which cleared people from the land in favour of sheep and deer, or simply nothingness. By the end of the eighteenth century, the Highlands were reinvented as a scenic game park filled with 'nature' and its game, but devoid of people. So powerful is this reinvention that we struggle to see the Highlands in any other way. They have, in Womack's words, been 'colonised by an empire of signs' (1989: 1). He observes that the Highlands as we know them are the result of a process 'at an identifiable point in time, in response to specific requirements and contradictions which are both exhibited and disguised by its eventual form' (ibid.: 2).

Accounts of Scotland are disproportionately dominated by this Highland, romanticised view of the country. The late Marinell Ash, in her book *The Strange Death of Scottish History*, accused Scots of a historical failure of nerve:

> The time that Scotland was ceasing to be distinctively and confidently her-self was also the period when there grew an increasing emphasis on the emotional trappings of the Scottish past . . . its symbols are bonnie Scotland of the bens and glens and misty shieling, the Jacobites, Mary Queen of Scots, tartan mania and the raising of Scottish statuary.
>
> (Ash, 1980: 10)

Ash was arguing that as Scotland was losing its distinctiveness, so it appropriated that which flourished in the currency of the late eighteenth-century Romantic movement – the Gaelic vision. These images have in turn become vital to the modern tourist vision of Scotland. The result was that whereas in the eighteenth century the Highlands had been invested with the symbolism of the exotic, the foreign, so by the end of that century all of Scotland was being colonised by that sign. Womack comments:

> Processes which promoted capitalist accumulation in the lowlands through economic integration with England simultaneously exaggerated Highland difference. . . . For the Scottish bourgeoisie, therefore, the Highlands had the aspect of a residual historical nation. So the Highlands acquired the role of representing Scotland 'for the English'.
>
> (Womack, 1989: 148)

One might add the rider that lowland Scots too were happy to acquire the role for themselves, despite the considerable irony that Highlanders had long been reviled by them as barbaric and savage (Hunter, 1999). Nevertheless, Scotland as a whole settled for a Celtic definition of itself in contradistinction to England, so that 'the face that Scotland turns to the rest of the world is, in many respects, a Highland face' (Chapman, 1978: 9). The end of the eighteenth century, then, was a crucial period in the 're-invention' of Scotland and the accoutrements of Highland imagery, which was reinforced by the likes of Walter Scott in the early decades of the nineteenth century. Scotland, and the Highlands in particular, became the focus for the 'rediscovery' of the wilderness. By the 1880s, visitors were remarking that 'the farther we went, the more we were reminded that to travel in Scotland is to travel through the Waverley novels' (M. MacArthur, 1993: 23).

What we are dealing with here is what Cosgrove has called 'terrains of power' (1994). He comments: 'Nature, landscape and environment are semiotic signifiers, deeply embedded in the cultural constitution of individual European nations, and integral to the distinctive identities of Europe's "peoples"' (p. 18). In other words, imagining the nation conjures up landscape signs of considerable cultural power (let us recall the example Schama gave of forests and Germanness). Each nation has an 'imagined geography' which acts as a physical representation of the Country as country. 'Nature' and 'nation' are closely bound together. In particular, as Cosgrove points out: 'Welsh and Scottish nationalisms have constructed their own meaning from mountain landscapes, valleys and glens, drawing as heavily on the natural world as upon their separate language to construct differences from England' (ibid.). This imagining of Scotland and Wales as lands of mountain and flood has helped to foster different versions of community from England which nourish distinctive national feelings.

It is significant, then, that in both Scotland and Wales the 'land' question is a live one, that the issue of land ownership and use has the capacity to mobilise political debate. For example, the first Scottish government elected in May 1999 let it be known that land reform was to be one of its key priorities, something which in England would cause considerable puzzlement. The Edinburgh

Parliament was drawn to the 'land' question in large part because it carries a political charge in defining what Scotland is. Calling for the democratisation of Scotland concerns itself with 'land' which is so fundamentally part of national identity. That is in part because it stands for the nation, for 'Scotland'. It is also because in Scotland the land question has never quite been settled. Again, it was Raymond Williams who pointed out that in Scotland, as in Wales and Ireland, the 'land' question somehow had never lost its cutting edge in politics.

The debate which is generated around land can be thought of as a form of 'discourse', namely the production of knowledge through language, so that we construct a topic in a particular way, and hence limit the other ways in which the topic can be discussed. The idea of discourse conveys the notion that what we may seek to present as 'real', as a one-to-one representation of how and what things are, is merely one way of representing 'reality' and actually carries an implicit set of power relations within it. The French writer Michael Foucault put it this way: 'We should admit that power produces knowledge . . . that power and knowledge directly imply one another; that there is no power relation without the corrective constitution of a field of knowledge, nor any knowledge that does not presuppose and constitute . . . power relations' (Foucault, 1980: 27).

Land and sovereignty in Scotland are intimately connected. In Scotland's feudal system of land tenure, under which nearly all Scotland's land is held, all rights of ownership are vested in the Crown as Paramount Superior (Callander, 1998: 8). All rights of land ownership are deemed to derive from the Crown, which is the ultimate owner in Scotland. As Robin Callander puts it: 'The Crown's identity in Scotland is dependent on the sovereignty of the people and the Crown's status is as the representative of the people or, traditionally, identified, of the Community of the Realm' (ibid.: 30). After all, he (or she) was referred to as King (or Queen) of Scots rather than monarch of Scotland. There is also an early representation of this in the Declaration of Arbroath of 1320 which seemed to give circumspect but limited allegiance to the monarch only on condition that he or she carried out the will of the people.

If Land and land are bound up with each other in Scotland, so one of the key aspects of its geography is vital for imagining the country: its shape. In referring to nations as 'imagined communities', Benedict Anderson argued that the map is to space what the clock is to time, namely a form of representation laden with power implications much as Foucault meant by the term 'discourse'. The effect is to reduce to a 'fact of nature' what is contentious and power loaded. Ways of measuring become the essence of the thing. Thus the clock is to time, and the map is to space, whereas these are simply ways of representing time and space for our purposes. We find it hard not to think of a map as 'of' somewhere, rather than 'for' a purpose. It is only in modern times that we conflate the representation (map or clock) for the concept (space or time). Anderson has pointed out that we have grown thoroughly used to the map as 'logo', as pure sign of the country in outline:

In its shape, the map entered an infinitely reproducible series, available for transfer to posters, official seals, letterheads, magazines and textbook covers, table cloths and hotel walls. Instantly recognisable, everywhere visible, the logo-map penetrated deep into the popular imagination, forming a powerful emblem for the anti-colonial nationalism to be born.

(Anderson, 1996: 175)

Anderson is observing that liberation struggles against occupying powers in the Third World were aided greatly by imagining their country in outline. Where the boundaries of the nation are fuzzy or contested, it becomes harder to rally a people around it; for example, Papuan nationalists only made progress when they agreed to a shared map of the nation in the 1960s. In this context, then, imagining Scotland in outline is easy because its shape has been virtually unchanged for over 500 years, even when it has been part of the bigger state, the United Kingdom. Oddly enough, what is fuzzy is 'Britain'. Whereas Scotland (and Wales) have clear logo-maps, 'Ireland' is more often than not portrayed as the island and not the state (itself a contested political entity). England as such rarely appears in territorial outline, despite Shakespeare's desire to describe it as an island set in a silver sea, a statement of political claim rather than geographical ownership. Maps, then, are more than their geographies, and have often taken on political personification. Maps offer unique and succinct opportunities to capture the essence of a cultural or political case.

Scotland as society

In this chapter, we have already explored the distinction between 'state' and 'society', and noted the tendency to confuse the two concepts such that they become interchangeable. In strict terms, of course, they belong to different realms: the state is in essence a political concept, and society belongs to the social realm. More precisely, society or 'civil society', as we shall call it, refers to those areas of social life, most notably the domestic world, the economy, cultural activities and even local political matters, that are organised by private or voluntary arrangements between individuals and groups outside the direct control of the central state. Society then is composed of an extensive though bounded network of self-activated individuals and groups who are frequently linked into the state but not coterminous with it.

In the modern age, state and society are not entirely independent, but are in fact shaped and maintained in the context of each other, which helps to explain the confusion between them. In effect, the state has encroached on society, and society on the state. Citizens demand more from the state, while in turn the state legitimates itself in terms of this demand. In Poggi's words, some encroachments on the state–society line result not from the state being 'pulled over' the line, as it were, but from its 'pushing' itself over it (1978: 131). This has occurred because the key domains of civil society, the familial/

domestic sphere, and the economy, have become thoroughly politicised. While classically they belonged to the 'private' sphere from which the state was excluded or excluded itself, it is now virtually impossible to disentangle them from the 'public' sphere. The marketplace is no longer self-equilibrating without state intervention in some form, despite the rhetoric of privatisation. After all, business spends a considerable amount of resources ensuring that the state provides a sympathetic environment in which it can operate profitably. In similar vein, the state is involved in the intimacies of domestic life, regulating and policing all forms of family life in a manner unthinkable to our Victorian forebears. The extension of the franchise has brought new pressures to bear on the state, which seeks its justification in meeting the needs of society. The domestic and economic spheres of life are no longer separated from the political realm in any meaningful way. The state does not and cannot stand outside the social, cultural and political relations of society. The empty state, bereft of a responsibility for social affairs, simply does not exist. The state constitutes society as well as being constituted by it.

How does this apply to Scotland? After all, it is not a state, and one might expect that its social institutions had increasingly been subject to rule by the state, in this case the United Kingdom. There is an important truth in this, for more and more of Scottish affairs have come within the ambit of West-minster. It is, however, precisely this greater involvement by the state that has brought about constitutional change in these islands. Put simply, just as the autonomy of Scottish social institutions has been eroded by greater demo-cratic accountability via the political process, so one can interpret the demand for a Scottish parliament precisely as a consequence of this.

What institutions are we referring to? While Scotland traded off its political sovereignty in 1707 in return for access to economic and political influence within the new British state, it retained much of the institutional apparatus of self-government through its different systems of law, the Church and educa-tion. Indeed, one might argue that the only kind of union which could be negotiated was one in which Scottish institutional autonomy was guaranteed. Historians tell us that accepting the Union was a close-run thing (Scott, 1979; Devine, 1999), and if anything, popular sentiment was against the new constitutional settlement for some considerable time. This was not an incorpor-ating Union as such, but a pre-democratic compromise between the English and Scottish political elites. Parliamentary politics were a fairly unimportant sideshow for much of the Union's history. It is highly doubtful if the Scots, even the undemocratic elite, would have agreed to submerge their institutional autonomy into the British state if it had incorporated Scotland into it in a thoroughgoing and modern fashion. In many respects this patrician bargain struck in 1707 allowed Scotland to survive as a sufficiently distinct civil society within the confines of the unitary British state. In Lindsay Paterson's words:

> The Union had left intact all that really mattered to daily life in Scotland in the eighteenth century. . . . the Union was, in Angus Calder's words,

'a rational solution to very dangerous economic and political problems', involving the abandonment of an already highly constrained foreign policy in the interests of maintaining independent control over domestic policy.

(Paterson, 1991: 105)

In many respects, Scotland remained self-governing in terms of its civil institutions, and the British state did not overly interfere except when it perceived the military–political authority of the state to be under threat (as in the Jacobite Rising of 1745–6), or at the behest of Scotland's ruling elites (as in the imposition of the laird's patronage over the appointment of Kirk ministers in 1712). Paterson argues that day-to-day life in Scotland and its governance remained in the hands of Scots, consolidated in the 1832 Scottish Reform Act, and in the setting up of ad hoc governing boards to administer, among others, prisons, Poor Law, health, schools and the crofting counties. These boards were incorporated into the responsibilities of the Scottish Office in 1886, ironically raising the complaint that the last vestiges of Scottish nationhood were thus being eroded. The rights of a distinct society were jealously guarded by those who thoroughly approved of the Union. Thus, Walter Scott in the 1820s strongly objected to a London plan to abolish distinctive Scottish banknotes by invoking the loss of national identity. He wrote: 'I think I see my native country of Scotland, if it is yet to be called by a title so discriminative, falling so far as its national, or rather, perhaps, I ought to say provincial, interests are concerned, daily more into more absolute contempt' (Ash, 1980: 136). Such nationalistic language did not contradict support for the Union, but rather underscored the point that to the Scottish middle classes it was a union of equals, and that London interfered with both banknotes and Union at its peril. The result was that Scottish banks retained the right to issue their own notes, something which strikes visitors to Scotland today as distinctive and a little odd. It is as if Scotland were an independent country but without an independent parliament.

As democracy slowly made its way into the governing structures of these islands in the nineteenth century, so it helped to consolidate Scottish civil society. The remarkable growth of separate political administration for Scotland since 1886 has undoubtedly helped to reinforce the sense of 'Scotland'. It is easier to visualise what a separate Scotland would look like precisely because by the 1980s the Scottish Office had become a Scottish semi-state with a powerful administrative apparatus. The proponents of devolution in the 1979 Referendum could set out their case for political autonomy in terms of the need to extend democratic accountability over this bureaucratic structure. Further, the emergence of distinctively Scottish media agendas from the 1960s rested on the administrative apparatus governing Scotland to which the media could address political issues. Along with law, the Church, education and banking, the media can be ranked as a key civil institution in Scotland which reinforces national identity. After all, the press is often referred to as the 'fourth estate', reflecting its role in social politics in modern societies. By the end of the twentieth century, the Scottish newspapers were being challenged by Scottish editions of London newspapers which themselves were having to address this distinctive agenda by putting out 'tartan' editions.

Throughout the twentieth century, increased agitation for reform in Scotland has resulted in increased responsibilities accruing to the Scottish Office to the extent that de facto Scottish self-government, or 'limited sovereignty' as Paterson calls it, has resulted. The demands for democratic accountability over this 'Scottish semi-state' in the late twentieth century represent recognition of the limits to which bureaucratic devolution was reached, and helped to bring about the devolved parliament in 1999.

At this level, Scotland undoubtedly exists as a political-administrative unit, as a governed system defined by the remit of the Scottish Office. In little over a hundred years of its existence, the Scottish Office has given a political meaning to Scotland. There is irony in this, because by treating Scotland as an object of administration, the Westminster government had to live with its political consequences. If the Scottish Office had never been created, it would have been much more difficult to address 'Scotland' as a meaningful political unit. The northern territory could have been handled as the North British regional province of the central British state, although the power and influence of civil society could never be ignored. What this highlights is that state and civil society are in fact difficult to disentangle. The Scottish Office, for example, was itself the expression of a complex network of social organisations – a Scottish 'civil society' – which have made political demands for democratic control of the bureaucratic machinery of Scottish government so much easier to effect than in, say, the north of England which lacks this administrative framework. Scotland (like Wales) retains important historical and cultural residues of nationhood, but also sufficiently separate networks of interaction around which social and political consciousness can form. Indeed, Scottish civil society was sufficiently strong to bring about a lawmaking parliament with tax-raising powers in contrast to what was on offer in Wales (Paterson and Wyn Jones, 1999).

The concept of civil society has operated in a number of ways in Scotland. It describes the dense networks of voluntary organisations and institutions which result from day-to-day interactions between people. Scotland is Scotland (and not England) in large part because associational life is distinctively Scottish. This is not a new development, for Scotland has always had this density of associational networks which 'Scotticise' everyday social interactions. As democratic accountability has grown in importance in Scotland as elsewhere, so another level of civic institutions has accreted to civil society. These are semi-state bodies, most obviously in the form of 'quangos' or quasi-non-governmental organisations that are to be found in all modern societies. The distinctive features of these is that north of the border these operate according to Scottish rules and with Scottish members. Particularly in the period of agitation for a parliament in the final quarter of the twentieth century, civic institutions became both the substitute for direct democratic accountability, and in turn the means for bringing it about. In other words, setting up non-elected boards was used as a way of buying off political demands, but also became the building blocks on which new democratic structures were erected.

'Civil society' has also had to do considerable political work in Scotland of a rhetorical sort. The political impasse in Scotland whereby the Conservatives were returned to power in the Scottish Office from 1979 until 1997 on the basis of a minority of seats and votes – what came to be called the 'democratic deficit' – helped to bring about the Scottish Constitutional Convention after the 1987 election. The Convention comprised a coalition of bodies in favour of 'Home Rule', including political parties like Labour and the Liberal Democrats who favoured devolution, but also the churches, trade unions, local councils, community and women's groups. Its legitimacy derived from this broad support. Its convener, the churchman Canon Kenyon Wright, captured this alternative source of legitimacy when he remarked in a speech that Mrs Thatcher as UK prime minister might observe: 'We are the state, and we say no (to a Scottish parliament).' Wright replied: 'We are the people, and we say yes.' The term 'people' here was used, rather than 'nation', to capture the breadth of organisational representation in the convention; in other words, to draw upon civil society as the root of political legitimacy.

Even with the election of a democratically elected parliament in 1999, there is still likely to remain tension between the new political institution and Scottish civil society as regards who speaks for Scotland (Paterson, 2000). The vocabulary of 'civil society' remains a powerful one especially in the early years of the new parliament. Significantly, the new Scottish constitutional settlement involves creating a 'Civic Forum' comprising the voluntary sector and voluntary organisations, possibly the business sector and other professional associations. The draft constitution of Civic Forum observed:

> Our vision is that Scottish Civic Forum will break the mould of old-fashioned politics. It will increase participation, find new ways to open up dialogue, raise awareness and stimulate debate on the many challenges facing Scotland. It will have a vital role in creating a more open and broadly based political culture.
>
> (Scottish Council for Voluntary Organisations, 1999: 6)

The implication was that the key role of the Forum was to avoid the political system narrowly defined being able to close down, rather than open up, the channels of communication. In short, this reflects the tension between notions of democracy as representation (through party politics), and democracy as participation (through social renewal).

The key role of civil society in Scotland is that it acts as the hinge between the political realm, the state, and the cultural realm, the nation. In other words, as we shall see in the next section, Scotland is a 'nation' because people identify themselves as Scots. They do so not because there is some ancient folk memory, but because national identity is carried by means of the plethora of associations and organisations we call by way of shorthand 'civil society'. To take an obvious example, a distinct school system encourages people to be Scottish not in any explicit and self-conscious way, but, to use Michael Billig's useful phrase, in a 'banal', that is, implicit way. In short, pupils learn to be Scots simply by being educated in Scottish schools and not because they receive lessons in 'civics'. It is of course the case that some institutional carriers such as the religious system matter far less than they have done in the past. Scotland is, after all, a secular society with relatively low levels of church attendance and affiliation. Nevertheless, the civil institutional apparatus of Scotland, whether it is the education system, the legal system, a distinctive press, financial system and so on, provides a social template which has not only sustained 'Scotland' as an idea, but has given it a social system of governance which only in the final year of the twentieth century reinstituted a formal parliament. Scotland is sustained as a nation through its institutional practices.

Scotland as nation

Whether or not Scotland is a nation evokes strong responses. On the one hand, the political nationalist takes it as axiomatic so that it is a self-evident truth. On the other hand, those who are opposed to political independence point out that there are too many deep and abiding differences across the country to sustain an argument for cultural homogeneity. What we see in this debate is its thoroughly political context. Asking the question seems to require that one reveals political preferences, that nationhood and statehood are inextricably linked. That is not our way here. We are concerned with decoupling these terms so as to argue that it is quite proper to treat Scotland as a nation without implying that it is or should be a state.

Let us take as our starting point the sceptic's view of Scotland as a nation. Put simply, this argues that there is little to distinguish Scotland and England in matters of language and religion, two of the conventional markers of nationality. For example, Benedict Anderson has pointed out that the Union of the two countries in the early eighteenth century came about precisely because of the lack of strong cultural markers, at least between lowland Scotland and England (Anderson, 1996). Others have commented on the considerable cultural diversity of Scotland: north/south; east/west; Highland/Lowland; Catholic/Protestant, etc. (Bruce, 1993), which has conspired to dissipate Scottish national identity, and to erode the case for Scottish self-government. In other words, on the face of it, Scotland seems a poor example of a single, coherent nation, and the lack of formal political independence a reflection of internal conflict.

Such a view, however, fails to take proper account of the difficulties in defining nations at all. The historical sociologist Charles Tilly commented: '"Nation" remains one of the most puzzling and tendentious items in the political lexicon' (1975: 6). The question 'What is a nation?' is the title of a famous lecture by Ernest Renan in 1882. He asked: Why is Holland a nation, and Hanover not? How did France continue as a nation when the dynastic principle which created it was swept away after the revolution? Why is Switzerland, with three languages, three religions and three or four 'races', a nation when Tuscany is not? Why, he asked, is Austria a state but not a nation?

Renan examined in turn the 'objective' bases of nations. It is plain, he said, that in modern nations blood is mixed, whereas in the tribes and cities of antiquity it was not. Nations, then, are not defined by 'race', though, most notoriously in Hitler's Germany it did not stop people trying to make it so. Just as race cannot define nations, neither can language, religion, physical or material interests. There are nations which speak the same language as their oppressors. English was the main language of nationalism in India and Ireland, despite the misgivings of some indigenous nationalists, and their failure to eradicate it from use. Max Weber pointed out that many states have more than one language group, and a common language is often insufficient to sustain a sense of national identity (Weber, 1978: 395–6). Neither can religion supply a sufficient basis for nationalism despite its ideological power. There is no simple mapping of God on to nation.

Nor is the nation defined by its economic boundaries. Material factors cannot be discounted, but, as Renan observed, 'a Zollverein [customs union] is not a patrie' (Renan, in Eley and Suny, 1996: 51). While material and economic interests cannot be ignored, there is more to nationalism than this. Chateaubriand commented: 'Men do not allow themselves to be killed for their interests; they allow themselves to be killed for their passions' (quoted in Connor, 1994: 206). Finally, 'nation' is not a matter of geography, of rivers, mountains, soil, for these ignore the fact that the nation 'is a spiritual family not a group determined by the shape of the earth' (ibid.: 52).

So, what is required? Renan observed that the nation is in essence a 'soul', a spiritual principle, a kind of moral conscience. He concludes: 'A nation is therefore a large-scale solidarity, constituted by the feeling of sacrifices that one has made in the past and of those one is prepared to make in the future' (ibid.: 53). Benedict Anderson shared Renan's view of these things when he defined the nation as 'an imagined community'. Like Renan, he took a 'spiritual' view of these things. In essence, says Anderson, the nation is an imagined political community, in the following ways (Anderson, 1996: 6–7).

- 'It is *imagined* because the members of even the smallest nation will never know most of their fellow-members, meet them, or even hear of them, yet in the minds of each lives the image of their communion.'
- 'The nation is imagined as *limited* because even the largest of them, encompassing perhaps a billion living human beings, has finite, if elastic boundaries, beyond which lie other nations.'
- 'It is imagined as *sovereign* because the concept was born in an age in which Enlightenment and Revolution were destroying the legitimacy of the divinely-ordained hierarchical dynastic realm.'

- 'It is imagined as a *community*, because, regardless of the actual inequality and exploitation that may prevail in each, the nation is always conceived as a deep, horizontal comradeship.'

Anderson is not saying that the nation is 'imaginary, but 'imagined'. He rebukes Ernest Gellner for his famous line that 'nationalism is not the awakening of nations to self-consciousness; it invents nations where they do not exist' (1964: 169). Anderson points out here that Gellner confuses 'invention' with 'fabrication' and 'falsity' rather than 'imagining' and 'creation'; in other words, the nation is imagined rather than imaginary. Anderson talks of nations being 'imagined communities' because they require a sense of belonging which is both horizontal and vertical, in place and in time. The 'nation' not only implies an affinity with those currently living, but with dead generations. The idea of the nation is to be conceived of, says Anderson, 'as a solid community moving steadily down (or up) history' (1983: 31). This idea of historical continuity is a vitally important part of the nation as imagined community. It implies links with long dead ancestors, and in Anthony Smith's words, 'the nation becomes the constant renewal and retelling of our tale by each generation of our descendants' (1986: 208).

There can be little doubt of the ideological power of 'Scotland' as a nation in these terms. It implies that Scotland is not simply a collection of rocks, earth and water, but a transcendent idea which runs through history, reinterpreting that history to fit the concerns of each present. In this respect, it is not unique. To say that Scotland (or Wales, Ireland or England for that matter) are 'figments of the imagination' is not to imply that they are 'false', but that they have to be interpreted as ideas, made and remade, rather than simply as actual 'places'. Above all, they are places of the mind. In this regard, the term 'the Scottish people' implies a historical idea stretching back over centuries, implying that fourteenth-century peasants and twentieth-century workers share some crucial identity. Nor is this unique to Scotland.

Consider the phrases 'the English people' or 'the German people'; these do not simply refer to those who inhabit the territory at one point in time, but to those who live elsewhere, and crucially those who once did (in 'history'). Such phrases have been used to include as well as exclude those who are deemed not to 'belong' – those born elsewhere, those whose racial or ethnic characteristics are not accepted. Most obviously in the German case, the nation is not coterminous with the state, because until 1990 there were two states, to say nothing of those 'ethnic Germans' who live in other states and who claim some linguistic or cultural affinity.

In the Scottish case, it presents problems of definition of those who would claim 'ancestry' some generations ago, over against those living but not born in Scotland. The Welsh case shows nicely how conceptualising the 'nation' can be time-bound and historically constructed. The late nineteenth century saw the remaking of 'Wales' as an ideological device for rousing 'the people' against the dominant foreigner – the English who were 'stealing the land'

(Williams, 1980). In this context, language became a crucial 'cultural identifier' in Gellner's phrase, which included some people, and, of course, excluded others. To borrow Anderson's comment: 'Seen as both a historical fatality and as a community imagined through language, the nation presents itself as simultaneously open and closed' (1983: 133).

It is not necessary for nations to be linguistically distinct, and there are many examples of nations setting about constructing or, rather, reconstructing 'national languages' for political purposes: Hebrew, Norwegian, Catalan and even Irish (previously known as Gaelic) which was given a political significance out of all proportion to those who could actually speak it. The 'real' or authentic Ireland demanded that it should be politically asserted. Scotland's failure to mobilise an oppositional nationalism in the eighteenth century has been identified by Anderson as partly the result of the hegemony of 'English' in lowland Scotland, so eliminating 'any possibility of a European-style vernacular-specific nationalist movement' (ibid.: 86), although the distinctiveness of the Scots tongue may well have provided fertile political conditions for the reassertion of nationalism (McClure, 1988). Anderson's is an important point, but implies that other identifiers are less significant in generating nationalism. Language, however, carries disadvantages as well as advantages, because it erects a threshold, a tariff, which has to be met if one wishes to participate. On the other hand, language is a clear and demonstrable tariff which can be met, unlike the subtle, even inscrutable processes which an incomer confronts in trying to become 'Scottish'. One might argue that the strength of nationalism in Scotland *vis-à-vis* that of Wales reflects the fact that, despite (or perhaps because of) a lack of linguistic differentiation, nationalism can present itself as more than protecting a cultural past under threat.

The debate about the importance of language to nationalism masks a more fundamental point. There is a conventional wisdom that nationalism is simply the expression of fundamental, preordained cultural and social differences. As Fredrik Barth put it:

> We are led to imagine each group developing its cultural and social form in relative isolation, mainly in response to local ecologic factors, through a history of adaptation by invention and selective borrowing. This history has produced a world of separate peoples, each with their culture and each organised in a society which can legitimately be isolated for description as an island to itself.
>
> (Barth, 1981: 11)

The point here is that nationalism is not the expression of 'objective' differences, but the mobilisation of those which the actors believe to be salient. Barth is arguing that cultural differences should be seen, not as primary and definitional characteristics, but as the outcome or implication of social struggles. In this regard, 'the nation' is not a primordial form of social organisation, but an idea, an aspiration. It should be considered not simply as 'place' but as 'process'.

In examining Scotland as a nation, then, it is important to ask what the mechanisms are which reproduce the necessary imagery. We have to ask not only 'When was/is Scotland?', but 'Where is Scotland?', and 'Whose Scotland?' There are, of course, competing versions of Scotland, using distinctions which have a mythological base: Scotland of the past and the present; Scotland of the Highlands or the Lowlands; small-town east-coast Scotland versus Scotland of the west-coast conurbation. At any point in history, for example, some versions of Scotland may win out over others. For example, the relegation of 'Catholic' history in eighteenth- and nineteenth-century Protestant Scotland (Ash, 1980: 129); the association of Scotland with Unionism in the nineteenth and early twentieth centuries, and in the late twentieth century their almost complete dissociation.

Other images of Scotland are associated with material and political interests: the rural Scotland of the lairds, the industrial Scotland of the urbanised working class, all are images which compete against each other in the political realm, and all are constructed out of partial interpretations of Scotland. If Scotland is a nation, we are entitled to ask whose nation?, whose image is being presented?, and what are its political implications? 'Scotland' is above all a set of meanings, as are England, France, Germany and so on. Much depends on whose meaning wins out.

Such images can, of course, be fought over and captured by social interests who seek to turn them to material advantage, but it would be a mistake to produce a simplistic association. One of the most interesting developments of the past two decades, for example, has been the way that the Scottish National Party has turned a rich and diverse cultural meaning of Scotland into a politically charged one, but one which frequently slips out of its grasp. The party's problem for long enough was that it could find no way of charging the idea of 'Scotland' into one of a politically independent nation. 'Scotland' remained associated with the music-hall, tourism and cultural organisations. It was not until the discovery of North Sea Oil that the SNP found the key which unlocked this rich source of political and cultural imagery. Similarly, the Conservatives in Scotland in the 1980s were genuinely perplexed that they had failed to mobilise what they saw as 'Scottish' values of thrift, hard work and enterprise. Their problem was that the Thatcherite project was largely perceived as an alien, an English, political creed, north of the border, and not an expression of indigenous Scottish values.

In many respects 'nation' is akin to 'community' in so far as the search for its 'real' parameters is less significant than the set of symbolic meanings which attach to it. In Anthony Cohen's phrase, community is essentially symbolically constructed; it does not reside in geographical or even social territory so much as in people's minds. 'People construct community symbolically, making it a resource and repository of meaning, and a referent of their identity' (1985: 118). The word 'nation' could just as easily be used instead of 'community' because the former is a version of the latter. Similarly, the notion of boundary or frontier takes on added significance, because these exist in the minds of the beholders rather than primarily as material artefacts. Cohen again: 'People assert community, whether in the form of ethnicity or of locality when they recognise in it the most adequate medium for the expression of their whole selves' (ibid.: 107).

'Nation', then, depends on people defining a community as such. If they withdraw their recognition from the totality, in theory it ceases to exist. Just as W. I. Thomas' 'definition of the situation' argued that something exists if people act as if it does, so a nation operates on a similar plane. This can be a troublesome thought, as if it represented the triumph of will over experience. Anthony Cohen (2000) has commented on the problem of the 'objective correlative' for the nation in so far as its existence requires some kind of affirmation in 'reality', some minimally shared content in order for the form of the nation to exist. That is why cultural markers such as language, religion, blood links and so on are frequently seized as the essence of what makes a nation. Simply to say that if a group of people claim that they are such, then the nation exists seems too nebulous a basis on which to erect such a powerful rallying notion. To be sure, some reality check is necessary, otherwise the symbolic account around which the idea of nation is woven falters and dies, or is superseded by alternative community ideas. One might say that the framing of social, cultural and political ideas around 'Scottishness' at the beginning of the twenty-first century is possible and indeed plausible because it is not at all at odds with social experience.

It is plain that over the final fifty years of the twentieth century, the concept of being 'British' was losing its symbolic power in Scotland in favour of the notion of being Scottish. This is not to say that it had been swept away by its alternative, but to indicate that what had been such a powerful symbolic context for at least two centuries had been eroding in favour of older, and strictly national identities. No longer were these subsumed or complementary to an overarching sense of Britishness. The publication of books with titles like *Britons: Forging the Nation* (Colley, 1992), *After Britain* (Nairn, 2000), and *The Day Britain Died* (Marr, 2000) indicate that British identity had become problematic by the twenty-first century. Such a notion simply could not have been sustained a century before. Scotland, we might say, is an appropriate imagined community because it fits and makes sense of the social realities as people see and live them in the new century. This frame of reference would appear to be gaining more explanatory power and purchase than a British one. In short, Scotland is sustained as a nation because people in Scotland treat it as a more appropriate social and cultural framework for making sense of their lives.

Conclusion

Nationalism is once more on the political agenda in Scotland and elsewhere, because rapid social and economic change has destabilised political conventions. The historic 'nation-state' of the mid-nineteenth to mid-twentieth century is losing its *raison d'être*: in economic terms, there is a diminishing correspondence between political and economic systems. The nation-state appears to be losing its rationale in a world dominated by multinational corporations and transnational organisations. Politically, the *raison d'état* of the nation-state, the control of violence and aggression, has been severely curtailed. In cultural terms, nations can no longer practise what Weber called 'Kultur politische', the political protection of cultural identity. Even in terms of language, it has become very difficult for the modern state to continue to insist on monocultural language. Multiculturalism becomes no longer merely desirable, but inevitable.

In this context, the claim to power of the nation-state is under pressure from two directions: from above from supranational organisations (like the European Union), and from below from national or regional autonomism. That such a phenomenon should happen within the United Kingdom simply reflects the special conditions which attach to British political and cultural life – its multinational legacy, the post-war paradigm of economic decline, the resurgence of English nationalism at the political centre, and Scottish and Welsh at the periphery. As Cohen puts it, the resurgence of ethnicity reflects 'the bankruptcy of the higher level entities as socio-psychological repositories of identity' (1985: 107).

The purpose of this chapter has been to examine the different levels of meaning which attach to Scotland – as country, as society and as nation. At each level, Scotland has a distinct identity, and considerable cultural and political capital attaches to them. Because Scotland is a nation which is not an independent state, conventional sociological models – premised on the fusion of nation and state – are of limited use. Nevertheless, as the nation-state loses its *raison-d'être* in a world economy, polity and culture, so Scotland seems to provide a glimpse into the future rather than the past. Given that in economic terms, it is locked firmly into an ever-expanding world economy, the assertion of national identity and cultural distinctiveness comes at a most interesting time in its history. As such, Scotland stands at the centre of sociological concerns in this late modern world.

3 Understanding Scotland's development

As a sociological oddity, a nation without an independent state, Scotland presents problems for sociologists and historians who would explain its economic and social development. Nevertheless, the case of Scotland has attracted much interest from those who see it as an exemplar of certain general models of change, and as a result a number of key debates have been generated around the issue of development and social change in Scotland. The main purpose of this chapter is to show how particular conceptual and theoretical vocabularies have shaped the study of Scotland.

As we saw in the previous chapter, the paradigm of modernisation focuses on the nation-state and its internal workings. This 'internalist' perspective seeks to relate social and economic change to the workings of the political system in such a way as to show how that system both reflects and drives social change. In this context, Scotland has not figured except as part of the broader ('homogeneous') British state, and as such has been judged as having little separate rationale for sociological study.

In many respects, conventional accounts of economic change are of limited applicability to Scotland. These are normally premised on the existence of a self-contained nation-state, a 'social system' within which satisfactory causes can be located, on assumptions about the linear character of economic development, and on the supposition that nation-states are the 'natural' units which develop. Clearly, Scotland does not fit easily into this mould, not only because it lost its formal political autonomy in 1707, but because even a superficial reading of its history reveals the extent to which its economic and social fortunes depended crucially upon external factors.

In terms of the development of the capitalist world economy. Scotland is doubly unique. First, Britain as a whole was the first state in the world in which a thoroughgoing capitalist revolution took place; second, Scotland's own capitalist revolution occurred within a country lacking the formal political and institutional structures of statehood. Further, as Tom Nairn has pointed out, such a transformation occurred before the emergence of the modern ideology of nationalism which was to inform the political and economic features of capitalist industrialisation in much of Europe (Nairn, 1977). Scotland, he says, crossed 'the great divide' to become an industrialised society without the benefit or indeed the hindrance of nationalism which usually acted as a political/ideological vehicle for the bourgeoisie in most other European countries. Further, Scotland's economy was rarely if ever self-contained and independent. It was an open economy, reliant on external capital and technology, and subject to the vagaries of the broader economic and political environment, whether of Britain or a wider European capitalist economy.

How, then, was modern sociology to understand Scotland? In the final quarter of the twentieth century, Scotland became the explicit concern of sociology in two ways. First, the long-standing debate about the relationship between religion and the rise of capitalism made Scotland and its 'Calvin factor' (MacLaren, 1974) an obvious subject for study. Second, the radical critique of modernisation theory, particularly by world-systems theory, opened up new models of development which seemed to fit non-states like Scotland much more appropriately. The lack of political statehood, the relative openness of its economy, and its reliance on external forces attracted a mode of theorising which one might term 'externalist', and, as a result, versions of theories of 'underdevelopment' and 'dependency' have been applied to Scotland. In the 1970s, it became part of the analytical discourse when talking about Scotland to refer to it as a 'colony' (without being too precise as in which respects this was true), as part of the 'periphery' of the developed world. Borrowed as these terms were from accounts of Third World development and underdevelopment, such models had difficulty explaining why Scotland had been 'developed' or part of the 'core' in the first place.

This debate has proved to be crucial because the assumption that Scotland is a colony has largely rested on presumed differences with the rest of Britain, with the inference that Scotland was permitted simply to develop as a specialised region. The argument here is that while the externalist perspectives of world-systems theory and models of underdevelopment have recognised the importance of a frame of reference wider than the nation-state, there is limited analytical value and not much empirical evidence for treating Scotland as a 'colony' of England. The key question which has underlain much historical and sociological analysis is why it was that a poor, northern territory of north-west Europe – 'la stérile Ecosse' (Lythe, 1960) – came to occupy such a place in the forefront of economic development.

Religion and the rise of capitalism

Religion has been one of the abiding cultural characteristics of Scotland which distinguish it from its southern neighbour. As the historian Callum Brown observed:

> religion in Scotland has had an important bearing on national consciousness. For a people whose sense of nationhood was removed early in the

18th century, religion remained one of the few facets of Scottish civil life in which a collective identity could survive.

(Brown, 1987: 6)

Furthermore, the role of Calvinism in Scotland seems to have played a major role in Scottish social and economic development, and in this respect it makes the connection between Calvinism and capitalism, especially in Max Weber's famous thesis, *The Protestant Ethic and the Spirit of Capitalism*. Gordon Marshall in his exploration of the Weber thesis, *In Search of the Spirit of Capitalism* (1982), has pointed out that while Weber only made passing mention of Scotland, there seems little doubt that he saw the Scottish case as corroborating his thesis. Historians have been less certain about the connection, at least in terms of Protestantism and capitalism. Christopher Smout observes:

> Max Weber's classic thesis suggests a close link between the rise of Calvinism and the rise of a capitalist economy in European societies. . . . Few countries were more completely Calvinist than Scotland, yet it is hard to see how any support can be found for Weber's thesis from the situation in this country between 1560 and 1690.
>
> (Smout, 1970: 95)

Smout nevertheless concludes that 'if we take the long view of Scottish history it does become difficult not to believe that Calvinism contributed certain things which could hardly help but favour the expansion of economic activity and the enrichment of cultural life' (ibid.: 96). On the face of it, however, it might seem that the Scottish case does refute the thesis because, while no one can deny that Scotland was infused with Calvinism as early as the late sixteenth century, that it was a 'theocracy', it was not until at least a century or more later that it became in any meaningful sense a capitalist country.

Gordon Marshall provided an exhaustive and critical examination of the applicability of the Weber thesis to Scotland in his book *Presbyteries and Profits* (1980). Weber, says Marshall, addressed two separate but related questions: that of determining the nature and origins of the 'spirit' of modern capitalism; and that of identifying the diverse origins of modern Western capitalism itself. On the first issue, Weber argued that the origins of the modern capitalist mentality may well have been located in a neo-Calvinist ethos in the seventeenth century, while the 'spirit' of modern capitalism was only one of many factors which might explain material-economic changes. Hence, Marshall is able to show that

> Scots Calvinist-capitalists were amply imbued with an appropriate capitalist mentality (deriving, it seems, from their Protestantism), but their efforts had few discernible consequences for economic development because of the unfavourable circumstances in which they were made and which they proved unable to transcend.
>
> (Marshall, 1982: 138)

The nub of Marshall's argument is that Weber never claimed that ascetic Protestantism was a sufficient cause for economic transformation, which was dependent on a series of economic, social and political factors (what he called 'conditions for action'). Scotland, then, is not a 'refuting instance'. Marshall's purpose, however, is not simply to defend Weber in a negative way against his critics, but to show how, by the late seventeenth century, certain Scottish entrepreneurs (notably Sir John Clerk of Penicuik) not only adhered to the principles of capitalist business practice, but did so through the values and ideals of ascetic Calvinism. That Scotland did not 'take off' until the late eighteenth century and beyond reflected a series of adverse social, economic and political circumstances such as 'severely detrimental economic and political relationships between Scotland and certain neighbouring states, inadequate supplies of suitably skilled labour and of liquid capital for investment, and the inappropriate fiscal and industrial policies pursued by the state' (ibid.: 138).

It is more difficult in modern (and secular) Scotland to grasp that Calvinism was not simply a religion in a narrow sense, but a social and political ethos rooted in distinct institutions. Calvinism was a highly flexible social ideology which could be used for diverse political purposes. The significance of 'Calvinism in one country', to use Harvie's apposite phrase, owed less to the all-pervasive appeal of such a religious belief than to its use by political and social factions as a means for grasping and legitimating power. By the second half of the eighteenth century, 'Calvinist' qualities of sobriety, frugality, industriousness and duty were stretched to some obvious material ends.

Allan MacLaren's study (1974) of the disruption of the Kirk in Aberdeen after 1843 showed nicely how new social interests and an upwardly mobile elite took to the new Evangelical Protestantism of the Free Church in part as a means to challenge the traditional merchants and the gentry. In many communities, Calvinism became what sociologists today would recognise as a hegemonic ideology, reinforced by the social power of the Kirk to issue a 'character' – a reference – for access to jobs, housing, poor-relief, and even criminal justice. At its height, many Scots were indeed 'keppit by fear'.

Nevertheless, by the late eighteenth and early nineteenth centuries the power of the Kirk was in decline, while at the same time Scotland was becoming a thoroughly industrialised society. It is this disjuncture which led Smout to conclude that 'Calvinism . . . seems to be released as a psychological force for secular change just at the moment when it [was] losing its power as a religion' (1970: 96). Such an apparent temporal disjuncture might seem to invalidate Weber's thesis, but as Marshall stresses, Weber was not pointing to a neat relationship between Protestantism and capitalism, but to an 'elective affinity' between the ethic of Protestantism and the spirit of capitalism. It was not necessary for capitalists to be Calvinists. The social type, the *berufmensch*, the man identified with his calling, belonged to an earlier age, but the secular legacy remained. In Weber's own words: 'The Puritan wanted to be a *berufmensch*. We have no choice but to be' (quoted in Poggi, 1983: 87). As Poggi pointed out:

A generation's moral project, embraced with a sense of its intrinsic validity (and perhaps of its religious significance) may become to later generations purely a set of tactical, expediential directives on how to adapt to objective constraints, followed purely because it would be impractical or foolish not to do so.

(Ibid.)

In sixteenth-century Protestant Scotland, the commercial classes did not, by and large, think or behave like capitalists. As Lythe points out: 'By and large the townsman had his capital tied up in goods, houses and ships; his economic thinking was encased in tradition; neither mentally nor financially was he equipped for great adventures' (1960: 35–6). The 'entrenched burghs' of Scotland were undoubtedly not the capitalist entrepôts of the sixteenth century, and the conservatism of the powerful Convention of Royal Burghs surfaced in opposition to the Union of parliaments in 1707. Before the last decades of the eighteenth century, there was little sign of indigenous capitalist enterprise from within Scotland. After 1780 – a substantial time-lag from 1707 – new opportunities afforded by the Union were taken up by existing low-cost, low overhead trades. The expansion of capitalism in Scotland seems to have owed more to external changes than to anything going on within its boundaries. From the late eighteenth century, the influx of foreign capital and talent was stepped up. As Lythe observes: 'the inflow of foreign skill and of some foreign capital was, not surprisingly, a concomitant to each surge of domestic enterprise' (ibid.: 37).

Although by the 1620s Scotland was trying to align her mercantile practices to those of more powerful and sophisticated trading nations like England, France and Holland, she was at a distinct disadvantage, and the 'notorious weakness' of Scottish government before the Union meant that no decisive and sustained commercial policy was followed. Even the nature of goods traded reflected the subordinate and semi-peripheral status of Scotland, especially the export of raw and semi-manufactured goods, and the import of finished and manufactured products. In the mid-sixteenth century, France was the major trading partner. Scottish merchants exported fish, raw wool, skins, some textiles and coal in exchange for quality textiles, provisions and wines. By the early seventeenth century, northern Europe formed the hub of trade, and in Lythe's words, 'to go to the Low Countries was to go to the emporium of Europe' (1960: 233). While the Scots exported essentially primary products to this core area of the world economy – skins, wool, fish, salt, lead and coal – imports consisted of crafted goods, manufactured products and 'groceries'. Important as trading links with northern Europe were, they do not seem to have represented the major factor in the penetration of capitalism into the Scottish economy. Scotland was a peripheral part of this central economy and probably would have remained so if new trading relationships had not been entered into with the burgeoning English economy.

A marriage of convenience

It became a truism that while the Union of 1707 was a military–political bargain for England, it was an economic one for Scotland. Much has been written about the causes and consequences of the Union, but in essence, for Scotland it was a matter of economics. In his book *The Scottish Nation, 1700–2000*, Tom Devine comments: 'It is not too difficult . . . to imagine a scenario in which, if the union negotiations had failed, the Scots would have been faced with the prospect of an English tariff wall at least as formidable as those which already confronted them in several parts of Europe' (1999: 54). This may not have been much of a choice as far as the Scots were concerned, but it ultimately gave them access to a free-trade zone of unparalleled size and extent. Because Scotland and England were at different stages of economic development, the Scottish economy ran the risk of being swamped by the superior technical and economic power of its southern neighbour, much along the lines of what happened in Ireland which took on the status of an economic satellite of England. Devine points out that the reason why this did not occur in Scotland is one of the key questions of eighteenth-century history. First of all, England's interests in the Union were largely military and political rather than economic; and second, the Scottish economy was at least developed to the extent that it was not wholly dependent on English markets. The Union led to development rather than underdevelopment because the Scottish ruling classes were committed to economic growth as a national goal; Scotland had unusually good natural resources in coal, iron deposits as well as developed urban markets; and the levels of cultural and educational capital were sufficient to take advantage of these new political and economic circumstances.

Trade with England in the early years of the Union continued to follow the traditional pattern: the exchange of Scottish raw materials for the more sophisticated products of England. The route to capitalism, however, lay through fuller participation in the English core economy, and the flow of ideas, of technology and of capital became the motor of Scottish capitalism. The failure of the Darien Scheme in 1700 had marked a significant turning point. Accordingly, the Union of 1707 took on an aura of inevitability despite the entrenched opposition of the merchants of the traditionalist Royal Burghs, who otherwise might have been expected to support it. Despite the fact that the burghs opposed the Union, the making of an indigenous class of capitalists began. In Smout's words: 'Both society and the economy would have been much more resistant to change in the 17th and 18th centuries if it had not been for the bourgeois leavening which such men provided' (1970: 172).

Why Scotland took off

Inevitably, the making of a capitalist economy was a fragmented affair. After the Union for a considerable number of decades, the Scottish economy was relatively backward, and the promised prosperity failed to materialise. The penetration of anything resembling a modern form of capitalism was sketchy and regionally specific. Much of the thrust towards economic development came from the traditional social structure, and as Bruce Lenman pointed out, 'Successful growth was achieved by exploiting low overheads and existing trends' (1977: 87). Much depended on the inflow of skills, capital and technology, and on the post-Union opportunities of new markets. Nevertheless, the Union had a longer term pay-off. Clive Lee comments: 'While the short-term effects of the Union were disappointing to some Scots, historians have generally agreed that in the longer term Scotland gained substantially from it' (1995: 13).

Scotland's unusual dependence upon external factors for its development has led some analysts to argue that this was development by 'invitation'. Immanuel Wallerstein has argued that 'Scotland was a classic case – Lowland Scotland, that is – of "development by invitation", the privilege (or the luck) of a very few, a case which offers few policy lessons for other states since it cannot be imitated at will' (1980: 633). He insists that the choice to develop or not was one made not by the Scottish elite, but at the invitation of the English, and concludes: 'Scotland's secret was not structural; it was conjunctural. The Lowlands were in a position after 1745, in Hobsbawm's phrase "to take advantage of the exceptionally favorable European and British conjuncture of the end of the eighteenth century"'(ibid.: 639).

A world-system perspective provided many of the theoretical answers to the 'problem' of Scotland. Scotland was invisible because it was no longer a nation-state, and the conventional paradigms passed it by. It had become a region of a homogeneous state of Great Britain. The notion of a 'world-system' – a unit with a single division of labour and multiple cultural systems, in Wallerstein's phrase – seemed to liberate Scotland from this analytical vacuum. National states, which had been conventionally treated as the organising categories of analysis, were relegated to bit-players in this system, because, according to Wallerstein, they are not 'societies that have separate, parallel histories, but [are] parts of a whole reflecting that whole' (1979: 53). Contrary to the prevailing wisdom of the time, all states are not in a position to 'develop' simultaneously, because the system functions by having core and peripheral regions.

Within this context, the notion of a 'nation-state' becomes problematic, because the idea of a 'nation' is essentially a political claim that the boundaries of a state should coincide with those of a given ethnic group. Hence, it is not very useful, according to world-systems theorists, to distinguish 'nations' from other kinds of ethnic groups. Further, says Wallerstein and his colleagues: 'if we are to use a strict definition of the concept "nation", we would be hard pressed to find even one "nation-state" in the entire world-system' (Arrighi *et al.*, 1983: 302).

Treating capitalism as a world-system rather than simply a characteristic of a national economy seemed, particularly in the 1970s, to provide a way of explaining Scotland's development. Some were far less certain. In 1980, a debate about the status of Scotland took place in the house journal of world-system theory – *Review* – between Christopher Smout and Immanuel Wallerstein. Smout expressed scepticism about how useful it was to describe some territories as 'dependent', pointing out that there were excellent examples in history (Australia, New Zealand, Denmark) of territories which launched themselves by trading primary products to 'developed' countries, and which ultimately 'made it' into the core of the capitalist world economy. In other words, 'dependency' was not necessarily a barrier to economic development (Smout, 1980a).

In this context, Scotland seemed to provide an interesting test-bed. Smout applied to Scotland the four criteria of 'dependency'; namely market dependency – a reliance on exporting a restricted range of goods to one richer area in return for the bulk of imports; technological dependency – a dependence on imported technology from richer areas; capital dependency – on injections of foreign capital; and cultural dependence – whereby the internal elite looked elsewhere for its cultural values.

On the face of it, eighteenth-century Scotland looked 'dependent'. It was significantly poorer than England, and if anything had grown more so since the sixteenth century. Scotland lagged significantly behind England on a whole range of social and economic indicators. Not only that, but it had grown more dependent on the four criteria by the sixteenth century. First, by the end of the seventeenth century, cattle and linen cloth represented the bulk of exports south of the border. The Union of the Crowns in 1603 still placed barriers on cross-border trade, but dependence had grown rather than diminished in the course of the seventeenth century. Second, similarly, virtually all new technologies came from the south, underlining Scotland's dependent position. Third, while there was some primitive internal capital accumulation before 1700, the dramatic failures of overseas investments (Darien was by no means the only one) spelled out in stark terms the dearth of capital. Finally, 'foreign tastes' – in fashions, life-styles, and even education – preoccupied the social elite in the late seventeenth century.

All in all, Smout argues, by the eighteeenth century Scotland was indubitably 'dependent' on virtually any criteria. He comments:

> Early 18th century Scotland was, indeed, as much a dependent economy as any country could be in that age, tied specifically to England in commerce and decision-making, more generally to the core countries of England, the Netherlands and France in technology and culture, and tending to look to the same countries on the rare occasions when it needed exceptional capital inputs.
>
> (Smout, 1980a: 612)

Nevertheless, Scotland, he claims, was not doomed to permanent 'underdevelopment'. By the nineteenth century, Scotland had embarked upon a programme of capital exports in per capita terms probably greater than

England's, and its cultural dependency – particularly in terms of education – had also been eroded. Smout continues: 'The dependent status so obvious in 1700 indeed turned out to be a symptom of an early stage in development rather than an obstacle to growth' (ibid.: 614).

Smout identifies six levers to economic growth. First of all, the cattle trade provided a limited opportunity for profits to be retained in Scotland, thereby helping to transform agriculture in the Lothians and the Border country in particular. Second, by means of the tobacco trade – a supremely 'colonial' activity – Glasgow was raised from the status of provincial centre to its later dominant position in the Scottish economy. Building on its native traditions, an indigenous bourgeoisie began to prosper in what was a considerably open system of social mobility. The linen trade, however, was probably, in Smout's view, a more powerful boost to proto-industrialisation in Scotland. It was spread, north to south, over the expanse of lowland Scotland; its entrepreneurs were clearly Scottish; and it employed a large labour force – an embryonic pro-letariat. The fourth lever to economic growth north of the border, the cotton industry, was more recognisably a 'modern' industry, and while the English connection was important, the Scots were able to win the initiative quickly. A similar situation occurred with regard to the mineral industry, the fifth lever. Finally, changes in lowland farming seemed to owe very little to English expertise and capital except in its early days. Scotland's exacting climate and topography allowed new indigenous developments to occur, with far-reaching consequences for its economic and social structures.

Smout concludes that 'dependency' *per se* did not block economic develop-ment in Scotland, but rather was beneficial and benign: 'Dependency in Scotland's case was far from being a crippling handicap. Trade was not an engine of exploitation, but a cause of growth' (1980a: 628). Scotland, it seems, had been able to move from peripheral to semi-peripheral to core status because of its early 'dependency'. Five specific factors helped to bring this about:

- in the eighteenth century, only small-scale external capital requirements were needed (in contrast to underdeveloped countries today);
- the English were not interested in developing Scotland as a 'colony' (like Virginia or the West Indies) because Scotland had limited raw materials, and because the 1707 Union had served England's political-military purposes;
- Scotland's civil society had not been smashed by invasions and colonisa-tions, unlike Ireland in the sixteenth and seventeenth centuries;
- Scotland's native culture remained strong, especially among its merchant class – the quintessential 'modernising' cadre;
- Scotland avoided over-rapid demographic growth (unlike Ireland and its own highland periphery) by means of emigration and the discouraging of sub-tenancies on the land. Scotland, claimed Smout, is a good exception to Wallerstein's rule that capitalism confines territories to peripheral

status, and he points to other exceptions to the rule – New Zealand, Finland, Japan and Singapore.

In response, Wallerstein argued that Smout's own data can be used to prove his own point, namely that between 1600 and 1750 Scotland was undoubtedly peripheralised, but that in the century after, the process was arrested and reversed. Of the factors which Smout identified as important in accounting for Scottish development, Wallerstein claimed that only two were significant. On the one hand, the fact that the native elite was not smashed, and on the other, that Scotland did not have resources worth having, both signify to Wallerstein that development by 'invitation' was operating. As to the six levers of economic growth, Wallerstein argued that while these may have been necessary, they were not sufficient.

It can be seen from this debate between Wallerstein and Smout just how difficult, even dangerous, it is to generalise to and from Scotland. While pinpointing lowland Scotland as 'development by invitation' is an important aspect of what happened, it does ignore the historical specificity of Scotland itself, and the double uniqueness of Scotland in its route to 'development'. Certainly, in its early stages, Scotland's conjunctural position seems to have been important; it found itself at a historic and geographical conjuncture which allowed it to pass into the core and away from the periphery.

At a conceptual level, the imagery of core/centre and periphery is unsatisfactory because its vagueness allows the defining characteristics of these terms to be precisely those found in what is to be explained. The characteristics of the cause are bound up inextricably with those of its effect. These terms have tended to overemphasise aspects of difference in economic and social development at the expense of those which are similar. Geographical imagery in itself does not provide an explanation. As Smout points out in a related article, also published in 1980:

> Neither the old slums nor the new got there because Scotland was a periphery; they were the consequence of the nature of Scottish Victorian capitalism and 20th century planning, just as the problems of Detroit or New York . . . are the products of the history of American capitalism and planning, not of any peripheral relationships within the USA.
>
> (Smout, 1980b: 269–70)

Not only does Wallerstein underplay contingency, he makes little room for the role of agency in explaining social change. What, then, are we to make of the analytical value of concepts like 'dependency' and 'underdevelopment'? In its strictest sense, 'underdevelopment' is inappropriately applied to Scotland because it implies – in its Third World sense – that some territories have been blocked or prevented from making the transition from feudalism to capitalism. Because Scotland shared in core status with England at the origin of the

Industrial Revolution, and unambiguously occupied 'core' status in the mid- to late nineteenth century, 'underdevelopment' *strictu sensu* is inappropriate.

The appeal of models of dependency and underdevelopment to the Scottish case was a reflection of the political and intellectual climate in Scotland in the late 1960s and early 1970s. The colonial metaphor seemed especially relevant at a time when the SNP was making headway with the electorate, and when concerns about Scotland having a 'branch-plant' economy were beginning to surface. Terms like 'dependency', 'underdevelopment' and 'colonialism' seemed to chime with the prevailing mood of the times.

Scotland and internal colonialism

Perhaps the most explicit (and contentious) attempt to employ the language of colonialism and dependency to 'ethno-nations' in Britain was that of the American sociologist, Michael Hechter. Published in 1975 and entitled *Internal Colonialism: The Celtic Fringe in British National Development, 1536–1966*, Hechter's book was an ambitious attempt – in both conceptual and methodo- logical terms – to apply an explicit Wallersteinian framework to Britain: 'It would not even have been attempted without his example', he acknowledged (1975: xvii). Hechter argued that orthodox 'diffusionist' models of develop- ment imply that strong core regions, through powerful central governments, are able to establish one national culture. To the contrary, an 'internal colony' model argues that a spatially uneven wave of modernisation creates relatively advanced and less advanced social groups and territories. The stratifi- cation system which emerges generates a 'cultural division of labour'.

Hechter acknowledged the origins of the notion of 'internal colonialism' in a Third World context – specifically Latin America – and refined it through its application to US race relations, before exporting it across the Atlantic to the 'Celtic fringe'. Like other versions of 'underdevelopment', internal colonialism implies that – contra a diffusion model – the 'backwardness' of the periphery can only be aggravated by systematic transactions with the core, not aided by them. Hechter borrowed from the anthropologist Fredrik Barth the notion of a 'cultural division of labour' whereby social roles are allocated to different ethnic groups. He adopted Ernest Gellner's idea of ethnic nationalism being generated by the uneven spread of industrialisation through territorial space so that cleavages of interest form around ethnic differences. Said Hechter:

> The superordinate group, now ensconced as the core, seeks to stabilise and monopolise its advantages through policies aiming at the institution- alisation and perpetuation of the existing stratification system. Ultimately, it seeks to regulate the allocation of social roles such that those roles commonly defined as having high status are generally reserved for its members. Conversely, individuals from the less advanced group tend to be denied access to these roles. Let this stratification system be termed

the cultural division of labour: it assigns individuals to specific roles in the social structure on the basis of objective cultural distinctions.

(Ibid.: 39)

This lengthy quotation gives the essence of Hechter's argument, and points out some of the problems in applying it to 'British national development'. Despite some sophistication applied to handling a range of social and economic indicators at the level of counties, his thesis seems methodologically forced into its theoretical frame. He adopted broad ethnic definitions of 'Anglo-Saxons' and 'the so-called Celts of Wales, Ireland and parts of Scotland' (ibid.: 47). This division corresponds to a 'radical split' down the middle of Britain between Highland and Lowland zones, divisions not simply geographical but reflecting 'types of social organisation' (ibid.: 58).

Celtic nationalism is the political response to the persistence of regional inequality, and in particular to the process of Anglicisation, especially in linguistic and religious terms. Industrialisation alone does not effect the national integration of Britain, as predicted by the 'diffusion model', but performs a mediating role for the persistence of regional identities on the Celtic fringe. While diffusion models predict the demise of peripheral ethnicity, the internal colonial model is justified in so far as it has persisted and grown. Industrialisation did allow a degree of integration, but its later effects were limited:

Though the partial industrialisation of Wales and Scotland did permit the structural integration of these regions into the national society, principally through the establishment of national trade unions and the Labour Party, persisting economic stagnation in the periphery has shaken much confidence in the class-based political organisation.

(Ibid.: 265)

Hechter's analysis generated considerable interest and controversy, not simply on the 'periphery'. Critics pointed out, moreover, that Scotland was a poor fit for his theory. While at times careful to refer only to the Gaeltachd of Scotland, at other times Hechter slid into a more general equation. Scotland was described as 'the sole Celtic land to have been politically united' (ibid.: 71). More generally, Hechter was careful to distinguish between the Highlands, indubitably Celtic, and the Lowlands which were 'culturally anglicised' (in language and religion, most evidently). Because of this, Scotland, he admitted, provides a 'more complex' case than do Wales and Ireland. His solution was to say that: 'Because the rulers of the Scottish state were themselves culturally anglicised, their English counterparts felt it unnecessary to insist upon total control over Scottish cultural institutions, as they had done in Wales and Ireland' (ibid.: 342–3).

This is a revealing statement, not simply because it implies, dubiously perhaps, that the version of 'English' spoken by Scots before 1707 was the same as that in the south, but because it employs much the same kind of explanation as Wallerstein did in his encounter with Smout – development by invitation. In other words, because lowland Scots adopted English manners and practices, they were 'allowed' to participate in British economic development. As such, while they were subordinate to wider British interests, they were dominant in their own territory, a point echoing Andre Gunder Frank's analysis of Latin American 'underdevelopment' in which a chain of metropolitan/satellite relations operate. This point of 'dependent development' is explicitly reinforced by Hechter a few pages later:

> Industrialisation did not diffuse into the peripheral areas in the same form as it had developed in the core. When industrialisation did penetrate the periphery, it was in a dependent mode, consequently production was highly specialised and geared for export.
>
> (Ibid.: 345)

We will return to this assumption of 'dependency' and 'regional specialisation' later, because it has become one of the key assumptions built into analysis of Scotland and other 'peripheral' regions of the UK. At the end of his book, Hechter has few doubts about the validity of his analysis. 'The Celts', he claimed, 'are an internal colony within the very core of this world system' (ibid.: 348). He was careful not to allocate them to the periphery, but to a special place in the cultural division of labour at the core. At this stage, Hechter proclaimed the homogeneity of 'the Celts' and the supremacy of 'the world system'.

Internal colonialism revisited

By the 1980s, Hechter had begun to modify his account of the Celtic fringe in the light of criticism, especially from historians. His basic theme survived, namely that nationalism was ultimately derived from the existence of a cultural division of labour – 'a stratification system giving cultural distinctions political salience by systematically linking them to individual life chances' (1982: 9). Southern Ireland remained, he thought, 'a stunningly clear example of internal colonial development' (ibid.), while Scotland – at least its Lowlands – had been more of an 'overdeveloped' peripheral region than an 'underdeveloped' one. The second and more fundamental criticism he admitted no answer to – that he could provide no direct evidence that a cultural division of labour existed.

Delving into US ethnic history, Hechter found a parallel to the Scots in the Jews (*vis-à-vis* the blacks, for example) who had become 'very highly occupationally specialised' (ibid.: 10). This led him to modify his theory, to say that the cultural division of labour has two dimensions, a hierarchical dimension in which groups are vertically distributed in the occupational structure, and a segmental dimension in which groups become occupationally specialised at different (theoretically, any) levels of the structure. In this way, ethnic groups may manage to retain a degree of occupational autonomy, even, as in the case of the Scots, of institutional autonomy, which generates what Hechter called a 'segmental cultural division of labour'. Similarly, he had to revise his theory of social action, of nationalism, by making it less dependent on common material interests, which are a necessary but not sufficient cause of action. Instead, support for nationalist movements varies according to the degree to which actors face limited sources of benefit.

Despite these revisions, or indeed because he has to make them, Hechter's account remains flawed. There is more than a suspicion that his sophisticated statistical gymnastics are insufficient to validate his theory because, ultimately, his data are not actually about the cultural division of labour on which his thesis rests. His revisionist interpretation of Scotland as an 'overdeveloped peripheral region', as is Catalunya, has a touch of desperation about it. Describing Scotland as 'overdeveloped' as an explanation for neo-nationalism when 'underdevelopment' does not do the job does not ring true.

Tom Nairn (1977) has also used, albeit in a more sophisticated way, the distinction between Scotland as 'underdeveloped' and as 'overdeveloped' (North Sea Oil provided at least the possibility) because his theory of nationalism is also classically 'externalist'. Nationalism is to be explained by the uneven development of capitalism at a world level. Nevertheless, Nairn does avoid the excesses of 'analytical Third Worldism' when it comes to Scotland. If 'underdevelopment' refers to a systematic blockage in development of the 'periphery', then Scotland does not fit, because, as Nairn points out, Scotland along with the rest of Britain made the great transition to industrial capitalism before it happened anywhere else in the world. To describe Scotland as 'underdeveloped' because it has been prevented from crossing, in Polanyi's phrase, the Great Divide, makes neither analytical nor empirical sense. What cannot be denied, however, is the powerful imagery which 'dependency' and 'colonialism' brought to academic study as well as to political practice. Its power is that of the metaphor rather than explanatory concept, and it is in this context that such assumptions have shaped academic work on Scotland, by both historians and sociologists alike.

The Highlands as periphery

If treating Scotland as a whole as 'peripheral' and 'underdeveloped' is somewhat problematic, the Highlands of Scotland perhaps most merit the description. More has probably been written by historians and social scientists on the Gaelic-speaking Highlands than on the rest of Scotland put together. There is the added irony that the Highlands provide many of the images and meanings for Scotland as a whole in the late twentieth century. In cultural terms, its imagery dominates. As the anthropologist Malcolm Chapman says:

> We are faced with the problem that a language not understood by 98% of the Scottish people, with a modern literary tradition that only begins to assume importance in the late 18th century and is still very small . . . and

spoken by a people who have been regarded for centuries by their southern neighbours as barbarians should now be regarded as the quintessence of Scottish culture.

(Chapman, 1978: 12)

The appeal of models of underdevelopment and dependency to the Highland case owes much to Ian Carter (1971), then a sociologist at Aberdeen University, who described the Highlands as an 'underdeveloped region'. Carter argued that the conventional way of seeing the Highlands was as an archaic, pre-capitalist, even feudal region whose future lay in opening up its traditional way of life to the market forces of the modern economy. He argued that such a model was fundamentally flawed, because it was premised on a very narrow conception as to what 'development' was, and was based upon assumptions of a 'dual sector' model, which set out two dichotomous economic sectors: the traditional and the modern. The classical economic stance implied in the dual economy model saw the Highlands as unequivocally 'backward'. Here, for instance, is the explanation by A. J. Youngson in his book *After the Forty Five* as to why the Highlands 'failed' in the nineteenth century: 'They [the peasants] clung to the land because it seemed their only guarantee of subsistence and of the continuity of life. These people were the remnants of a feudal system which had ebbed away, leaving them stranded in remote glens and straths' (1973: 179). Committed, as he saw them, to 'traditional' ways of life, the answer to their plight lay in embracing modern practices. Youngson goes on: 'The Clearances to which so much attention has been paid in Highland history were important; but they were no more than the visible, breaking crest of a long-travelling, irresistible wave' (ibid.: 185), or, if one can change the metaphor, the impact of the hidden hand of the marketplace. 'Progress' requires the setting aside of 'status' and 'tradition' (ibid.: 201).

Radical revisionists like Ian Carter and James Hunter took issue with this characterisation. Hunter replied that 'the crofter has never been immune from the pressures generated by capitalist civilisation. Indeed, he has suffered from them more than most' (1976: 2). Hunter later developed this argument in *Last of the Free: a Millennial History of the Highlands and Islands* (1999) in which he argued that the Highlands had been systematically oppressed in both economic and political terms by 'outsiders', first by the Scottish and then, after 1746, by the British state. There was little question that outsiders rather than insiders were to blame for the underdevelopment of the Highlands. Hunter and Carter both argued that crofting was by no means a 'traditional' means of livelihood, but the rational response of a people moved off the more fertile land in the glens to the marginal land of the coast. Farming with a little fishing (or vice versa) became a sensible adaptation to circumstances over which the crofter had little control.

Carter's analysis (1974) of the black cattle and kelp (seaweed) industries showed that both of these were market-oriented, organised on capitalistic lines. The cattle trade was essentially a commercial operation with Lowland or even English markets. The kelp industry – which involved obtaining alkaline for the making of glass, fertiliser and soap – came into its own during the Napoleonic wars when the traditional sources in Spain were cut off. The escalation in price allowed Highland landlords to organise their people in what was a labour-intensive industry, largely because they held monopolistic control over their tenants' output. The driving force behind the kelp industry was the desire of the landlord to maximise profit. Kelp, said Carter, was a paradigm case of what Barrington Moore Jun. called 'conservative modernisation'. In Moore's words: 'the landed upper class will use a variety of political and social levers to hold down a labour force on the land and make its transition to commercial farming in this fashion' (Carter, 1974: 301).

Applying a sociology of underdevelopment to the Highlands, Carter concluded that characterising them as 'backward' is historically inaccurate and sociologically limiting. He concluded that 'Any attempt to strengthen the links between the Highlands and the "modern" economy through a large-scale exploitation of indigenous Highland raw materials . . . will increase the underdevelopment of the area by reinforcing the satellization of the Highlands' (ibid.: 302). Crucially, whether or not a region is defined as 'backward' is, he said, a matter of definition. The Highlands had embraced economic change with new trades (cattle, kelp, crofting), and had long since left the traditional communal runrig system of land tenure behind. Nevertheless, because they had not produced a polarised social structure of capitalist farmers and landless wage labourers, such change could not count, in official circles, as 'improvement'. All in all, said Carter, 'it all depends what you mean by development' (ibid.: 303).

What is sociologically interesting about Carter's analysis is that it explicitly attempted to import modes of analysis based upon 'underdevelopment'. Hence, he prefers to define capitalism as a system of exchange, as a market system rather than as a mode of production. Latifundias in Latin America and cattle-rearing in the Scottish Highlands were therefore defined as forms of capitalistic activity in this way rather than because these systems employed free, waged labour. In his later book *Farm Life in Northeast Scotland* (1979), Carter used a more 'orthodox' definition of capitalism in analysing the articulation of capitalist and pre-capitalist modes of production in the countryside. A peasant population existed in late nineteenth-century north-east Scotland because capitalist or 'muckle' farmers needed essential supplies of hired labour power, and because peasant farmers supplied quality lean cattle for fattening. Their demise by 1914 resulted from the removal of these two necessary conditions for generating profit.

Carter's work represented an important attempt to apply a new revisionist Marxism to northern Scotland or, more explicitly, to the Highlands of Scotland. Carter was careful not to imply that what is true for that region of Scotland is true for the country as a whole. Nevertheless, he, like Wallerstein, argued the case for 'development by invitation' for Scotland as a whole:

Lowland industrialisation was the result of the English allowing a place in the metropolitan sun for certain specialised heavy industries, provided that they were *complementary* with the English economy and *not competitive* [my emphasis], and Scottish capital was invested abroad – three-quarters of the foreign investment in ranching in the United States in the 1870s and 1880s was Scottish.

(Carter, 1974: 306)

Such a view that Scotland's economic trajectory was shaped explicitly by its relationship with England has proved to be a powerful if somewhat flawed analysis. It has implied that certain forms of economic activity were forbidden to the Scots, that Scotland's economy developed in a highly specialised form, and that its class structure was somehow deformed by an essentially 'colonial' relationship. The notion that capitalism in Scotland had a 'complementary' rather than a 'competitive' form proved to be a powerful motif from the 1970s.

Industrial change in Scotland

Between 1750 and 1850, Scotland became not simply an industrial society but one of the world's foremost examples. In particular, as Christopher Smout points out:

the central belt of Scotland became . . . one of the most intensively industrialised regions on the face of the earth. By 1913, Glasgow, claiming for
herself the title of 'Second City of the Empire', made, with her satellite
towns immediately to the east and west, one-fifth of the steel, one-third
of shipping tonnage, one-half of the marine-engine horsepower, one-
third of the railway locomotives and rolling stock, and most of the
sewing machines in the United Kingdom.

(Smout, 1987: 85)

Given that prosperity (for a few) rested upon a small number of industries, it is tempting to conclude that Scotland's development depended on its becoming regionally specialised. The dominant image of Scotland's industrial structure was, in the words of the historian Bruce Lenman, that 'by the 19th century, Scotland had developed a very specialised regional branch of the British economy, heavily oriented towards the manufacture and export of capital goods and coarse textiles' (1977: 204).

We find this assumption of regional specialisation in Marxist and non-Marxist accounts alike. For example, one of the most influential and comprehensive histories of capitalism in Scotland, *Scottish Capitalism*, underlines 'the commitment of Scottish industry to the production of a relatively narrow range of specialisms, like ships and other heavy engineering equipment, which were so essential to the growth of world trade' (Dickson, 1980: 194).

The authors of this book explain this specialisation in terms of the way capitalism developed in Scotland:

> In relation to Britain as a whole, what were to emerge in Scotland were complementary rather than competitive forms of capitalism, their inter-dependence being regularised under the political domination of West-minster. Such were the roots of the dependent or client status of the Scottish bourgeoisie.
>
> (Ibid.: 90)

This distinction between 'complementary' and 'competitive' forms of capitalism echoes exactly that made by Carter in his analysis of the Highlands of Scotland. In each, the supposition is made that Scottish capitalists were allowed only to develop those forms of economic activity which did not conflict with those of their more powerful counterparts in the south. However, this distinction seems somewhat superfluous, even misleading, as an account of the development of capitalism in Scotland (or even in England, for that matter). In what was perhaps the quintessential free-market economy, there is little need to import the notion that economic activity was managed by the state (or 'Westminster', in the words of the above quotation). In so far as capital would flow into those sectors where profits were to be made, that capitalists would invest in areas on strictly economic terms, the notion of 'complementarity' (with its implication of explicit intervention in the workings of the market) does not ring true. Such a perspective seems unduly influenced, albeit implicitly, by Wallerstein's notion of 'development by invitation', that Scottish capitalists were permitted to take on certain forms of economic activity which would not 'compete' with those of English capitalists. It is difficult to see what the mechanism would be for permitting or forbidding such activity.

While it is true that simply comparing the industrial structures of Scotland with those of the rest of Britain will not of itself tell us whether or not Scottish capitalism was 'complementary' or 'dependent', such an exercise does give a much more accurate guide to industrial development in Scotland *vis-à-vis* England and Wales. Using the reclassified data in the work of the economic historian Clive Lee (1979), it is possible to estimate more precisely than hitherto the differences in the industrial structures of Scotland and Britain. To do so is not to betray a sense of insecurity that Scottish economic development cannot stand on its own, but to set this development in the firm context of British patterns. If, for example, the structure of industrial employment in Scotland was significantly different from Britain as a whole, we might conclude that it had a more specialised economy, fitting into the broad parameters of the British economy.

In the period between 1851 and 1911, for example, it is clear that while there are differences between Scotland and Britain, they are nowhere as great as those between Wales and Britain. For example, while 37 per cent of total employment in Wales in 1851 was in mining and quarrying, and a massive

52 per cent in 1911, the figures for Scotland were 9 per cent and 17 per cent, respectively, and for Britain as a whole, 10 per cent and 15 per cent. The simplest way of comparing industrial employment structures is the positive percentage difference, or the index of dissimilarity. To calculate this index for Britain and Scotland in 1851, one simply adds together the differences between the British and Scottish percentages for those industries for which the British figure is higher. If the structures were identical, the index would be zero. If there were no overlap at all, the value would be 100. In 1851, the index of dissimilarity between Britain and Scotland was 12.3, and in 1911, 10.2. The comparable index for Britain and Wales, on the other hand, was 37.6 in 1851, and 41.9 in 1911.

The positive percentage difference (ppd) has to be interpreted with care, because its size is determined by the number of categories, not just by the degree of dissimilarity. Nevertheless, because we are making comparisons based on a fixed number of categories, it is an appropriate measure to use in these circumstances. Similarly, while we can make comparisons between Scotland (and Wales) and Britain, it makes little sense to compare England and Britain because, given its relative size, it would be bound to show very low positive percentage differences. Nevertheless, the ppd does provide an intuitively straightforward measure for our purposes here. In fact, if one calculates the indices of dissimilarity between the industrial structures of the ten Standard Regions of Great Britain, Scotland appears to be the closest to the overall British structure in both 1851 and 1911. In 1851 the mean value of the index between the regional structures and that of Britain as a whole was 25.4, compared with the figure for Scotland of 12.3, and in 1911 the mean was 25.7, compared with 10.2 for Scotland.

On this evidence, there are no grounds for saying that Scotland in the nineteenth century had an industrial structure which was particularly specialised with regard to the British economy. If anything, Scotland mirrored Britain's industrial structure, and was more 'British' than the other economic 'regions'. We should be careful in noting the point we are making here. Clearly, Scotland did not become 'British', but rather 'industrial' and 'capitalist'. As such, it remained a country within the British state with a high degree of civil autonomy within the structure of that state, and was not reduced to a region of England (as was the North of England, for example). Scotland was simply especially well adapted to take advantage of Britain's highly advantageous structural position within a world economy itself shaped around Britain's interests. As Kirby put it:

> The distinctive nature of Britain's industrial structure was in fact one of the most outstanding features of the pre-1914 economy. In 1907 the old-established staple trades of textiles, coalmining, iron and steel, and general engineering accounted for approximately 50% of net industrial output and employed 25% of the working population. Most were heavily dependent upon an increasingly narrow range of export markets located mainly

within the British Empire, South America and Asia, and coalmining, textiles and iron and steel alone contributed over 70% of the country's export earnings.

(Kirby, 1981: 3)

In so far as Scotland was so well adapted to imperial opportunities in the nineteenth century, the collapse of the post First World War economy was more catastrophic for Scotland. The roots of Scotland's decline are to be found in a 'surfeit of imperialism' rather than, as is more commonly supposed, in a position of clientage or dependence. When the international order collapsed, Scotland – locked firmly into it – suffered in the way experienced by Britain as a whole.

The extreme localisation of the effects of this collapse within Scotland in the 1920s and 1930s stemmed from the degree of regional specialisation which had occurred within Scotland prior to the war. Significant specialisation had taken place within Scotland in the nineteenth century. Thus it was that counties dependent on engineering and shipbuilding such as Lanarkshire, Renfrewshire and Dumbartonshire which suffered most from the economic downturn, as well as the coal-mining communities of West Lothian, Fife and Stirlingshire.

Largely because of the switch in 1921 from an occupational- to an industrial-based classification in the Population Census, it is much more difficult to trace industrial employment changes from 1911 to 1931. Campbell's work on the Census of Production of 1907 and 1924 conveys a picture of stability, in which the industrial structures of Scotland and the UK changed rather little, and on the whole remained alike (Campbell, 1980). However, such differences as did exist in this period were to prove highly significant in the future. In 1907, 27 per cent of Scotland's industrial workforce was employed in 'iron and steel, engineering and shipbuilding' compared with 22 per cent for the UK as a whole.

In the four decades in the mid-twentieth century from 1931 to 1971, the industrial structure of Scotland appears to have been marginally more differentiated from that of Britain as a whole than was the case in the nineteenth century. The indices of dissimilarity between Scottish and British industrial employment structures were as follows: 1931, 15.4; 1951, 16.1; 1961, 18.2; 1971, 14.6. In 1931 and 1951, Scotland remained the region with the industrial structure closest to the British mean, and in 1961 and 1971, only north-west England was closer. In general terms, the other British regions were converging with Scotland. Nevertheless, the general process of convergence in the industrial regions of Britain in the twentieth century is not mirrored (up to 1971) within Scotland.

In many respects, the traditional specialisations of the nineteenth century remained in the regions of Scotland well into this century. The temporal trajectories suggest that in the twentieth century the regions retained the relative positions bequeathed to them by the nineteenth century. In most respects, industrial differentiation within Scotland has been of a higher order of magnitude than the industrial differentiation of Scotland from the rest of Britain. Perhaps the tendency to write the economic history of Scotland from the standpoint of one region – usually west-central Scotland – reflects itself in the belief that all of Scotland is, accordingly, regionally specialised. Far from being a specialised 'region' of Britain, however, Scotland throughout its industrial history has shared a very similar profile to Britain as a whole, while containing considerable internal specialisation, reflecting its position as a distinct country within the United Kingdom.

In terms of understanding occupational change, change at the broader sectoral level has been much more important than change in the industrial structure. Although it is from 1951 onwards that the 'occupational transition' – the shift from manufacturing to service employment – is thought to have occurred in advanced industrial societies, only in the 1970s does this happen in a fairly unequivocal way. The accelerating increase in the share of the service sector – from 24 per cent in 1951, to 33 per cent in 1971, to 66 per cent in 1991, and to 70 per cent by the turn of the century – is undoubtedly the greatest single shift in sectoral employment which Scotland has experienced in modern times. The growth of the service sector has been by far the greatest single identifiable motor of social change in Scotland since 1945. The changes in occupational structure, patterns of female employment and social mobility right through to household structure, demographic behaviour and political orientations can be traced back to this single transformation. These will be analysed in the following chapters.

Changing ownership and control

The final quarter of the twentieth century saw a new concern emerge: the increasing external ownership of much of Scottish business. The influx of foreign-owned plants began to generate concern over Scotland becoming a 'branch-plant economy' (Firn, 1975; Young, 1984). Since the mid-1980s, the following major Scottish companies have been subject to takeover: Distillers (by Guinness), Coats Paton (by Viyella), House of Fraser, Yarrow (Trafalgar House), Bell's (by Guinness). By the early 1990s, a mere five of the top fifty manufacturing companies were controlled from Scotland (*Glasgow Herald*, 15 January 1990). The shift of decision-making furth of Scotland has been a notable feature of the post-war economy. The trend towards external ownership, and hence control, is especially noticeable among the major employers (STUC, 1989). Takeovers have swallowed up Distillers, Britoil, Coats Paton, Govan Shipbuilders and Anderson Strathclyde, and threatened the major Scottish clearing banks. The problem is particularly acute among Scotland's major employers, while among companies operating in Scotland, 61 per cent remain Scottish-owned independents. During 1985 and 1986, external takeovers cut the amount of capital controlled by Scottish-registered commercial and industrial companies from £4672 million in 1985 to £2278 million at the beginning of 1987 (ibid.).

The decline in manufacturing employment would undoubtedly have been much worse were it not for the contribution of incoming multinationals like Motorola, IBM, Hoover and NCR, and the efforts of government agencies like Locate in Scotland and the Scottish Development Agency. The issue of external ownership and control became part of Scottish political discourse from the early 1970s, when John Firn's work on the 1973 database showed that large and fast-growing enterprises operating in advanced sectors of manufacturing were more likely to have their headquarters outwith Scotland, notably in England or North America (Firn, 1975). Since Firn carried out his work in 1973, the trend towards foreign investment has continued, and Scotland has taken on the characteristics of a branch-plant economy. Work by the Scottish Office in the 1980s confirmed the trend (Taylor, 1986). While in 1950 only 4 per cent of Scottish manufacturing employment was provided in overseas-owned plants, by the mid-1980s it stood at 19 per cent, some 72,000 jobs in over 300 foreign-owned plants. Overseas ownership of Scotland's manufacturing base is compounded by ownership by British conglomerates controlled via the City of London, which controls well over half of Scottish manufacturing capital. As a result of government policy of privatising major companies like Yarrows, Scott Lithgows and Britoil, the share of manufacturing employment provided by Scottish-owned companies was less than 40 per cent by the late 1980s (STUC, 1989; Lee, 1995).

To be sure, the loss of local economic control in Scotland had been taking place since the early part of the twentieth century, as bank mergers and the amalgamation of railway and chemical companies took place after the end of the Great War. It was, however, the 1970s and 1980s which saw the branch-plant phenomenon becoming a political issue. In the final years of the twentieth century, however, the steam had gone out of the issue, possibly because it was becoming a fact of global economic life. Clive Lee commented: 'Small, open economies, and Scotland is smaller than the United Kingdom and as open, cannot really dictate effectively to multinational corporations which have numerous alternative venues from which to select bases for their operations' (1995: 125). Studies of external takeovers between 1965 and 1980 found that firms were, by and large, better managed, though managerial functions such as marketing and research and development were located furth of Scotland. Despite high-profile closures by multinational companies such as Singer in 1980 and Timex in 1993, there was little evidence that these were the result of foreign ownership *per se*, and much more to do with diminishing markets for outdated products (Hood and Young, 1984).

By the 1990s, the transformation of the Scottish economy, notably the concentration of electronic expertise in what became known as 'Silicon Glen', was something to be celebrated rather than feared. Information industries have come to dominate Scottish manufacturing output and exports. By the late 1990s, there were over 200 manufacturers employing 46,000 people, one in seven of Scottish manufacturing employment, with 80 per cent of products exported to the rest of the European Union and beyond. Almost two-thirds of employment in electronics manufacturing is provided by multinational enterprise subsidiaries, and fully half in American multinational enterprises (MNEs) alone (Hood, 1999). The success of inward investment into Scotland was disproportionately high. As Neil Hood commented: 'During the 1990s, the Scottish share of foreign inward investment projects coming into the UK typically averaged between 15 and 20 per cent of the annual total' (ibid.: 44).

By the end of the twentieth century, the Scottish economy had been transformed. In the fifteen-year period between 1979 and 1994, employment in banking, finance, insurance and business services had increased by a massive 66 per cent, whereas employment in agriculture, fishing and forestry had declined by 46 per cent, and manufacturing by 41 per cent. This period also saw the transformation of employment in gender terms. Male employment had fallen by almost 20 per cent, and female employment had risen by over 10 per cent, with the effect that by the mid-1990s there were actually more women than men in Scotland's labour force, albeit that most women worked part-time (Brown *et al.*, 1998: 86). One of the effects of this transformation was that Scotland caught up with the rest of the UK in terms of differentials such as gross domestic product (GDP) per head, and rates of unemployment. By 1996, its GDP per head stood at 98 per cent of the UK average, with only London and south-east England having larger shares per capita (*Regional Trends*, 1999: Table 2.3, p. 33). Scotland's official unemployment rate of 8.5 per cent in 1997 was marginally ahead of the UK's 7.1 per cent, but the differential had been considerably reduced since the 1950s and 1960s. Taking the century as a whole, Scotland, it seems, 'has occupied a position in the middle range of the United Kingdom per capita income distribution' (Lee, 1995: 54).

Conclusion

Much of the discussion about Scotland in the final quarter of the twentieth century has focused on the relationship between Scotland and England, and, more specifically, on the extent of divergence, parallelism or convergence between the two countries. The debate over the similarities and differences between Scotland and England with regard to patterns of social and economic development is in many ways a proxy for a deeper debate about Scotland's status as an object of sociological study. Much of this debate has focused on how much divergence there has been with other parts of the United Kingdom, and if so, why. The argument here, however, is that it is not necessary for Scotland to be 'different' in terms of its social structures to be a proper object of sociological study. We do not negate its existence by pointing out that it shares far more similarities with other advanced industrial countries (including England) than differences. As such a society, it will share common mechanisms of social change, while its particular structural position within the international division of labour will be distinctive. Above all, how these changes are interpreted, what they tell Scotland's inhabitants about themselves and their country will depend much more on cultural and ideological systems of understanding. We will explore this in detail in the next chapter when we examine social class and social mobility in Scotland.

4   Getting on in Scotland

That Scotland is a class society would seem to be unarguable. After all, social class has underpinned most of the popular political movements of the past hundred years: Scotland's history can largely be written in terms of class conflict and class politics. In the first half of the twentieth century, the political milestones of 'Red Clydeside' around the Great War, the events of the General Strike in 1926 and the Labour landslide of 1945 were matched by class struggle on the Clyde in the 1970s, labour resistance to Thatcherism in the 1980s and Labour's disproportionate success north of the border in the final quarter of the century. If Scotland was stony ground for the New Right in the 1980s and 1990s, most would explain that in terms of a quite different sort of class politics than south of the border. In similar vein, Scotland has always seemed to generate disproportionate support for socialist parties and movements, for the communists and Independent Labour Party, and in the 1999 Scottish Parliament for the Scottish Socialist Party. Scotland was not only configured by class conflict, but some even spoke of the country as a class in and of itself.

Describing Scotland as an "ethno–class colony" of England has been a rhetoric of leftist and nationalist movements alike. We have already seen in the previous chapter just how powerful such claims have been, especially in the 1970s and 1980s when writers on colonialism such as Wallerstein and Hechter were attributing oppressed status to Scotland. While such theses have effectively been disproved by academic analysis, the thesis of dependency and colonialism still retained a political and rhetorical force in the 1990s. In short, Scotland and class seem to go together. If political movements flourish here, then is it not because Scotland is configured by the politics of class? Even non-Scots are willing to help keep the egalitarian belief alive. Eric Hobsbawm (1969), for example, points up the different historical experiences of Wales and Scotland, and makes their commitment to political radicalism in Liberal then Labour voting a key feature of his opposition to independence for these nations. If nothing else, separation, he judges, would condemn the English to the folly of their own political conservatism.

There is, however, another set of ideas which appear to be at odds with this view of Scotland as a class society. It is the one which stresses that Scotland, far from being closed, is an open society, with few apparent barriers to social mobility. Put simply, the Scottish myth that talent and hard work will out retains a direct parallel in the better-known American Dream of the potential from rags to riches. It is perhaps significant that there is no English equivalent of such force. Some historians have even argued that social class was actually an alien intrusion into Scotland from a much more class-conscious England. The late Gordon Donaldson, historiographer-royal, once commented: 'It is true to this day that Scotland is a more egalitarian country than England, but as a result of class consciousness horizontal divisions into classes have become . . . more important than vertical divisions into nations' (1974: 117). Donaldson was referring to the powerful 'lad o'pairts' myth which takes as axiomatic that social mobility – 'getting on' – is significantly easier in Scotland than in England. Scotland is portrayed as a more socially egalitarian country in which people relate to each other on the basis of merit rather than status, reflected in Robert Burns' 'A man's a man for a' that', chosen, significantly, to be sung at the official opening of the Scottish Parliament in July 1999.

This myth of egalitarianism – myth used here as a truth held to be self-evident – is similar in content and function to the American Dream. In the American context the Dream is a story, a narrative, which helps to define Americans to themselves and others. It is, in other words, an identity myth saying who 'we' are and what are the intrinsic values of a people. Such beliefs – held as in the USA as self-evident – are sustained by the institutions of civil society such as education as well as by wider notions of social opportunity. An appeal to a mythic past has radical as well as nationalist roots. In the 1970s, Stephen Maxwell, a prominent nationalist commented:

> The idea that Scottish society is egalitarian is central to the myth of Scottish Democracy. In its strong nationalist version, class division is held to be an alien importation from England. In the weaker version, it describes the wider opportunity for social mobility in Scotland as illustrated in 'the lad o'pairts' tradition.
>
> (Maxwell, 1976: 5)

In like manner the myth takes on a more radical guise for socialists: 'the myth that the Scottish working class has an instinct for radical if not revolutionary socialism lacking in its Sassenach counterpart' (ibid.)

The Scottish myth persists, then, and lends itself to a variety of uses and interpretations. In many ways, the ambiguity and ambivalence of the myth helps to explain its persistence. In various contexts it has continued to act as a partial interpreter of social reality and social change. Further, as Allan MacLaren has pointed out: 'The belief that Scotland was an open society whose fundamental egalitarianism was gradually eroded, in part by contact with its more powerful neighbours is not just a piece of popular nationalism but has penetrated and been propounded by works of academic scholarship' (1976: 2).

These two dominant accounts, on the one hand that Scotland is irredeemably a class society, on the other that it contains unrivalled openness, at least compared to England, have helped to shape how Scotland sees itself and portrays itself to others. The task of this chapter is not to reconcile what appear to be opposite myths, but to show how they sustain a dialectic which configures to present Scotland as a separate nation, and, crucially, quite unlike its southern neighbour.

While on the face of it such notions of class seem at fundamental odds with each other, the American experience suggests to us that they are not impossible to reconcile. On the one hand, the idea of Scotland being driven by a social class dynamic belongs to features of the social structure and economic relationships, while on the other, the ideology of mobility and openness derives from social values and beliefs. It is not difficult even to show that one sustains the other, for example, that, as in the USA, deep social inequalities can coexist with merito-cratic ideology such that the latter helps to sustain the former (Kluegel and Smith, 1986). Put simply, if everyone has the opportunity to 'get on', then a lack of achievement must result from personal failings rather than structural obstacles, with the effect that people blame themselves for failure (Sennett and Cobb, 1977).

What is social class?

To begin with, let us be a little more rigorous in defining what we mean by social class. First of all, social class implies a relationship; it is not a category as such. In other words, classes only exist in juxtaposition to others. The English historian E. P. Thompson in his classic study *The Making of the English Working Class* commented: 'class is a relationship and not a thing. . . . "It" does not exist, either to have an ideal interest or consciousness, or to lie as a patient on the Adjustor's table' (1968: 11). Second, social class has key dimensions: class struc-ture – how class is 'objectively' constructed and reproduced; class consciousness – the level of culture and meaning which surrounds class and other systems of inequality; and class action, how people mobilise, usually but not exclusively in terms of political and/or social movements. Thus, 'class' can exist at any or all of these three levels, and the relationship between them is complex. Similarly, social classes are not static. In the words of Therborn: 'classes must be seen, not as veritable geological formations, once they have acquired their original shape, but as phenomena in a constant process of formation, reproduction, re-formulation and de-formation' (1983: 39).

Social class refers to the ways power is structured, largely but not exclusively with reference to the economic realm, which differentiates people in the marketplace according to the skills and resources they are able to bring to that market, as well as the rewards they derive from it. All advanced industrial or capitalist societies share similar features. After all, the private ownership of economic resources coupled with the capacity to transmit such property by sale or by inheritance supports the broad power structures within them. For most people their life-chances are determined by what they do for a living, what they work at, because that is the source of their income. It characterises their life security, gives them access to housing, education, social goods and so on. In modern market societies, then, there tend to be three main classes – a dominant class whose power is based on the capital it owns; an intermediate class whose power derives from the educational or organisational skills it possesses; and a subordinate class whose power, such as it is, tends to be based on its physical labour. It is this relationship to the labour market which determines to which social class people belong. Runciman (1990), for example, argues that three key criteria matter: 'control' – an ability or otherwise to control or organise the work process; 'ownership' – the legal title to some productive property; and 'marketability' – the institutionally recognised possession of an attribute, skill or asset with income-generating powers.

In modern times, the conventional rankings are those of the Registrar-General, whose socio-economic groups are 'differentiated by life-style' (Marsh, 1986), and a more sociologically derived schema by Goldthorpe which brings together 'market' and 'work' situations (Runciman's marketability and control aspects respectively). These are described as

> Occupational categories whose members would appear, in the light of the available evidence, to be typically comparable, on the one hand, in terms of their sources and levels of income and other conditions of employment, in their degree of economic security and in their chances of economic advancement; on the other hand, in their location within the system of authority and control governing the processes of production in which they are organised.
>
> (Goldthorpe, 1987: 40)

Scotland's class structure

At the beginning of the twentieth century, around three-quarters of the labour force were manual workers, with the upper and middle classes accounting for around 15 per cent between them. The rest belonged to what would be termed the 'underclass', namely those in very short-term employment or, more usually, long-term unemployment. In other words, the Scottish class structure represented the classic pyramid, with the bulk of the labour force in manual jobs, a small group of non-manual managers and professionals, and at the top a self-contained elite. By the second half of the century, the manual working class had shrunk in size to less than 50 per cent of people in employment, while the middle or service class had grown concomitantly. From 1951 what sociologists call the 'occupational transition', the shift from manufacturing employment to services, has occurred, in line with other advanced industrial societies. The growing share of services, from 19 per cent in 1911 to 43 per cent by 1981, and over 70 per cent by the turn of the century, has been the major motor of economic and social change. It is important to note that what is meant by 'services' has changed considerably over the twentieth century, from domestic service employment to occupations concerned with state service functions like education and social services, and private sector functions such as banking and finance. The changing occupational structure and concomitant patterns of social mobility, coupled with new opportunities for women, have ushered in major political and social change.

The trend for women to participate in the labour force has been a feature north and south of the border. In Scotland, however, as far as married women are concerned, the trend has been one of convergence. Until well after 1945, the economic activity rate for married women in Scotland was only two-thirds that of the rest of Britain, and it was not until the late 1970s that Scotland caught up. By 1981, 57 per cent of married women in Scotland under age 60 were economically active. The expansion of new occupations for women runs alongside the feminisation of certain occupations such as clerical work, in which the percentage of clerks who were female rose from about half in 1961 to three-quarters by 1981. Women are not, however, becoming 'middle class' simply because more are in non-manual jobs, because female pay and conditions remain substantially poorer than those of men.

By the 1970s, the trends, which Scotland shared with the rest of the UK, were for the expansion of white-collar work, notably professional employees, and intermediate non-manual workers (teachers and non-managerial workers). Manual workers declined as a percentage of those in employment, from just over half (52 per cent) in 1961, to just over 40 per cent in 1981. In comparison with the rest of the UK, while Scotland had a higher share of manual workers in employment, the general decline was in line with the decline in the United Kingdom. In comparison, Scotland had a lower share of non-manual workers, notably in the private sector, and of own-account workers.

In the 1970s, paralleling the belief that Scotland's industrial structure had been characterised by 'regional specialisation' (reflecting its 'dependency') was the view that its occupational structure had also been shaped by external relationships with England. Specifically, there was the view that Scotland had undergone a process of 'deskilling' or 'proletarianisation' *vis-à-vis* its southern neighbour. This was often linked to the increasing dominance of Scottish manufacturing industry by foreign multinational companies in the post-war period. These elements were appropriately fused in the following:

> in importing production line branch plants requiring, in the main, semi-skilled workers and a disproportionately low number of technical and skilled workers as against indigeneous employers, US firms reinforced the de-skilling processes already at work in the economy. This de-skilling led one writer to conclude that by the mid 1970s, Scotland was 'more working class, and its population . . . less skilled, visavis England, than at any time since the First World War'.

(Dickson, 1980: 246)

The claim that Scotland was being deskilled compared with England in the 1970s was taken up by some writers as the most significant characterisation of the Scottish occupational structure (Watson, 1980: 154; Watt, 1982: 222). The problem was, however, that 'deskilling' was being used to mean different things. On the one hand, it was used to refer to deskilling within the manual labour force, principally in the form of a swing away from skilled manual to semi-skilled manual work (Dickson, 1980). On the other hand, the term was also used to refer to a change in the relative balance between non-manual ('more skilled') and manual (less skilled, but, crucially, including skilled manual workers) (Payne, 1987). In other words, deskilling was taken as referring to a relative diminution of skilled manual workers as a proportion of the *manual* workforce, whereas it was also being used by others to refer to the fact that Scotland has had relatively more skilled and unskilled manual workers as a proportion of the *total* workforce.

The fact that Scotland's industrial structure has been close to the British mean for much of its industrial history suggests, however, that so too would its occupational structure, and this is reflected in the data. Only that of the north-west of England was closer to the British mean in the 1970s, and Scotland's proportion in most socio-economic groups occupies a fairly median position with regard to the other standard regions. Scotland did have the highest proportion of unskilled workers as well as the lowest proportion of *petit bourgeois* groups, employers and managers in small establishments, and own account workers. In terms of white-collar employment, however, the divide was not between Scotland and the rest, but between the south-east of England and the rest. In Scotland, as in other standard economic regions of Britain, the expansion of white-collar employment has been by far the most important transformation since the Second World War.

The expansion in non-manual employment was occurring before 1961, but has continued subsequently, notably for professional employees and intermediate non-manual workers (such as teachers, nurses and 'non-managerial', non-manual workers). Manual work continued to decline, especially the skilled manual group, down from 28 per cent in 1961 to 20 per cent twenty years later. However, Scotland was by no means extreme in this regard, lying in a middle band along with Wales and the north-west of England. It is once again difficult to escape the conclusion that Scotland's occupational structure has largely mirrored that of Britain as a whole.

Scotland's class structure has changed in much the same way as that of the rest of Great Britain. We can compare change over time by comparing generations. For example, the British Election Survey of 1997 allows us to compare respondents' occupations with those of their fathers.

What did Scotland's class structure look like at the end of the twentieth century, and how different is it from England's? We can see from Table 4.1 that convergence is virtually complete. While Scotland has marginally fewer routine non-manual workers, its salariat or 'service class' is slightly bigger in proportional terms. In like manner, and in the context of the debate about

Table 4.1 Occupational distributions, England and Wales, and Scotland, 1997

Class	Fathers (percentages)		Respondents (percentages)	
	England and Wales	Scotland	England and Wales	Scotland
I	13.3	12.3	14.3	10.9
II	10.5	10.5	17.4	14.7
III	4.2	3.0	21.6	23.2
IV	15.6	13.4	9.1	6.8
V	15.5	15.0	6.7	8.7
VI	17.1	18.8	9.1	9.1
VII	23.8	27.1	21.8	26.6
Sample sizes (= 100%)	2335	719	2618	821

Notes:

Class	Description
I	'Service class': all higher grade professionals, self-employed or salaried; higher grade administrators and officials in local and central government, and public and private enterprises; managers in large industrial establishments.
II	'Subaltern or cadet levels of service class': lower grade professionals and higher grade technicians; lower grade administrators and officials.
III	'White-collar labour force': routine non-manual employees in administration and commerce; sales personnel; other rank-and-file employees in services.
IV	'*Petite bourgeoisie*': small proprietors, including farmers and smallholders; self-employed artisans; all other own account workers except professionals.
V	'Blue-collar elite': lower grade technicians (largely manual); supervisors of manual workers.
VI	Skilled manual workers.
VII	Semi- and unskilled and agricultural workers.

Source: British Election Survey, 1997

deskilling alluded to earlier, it has a marginally bigger manual working class, but somewhat more skilled manual workers. What these data show is the growth in non-manual employment in all parts of Great Britain, especially in the white-collar labour force (class III). There are, of course, important gender effects in these changes, such that white-collar work is the largest occupational category for women, as we can see from Table 4.2.

It is difficult to escape the conclusion that the considerable divergence in political behaviour between Scotland and England since the 1970s cannot be explained by the fact that the two countries have distinctly different class structures. As we shall see, the explanation lies far less in difference of class structure and much more in the realm of class culture and political action.

Social mobility in Scotland

Simply describing the class structure at different time-points is valuable, but limiting. It tells us nothing about social mobility, that is, how people move, if they do, between social classes, especially across the generations. This is

Table 4.2 Occupational distributions by gender, England and Wales, and Scotland, 1997

Class	Male respondents (percentages)		Female respondents (percentages)	
	England and Wales	Scotland	England and Wales	Scotland
I	19.4	18.0	9.3	4.4
II	14.8	12.8	20.0	16.4
III	6.5	7.5	36.6	37.5
IV	14.2	9.5	4.1	4.3
V	9.8	13.7	3.5	4.1
VI	14.3	15.8	3.9	2.9
VII	21.0	22.6	22.6	30.3
Sample sizes (= 100%)	1229	363	1389	458

Source: British Election Survey, 1997

what sociologists call inter-generational social mobility such that individuals can move up or down the social class ladder in comparison with their families of origin. In the mid-1970s there were major British and Scottish studies of social mobility, and while these studies were explicitly sexist – women's class positions were deemed to be best read off those of their partners – they do clearly show the social mobility implications of the continuing expansion of non-manual work in the post-war period.

We should keep in mind that any study of social mobility in Scotland is likely to underrate the true rates of mobility because of disproportionately high rates of out-migration north of the border. Nevertheless, we would expect Scottish patterns to be similar not just to England and Wales, but to most other European countries in so far as it has a market economy, and its social structure is founded on the nuclear family:

> these are all countries with similar forms of capitalism and a shared recent history. However, we would not expect precisely the same patterns of mobility because Scotland has not shared an identical history. Its separate culture and historically subordinate relationship to England mean that its employment opportunities have been distinctive.
>
> (Payne, 1987: 2)

Looking at the pattern of recruitment as a whole, Payne's conclusion from his own analysis of the Scottish data still holds, both north and south of the border: 'Although this is not to say that Scotland is an "open" or egalitarian society, it does show that direct inheritance of occupations is relatively rare' (ibid.: 65). These data do seem to confirm the relative openness of social mobility in Scotland (and in England and Wales, for that matter). The significant changes in the employment structure of Scotland, Wales and England since 1945 have helped to create, at least in non-manual occupations, heterogeneous groupings drawn from across the social spectrum. We should bear in mind, however, that social opportunity is by no means equally distributed. For example, while 22 per cent in the service class (I) had class I fathers, this group represented only 5 per cent of the population; hence the opportunities for class I sons to 'self-recruit' were over four times greater than perfect mobility expectation (reflecting the raw marginal distribution), while the inflow into class I from classes VI and VII was only about half of what might be expected if life-chances were distributed equally.

The 1970s

The dominant impression from the analysis of social mobility patterns in the 1970s was one of similarity between Scotland and the rest of Britain, rather than difference. The significant differences occur among the *petite bourgeoisie* (class IV), although it seems that fewer sons of class II fathers made it into class I compared with England and Wales, and there was a higher degree of class retention in class II. Given the differences in employment structures north and south of the border, the similarities in social mobility patterns were what is striking, not the differences. Goldthorpe's remark in this respect was sound: 'On the basis of such comparison, it would seem clear enough that, had our enquiry been extended to Scotland, no substantially different results would have been produced so far at least as the pattern of de facto inter-generational rates is concerned' (1980: 291). He concluded that the mobility model for England and Wales had a tolerably good fit with the Scottish data, the model accounting for over 95 per cent of the association between class of origin and destination.

In the later edition of his social mobility study (1987), Goldthorpe set the Scottish experience in the wider context of other industrial nations – England and Wales, France, West Germany, Republic of Ireland, Sweden, Hungary and Poland. As regards relative rates of mobility:

> England and Wales, together with France, turn out to be the most central nations with the configuration that emerges. Scotland and Northern Ireland, along with Hungary, fall into the intermediate band, and it is Poland, Sweden, West Germany and Ireland which, in that order, represent the most outlying cases.
>
> (Ibid.: 309)

As regards absolute rates of mobility (reflecting structural or exogeneous factors), Scotland, England and Wales shared common characteristics by virtue of early industrialisation and the demise of a peasantry. Hence, in terms of comparative inflow rates, Scotland, as well as England and Wales, had the highest percentage in classes I and II who originate from manual working classes, and the lowest recruitment from farm origins (unlike the Republic of

Ireland, for example). On the other hand, the British nations showed the highest proportions of self-recruitment into the manual working classes, with Poland and Hungary the lowest. These patterns are the result of a shared economic history of industrialisation. In Goldthorpe's words:

> Britain's early industrialisation and the unique path that it followed can be rather clearly associated, first, with a service class recruited to an unusual degree from among the sons of blue collar workers, and secondly with a broadly defined industrial working class which is to an unusual degree self-recruited or which, one could alternatively say, is highly homogeneous in its composition in terms of its members' social origins.
>
> (Ibid.: 316)

Britain, he concludes, does not possess any kind of historical legacy or institutional barriers (reflected in these data) either to impede or to promote social fluidity. In this context, Scotland together with England and Wales are the nations in which the distributions of social origins and destinations differ least. On reflection, we should not be surprised at this finding, because Scotland, England and Wales share common features as industrialised countries. Plainly, it would be perverse to conclude from the general data on social mobility patterns that Scotland had taken a different mobility route from the rest of the UK. Scotland has a slightly smaller middle class, and a slightly larger manual working class, but the processes of upward and downward social mobility which created these structures of opportunity are remarkably similar on both sides of the Tweed.

The picture of inter-generational social mobility in Scotland in the 1970s, then, was of a society similar in many ways to England and Wales, with a substantial proportion of the service class drawn up from manual working-class backgrounds. For example, fully one-third of the top salariat had fathers who had been in manual jobs, and for class II, the figure was 43 per cent. On the other hand, the manual working classes (VI and VII) were much more homogeneous and self-recruiting. In other words, while there was considerable upward mobility into the social classes at the top, there was little corresponding downward mobility into the lower social classes. This lack of correspondence was due to the fact that while the size of the manual working class had shrunk, that of the service classes had grown, thus allowing those who were already there to stay there, as well as permitting considerable upward social mobility from below. In other words, the changing shape and size of social classes within the class structure was permitting class retention at the top and class mobility from the bottom.

The 1990s

The social mobility studies of the 1970s depicted a post-war society in which the expansion of non-manual occupations reflected the growing public as well as private sectors. What was the impact on social mobility of the election of the first of the Thatcher government in 1979, dedicated to 'rolling back the state', particularly into public sector service class employment? There have, in truth, been no systematic studies of social mobility along the lines of the 1970s studies, but the British and Scottish election studies of the 1990s in particular provide important clues as to the answer. Taking the 1997 studies at which Scottish numbers were enhanced so as to provide comparisons between Scotland, and England and Wales, we find a considerable degree of continuity with the post-war period. Given that we have information on all respondents rather than simply males as in the 1970s studies, and taking fathers' occupations as the benchmark, we find continuing upward mobility implied in the 1990s, as Table 4.3 indicates. Table 4.4 confirms that much of the upward social mobility was into middle-class jobs, thereby helping to construct a larger and much more socially diverse middle class, at least in terms of social origins.

Once more, the similarities between Scotland, and England and Wales are far more striking than the differences. It is simply not possible to sustain an argument that somehow Scotland and England were diverging in terms of social, that is, occupational mobility. The structural similarities between the main parts of the United Kingdom were following similar patterns. This is not to suggest, however, that because both in terms of class structure and social mobility patterns Scotland, and England and Wales were converging, their populations were perceiving these patterns in the same way. We began this chapter by pointing out that social class had to be disaggregated into the components of structure, consciousness and action. We also need to remember that

Table 4.3 Inter-generational social mobility, Scotland, and England and Wales, 1975 and 1997

	1975 Men	1997	1997 Men	1997 Women
Percentage of whole sample who have been upwardly mobile				
Scotland	42	47	47	48
England and Wales	43	47	45	50
Percentage of whole sample who have not been mobile				
Scotland	30	24	27	22
England and Wales	28	24	28	19
Percentage of whole sample who have been downwardly mobile				
Scotland	29	29	27	30
England and Wales	28	29	27	31

Notes
Unweighted sample sizes (= 100%); Scotland 1997: Men 304, Women 387; England and Wales 1997: Men 1094, Women 1162.

Source: Goldthorpe, 1980: 289, 290; British Election Survey, 1997

Table 4.4 Inter-generational social mobility into and out of the middle class,[1] Scotland, and England and Wales, 1975 and 1997

	1975 Men	1997	1997 Men	1997 Women
Percentage of whole sample who have been upwardly mobile into the middle class				
Scotland	20	29	22	35
England and Wales	22	30	25	35
Percentage of whole sample who have been stable middle class				
Scotland	8	28	27	30
England and Wales	9	32	31	34
Percentage of whole sample who have been downwardly mobile out of the middle class				
Scotland	11	10	11	8
England and Wales	12	10	12	8

Notes
[1] Classes I, II, III and IV.
Unweighted sample sizes (= 100%); Scotland 1997: Men 304, Women 387; England and Wales 1997: Men 1094, Women 1162.

Source: Goldthorpe, 1980: 289, 290; British Election Survey, 1997

there need not be a necessary correspondence between people's occupational class position, what we might call their 'objective' class, and how they make sense of that, their 'subjective' class. This is brought out very clearly in Table 4.5, which focuses on how people describe their current class. This table focuses on social classes I and II ('professionals') so that we can draw inferences about the upper reaches of the class structure.

While those in non-professional positions in both Scotland, and England and Wales are just as likely to describe themselves as 'working class', regardless of class of origin, the differences among professionals are very striking. For

Table 4.5 Self-assigned class, by own class and father's class, 1997

Respondent's objective class	Father's objective class	Scotland	England and Wales
Not professional	Not professional	85 (443)	76 (1249)
Not professional	Professional	49 (52)	53 (233)
Professional	Not professional	59 (109)	50 (433)
Professional	Professional	28 (68)	25 (279)

Notes
The figures show the percentage describing themselves as 'working class'.
Unweighted sample sizes (= 100%) are in brackets.
Objective classes: professional is classes I and II.

Source: British Election Survey 1997.

example, those who are mobile out of the working class into the professional classes in Scotland are significantly more likely to describe themselves as 'working class' than are similar people south of the border, while a similar differential operates even among those who are professionals from professional origins. What might this be telling us? Put simply, it seems to indicate that the culture or meaning of class operates differently, that people in Scotland are much more likely to say they are working class, regardless either of class of origin, or class of destination.

We cannot be sure just why people in Scotland are more likely to do this than their counterparts in England (one might expect Wales to be different, but the data are unaggregated for England and Wales), and cross-sectional surveys are probably not the best sort of medium for getting at the nuances of meaning which must be involved. Most sociologists recognise Marx's distinction between '*klasse an sich*' and '*klasse für sich*', that is, that the existence of classes objectively does not determine how their members see themselves. Whether or not people use class categories and what they mean when they do so depends on an array of social and cultural forces impacting upon how they view and make sense of the world around them. It does, however, draw us back to important matters of culture which are underpinned by institutional differences. Let us assume that we were interested in studying social class in different societies, say in Germany and France. We would have little quarrel with the view that, by and large, their class structures were quite similar, and yet the meanings of class, generated by distinct political cultures and histories, were different. We would acknowledge, for example, that these cultures are historically constructed and refracted through, for example, the political agendas in the two countries. While this might seem an obvious point to make in this context, it is frequently unobserved when looking at differences within the societies of these islands. Put simply, we should not expect that social class in Scotland will be interpreted and explained in the same way as in England, because key institutions such as the legal system, religion and the education system will evidently mediate structures and experiences to produce different political and social outcomes.

The Scottish myth

This is the context, then, for re-introducing the conundrum we set out at the beginning of this chapter, namely, the existence of what we called the 'Scottish myth'. We use this term 'myth' not to imply that it is untrue, but that it refers to a set of self-evident truths which are not amenable to 'proof'. Myths of this sort, and this includes its comparator, the American Dream, are not meant to be open to proof or disproof. The notion that hard work coupled with ability will lead to achievement unless you are particularly unlucky is a powerful value in the USA. It is a story, a narrative of considerable power which helps to define Americans to themselves, and they hope to other people. It is an identity myth, saying who they are and who they are not. In like manner, the Scottish myth – with interesting parallels with the American one – is a truth held to be self-evident, that all people are created equal, that 'we're a' Jock Tamson's bairns', and 'a man's a man for a' that'.

Myths are notoriously difficult to examine. By their nature, they represent a collection of symbolic elements assembled to account for and validate a set of social institutions. In Mitchell's words, myths operate 'to record and present the moral system whereby present attitudes and actions are ordered and validated' (1968: 122). 'Myth' here does not refer to something which is manifestly false but to a perspective, a guide to help interpret social reality. As guides, myths are of little help in predicting or explaining actual features of the social structure.

In so far as myths are drawn from the past, they are akin to 'traditions', and like traditions have an active, contemporary significance (Williams, 1977: 115). Like traditions, myths connect with past realities. They do, however, draw selectively from the past, a process which involves selective exclusion as well as inclusion. In so doing, myth becomes a contemporary and active force providing, in most instances, a reservoir of legitimation for belief and action.

In the Scottish myth, the central motif is the inherent egalitarianism of the Scots. This motif operates in different ways and at different levels. While there are social structural factors such as the system of education or forms of democracy which are judged to have contributed to the relatively open and democratic ethos of seventeenth-century Scotland, the myth of egalitarianism has at root an a-sociological, almost mystical element. It is as if Scots are judged to be egalitarian by dint of racial characteristics, of deep social values. Man (or at least Scots-man) is judged to be primordially equal; inequality is man-made, created by the social structure he (for the myth has historically been male-centred) erects, or which is erected by others around him.

The myth is ambivalent, and it lends itself to two interpretations. The first, which might be called the activist interpretation, takes the coexistence of man-made inequality and primordial equality, and argues for an active resolution of this apparent anomaly in favour of social equality. A second interpretation, which might be labelled 'idealist', adopts a more conservative response. If man is primordially equal, social structural inequalities do not matter, so nothing needs to be done. In this way, the egalitarian myth lends itself to conservative as well as to radical interpretations.

These levels can be seen in at least two forms in Scots vernacular: the allusion to common humanity in 'we're a' Jock Tamson's bairns', and in Burns' poem 'A man's a man for a' that'. The former phrase seems to have no precise origin in literature, whereas Burns' title so struck a chord in his own society that it entered immediately into the language (Craig, 1961: Ch.4). 'Jock Tamson's bairns' has a curious and fascinating set of meanings associated with it. According to David Murison's authoritative *Scottish National Dictionary* (1986, Vol. V: 337), the most common meaning is 'the human race; common humanity; also with less universal force, a group of people united by a common sentiment, interest or purpose' – innocuous enough, and fitting in with its usage by Presbyterian ministers to refer to 'God's children'. There are, however, darker meanings: 'Jock Tamson' can also refer, jocularly, to whisky; more darkly, to a Scottish version of 'John Thomas', which certainly conveys more force to the 'common humanity' reference.

In the same way that 'we're a' Jock Tamson's bairns' touches upon the essential common humanity, Burns' A Man's a Man for a' that' seems to strip away the differences which are essentially social constructions. In spite of these (the 'a' that') Burns is saying that people are equal. His message of equality, however, is ambiguous. He is calling not for a levelling down of riches, but for a proper, that is, moral appreciation of 'the man o' independent mind'. It is 'pith o' sense and pride o' worth' which matters, not the struttings and starings of 'yon birkie ca'd a lord'. The ambiguity of his message is retained to the last stanza: 'that man to man the world o'er shall brothers be for a' that' – an appeal to the virtues of fraternity rather than equality in its strict sense.

There are two sets of implications to be drawn. In the 'idealist' version, the objective facts of social inequality, status and poverty melt into insignificance alongside the common humanity (and Scottishness) of people. In the 'activist' version, Burns is making a revolutionary appeal. In his own time, the French Revolution and the appeals for democracy gave a heady political flavour to such poetry, and in David Craig's opinion 'the significant Scottish literature of that time was popular, entirely so, and furthermore, the polite public tended to hold aloof from such work' (1961: 111). Burns may simply have adopted 'a man's a man . . .' from the vernacular, but there is no doubt that such works had an immediate popular impact, finding their way into popular parlance, reinforcing the imagery of egalitarianism.

Although egalitarianism was, in essence, a set of social values, a body of sacred truth, it has often connected with features of the social structure. 'Facts' about the social structure can provide prima facie support for the myth, or, more likely, a set of data requiring interpretation. Nevertheless, myths do not depend on 'facts' to sustain them. Egalitarianism refers essentially to a set of social values, an ethos, a celebration of sacred beliefs; social inequality, on the other hand, is a characterisation of the social structure referring specifically to the distribution of resources, rewards and opportunities. In Scotland, the egalitarian myth has proved largely impervious to falsification, not because appropriate data are not always available, but because 'myth' in essence cannot be 'disproved'. Nor should they be cast out as 'unscientific'. As Andrew McPherson has pointed out: 'The demythologiser is as likely to de-historicise, to discount the significance of the interplay over time of changing forms and ideas, as is the prisoner of myths who interprets present institutions as the unchanged expression of a timeless ideal' (1983: 217).

In a similar way and for similar reasons, sociological evidence has made little impression on the American Dream – the idea that hard work and ability will lead to achievement. Plainly, myths and legends of this sort could not be sustained if they had no connection whatsoever with what people recognised as reality. However, the Scottish myth and the American Dream belong to the realm of those 'truths we hold self-evident, that all men are created equal'. The coexistence of egalitarian beliefs and socially created inequality need not be a contradiction in either society. The conservative may use it to justify the social order; the radical may seek to rectify the anomaly in political and economic ways.

Education and the Scottish myth

One of the key carriers of that identity has been the education system. In this regard, the ideology has been kept alive by the experiences and beliefs of those who have led that system. Andrew McPherson has spoken of the 'Kirriemuir career', both moral and secular, and a 'symbolic world bounded by Angus, standing for the East and North and with Kirriemuir at its heart, by Dumfries in the South and, in the West by a Glasgow academy, perhaps The Academy' (1983: 228).

McPherson's analysis of the Scottish Advisory Council on Education between 1957 and 1961 shows that only four out of minimally sixteen members came from the west of Scotland, and most articulated an image of Scotland 'as a nation of small towns, and implicitly therefore, a Protestant nation' (ibid: 233). As many as nine of the sixteen held posts in independent, semi-independent or fee-paying schools, so the lad o'pairts ideology was mobilised in the late 1960s in defence of the local authority fee-paying system. The debates about educational change in the 1960s took on a particular Scottish flavour with the publication in 1961 of George Davie's *The Democratic Intellect*, which, observed Andrew McPherson, 'served, in the context of English debates of the time about social class inequalities of access to educational opportunity in England, only to confirm to Scottish opinion the egalitarian pedigree of the national institution that Scotland had substituted for English gentility' (ibid.: 225–6).

Robert Anderson's work on the university system also adds some evidence that the myth is supported by reality. He observes: 'The evidence suggests that the Welsh and Scottish "democratic myths" had some substance, and that members of the British elite recruited there may have had broader social origins than their English colleagues' (1991: 12). Robert Anderson's re-analysis of data from the 1860s Argyll Commission on Scottish Education shows that as late as the third quarter of the nineteenth century many of working-class and peasant origin attended Scotland's universities. Taking a sample of 882 students (a quarter of the total) the Commission showed that 50 per cent came from professional or business families, 127 were sons of farmers, others were from *petit bourgeois* backgrounds, but that 200 (23 per cent) could be described as 'working class'. They were largely the sons of skilled artisans (carpenters and joiners, masons and shoemakers), or miners. Only two were the sons of crofters, three of shepherds, two of farm-hands, one of a fisherman, and thirteen of labourers. He concludes: 'It was thus the skilled urban elite of the working class from which university students came rather than from the families of factory workers or the really poor' (1985: 92).

Working-class students in the late nineteenth century were usually mature men who had prepared through private study or evening classes, and a few were qualified teachers. Although the Scottish system (one in 1000) had more university places than England (one in 5800) or Germany (one in 2600), it was based on the tradition of competitive individualism, or, in the term of Ralph Turner, 'contest mobility' (1960) in which individual failure or success maintained the system ideologically. Lasses o'pairts were barely recognised, and Catholics were virtually non-existent in the university system (only two could be found in a sample of 1779 students between 1860 and 1900, at a time when Catholics numbered about 8.5 per cent of the Scottish population in 1891 (Brown, 1988)).

Nevertheless, both Aberdeen and Glasgow universities had unusually large numbers of the 'disadvantaged'. While Aberdeen took in a large proportion of students from agricultural backgrounds (16 per cent in 1860 and 20 per cent in 1910), Glasgow had a higher percentage of students from manual working-class backgrounds (19 per cent in 1860 and 24 per cent in 1910). For Aberdeen, 'the majority of those who went to the university from a parish school were not poor boys but the sons of the rural middle class – of the minister, of the schoolmaster himself, of farmers, often described as prosperous although this category could cover different levels of wealth' (Anderson, 1983: 124).

Glasgow, on the other hand, catered for the sons of skilled artisans, but with a much larger pool of students to draw on. Nevertheless, 'by the eve of the First World War, the proportion of working class students was as high at Glasgow as it was later in the 20th century' (Anderson, 1983: 309). As the nineteenth century wore on, the proportion of university students from parish schools was in decline, while those from burgh schools increased. The traditional urban high schools catered for the professional and commercial classes, in which, says Anderson, 'both peer and peasant were conspicuous by their absence' (ibid.: 140). The idealisation of the rural parish school began in the 1890s (in the Kailyard literature, for instance,) just as it was vanishing in practice, generating a rearguard defence of the institution and its culture, and lending validity to that version of the myth which sees it as a Scottish characteristic which has been eroded by Anglicisation (Davie, 1961).

In his fine study of farm life in north-east Scotland, Ian Carter charts the decline of the peasant stock in the late nineteenth century, who were in many ways the ideal type for the lad o'pairts. Leasing marginal land from landlords who were themselves sweirt to bring it into cultivation, the peasant class struggled to make a living until their labours were no longer required. However,

> The crofter's son who stayed on the land might hope to climb some way up the farming ladder. His chances were not very good after the middle of the nineteenth century – it is clear that relatively few peasant farmers made it in these years into the ranks of the larger farmers – but the ideology of the

lad o'pairts asserted the opposite and moulded the aspirations of the peasant children.

(Carter, 1979: 94)

As Anderson points out, myths do not survive and flourish unless they express some fundamental truths, unless they connect with the realities of life. The Scottish myth of egalitarianism survived because it kept alive a sense of national identity, as I shall show later in this chapter. In the shorter term, the lad o'pairts ideal survived because it was transposed on to other social groups than those for whom it had been intended. In Anderson's words:

The lad of parts did exist, but they were drawn from the middle rather than the lower ranks; the children of ministers, teachers, farmers, shopkeepers and artisans enjoyed opportunities, especially for entry to the professions, which long had no equivalent in other countries. Scotland was also unusual in providing such opportunities even in remote areas, and it was the rurality as much as the social origins of the lad of parts which attracted attention.

(Anderson, 1985: 100)

We should remind ourselves in dealing with the egalitarian myth that direct proof is hard to come by. However, its survival as a cultural construct depended perhaps less on what people actually believed and more on what institutional carriers were available. The Scottish educational system has provided such a carrier, and its administrative elite gave voice to it right down to modern times (McPherson and Raab 1988).

The mythology of the lad o'pairts does appear to have survived well into the twentieth century, and in his re-analysis of the 1947 Scottish Mental Study, Keith Hope argues that the notion of educational opportunity – or 'merit-election' as he calls it – has some basis in fact. Recognising that 'the native tradition of meritelection, in which educational selection of the "lad o'pairts" was a recognised mode of social ascent of the poor [*sic*]' (1984: 19), Hope studied 590 males who were 11 years old in 1947 in order to find out the main determinants of their occupational position as 27- to 28-year-olds in 1964. Using path-analytical techniques, he concluded that 'Scotland, as we would expect, is more meritelective than the United States' (ibid.: 30) even during this period when selective education was operating. Admitting that the concept 'equality of opportunity' has different meanings in each system, he is convinced that the Scottish system offered greater equality of opportunity in this period than its US counterpart. While the Scottish myth does seem to receive some confirmation in these studies (English data were not available to Hope), we will see that its survival does not rely on material confirmation, but on its capacity to provide a reinforcement of the Scottish identity.

Further support for the 'myth' can be found in the analysis of social selection in European educational systems. Mueller and Karle (1990) showed that the skilled working class in Scotland after 1945 had similar educational

opportunities to mainland Europe whereas this class was noticeably disadvantaged in England. Nor was this comparative advantage confined to the
skilled working class. They point out: 'Scotland . . . deviates from the cross-
national average in another respect: the offspring of the petty bourgeoisie
have much better opportunities to survive in the Scottish educational system
than in any of the other countries' (ibid.: 22).

   The Scottish myth, then, is kept alive not simply because people believe it to
be founded in fact, but also because there are institutional mechanisms, like the
education system and its ideology, which provide sufficient affirmation of its
validity. Scottish education even carried its own personam, the lad o'pairts
who was, in David Murison's phrase, a 'talented youth', often the son of a
crofter or peasant who had the ability but not the means to benefit from education. The term itself seems to have originated, according to Murison, in the late
nineteenth century, and its first citing appears in the story 'Domsie' by the Kailyard novelist, 'Ian MacLaren'. This story of thirty-three pages overtly describes
the short life of George, a talented pupil who wins prize medals in Latin and
Greek, ending up with a double-first degree at university. The real 'hero' of
the story is Domsie, the dominie or schoolteacher, whose task it is to spot
likely talent and persuade the local farmer, Drumsheugh, to put up the
money for the boys' fees at university. So successful was this village dominie
that: 'Seven ministers, four schoolteachers, four doctors, one professor and
three civil service men had been sent out by the auld schule in Domsie's
time, besides many that "had given themselves to mercantile pursuits"'
(MacLaren, 1940: 8).

   MacLaren's careful accounting of the 'professions' contrasted with his vagueness about the number going to trade (the quotation marks seem to withhold
approval for such a career) indicates the social values being celebrated. Teaching, ministering and administering are the prime goals; Latin and Greek (with
some maths and philosophy) plainly echo the old Scottish curriculum.

   The teacher's obsessions are shared with the community. MacLaren leads us
to believe that:

> There was just a single ambition in those humble homes, to have one of its
> members at college, and if Domsie approved a lad, then his brothers and
> sisters would give their wages, and the family would live on skim milk
> and oat cake, to let him have his chance.
>
> (Ibid.: 10)

   The mawkish, sentimental tone comes into its own as MacLaren takes four-
teen out of thirty-three pages to describe the final illness and death of Domsie's
protégé. There is no doubting, however, the real hero in these Kailyard stories:

> Domsie, as we called the schoolmaster, behind his back in Drumtochty,
> because we loved him, was true to the tradition of his kind, and had an
> unerring scent for 'pairts' in his laddies. He could detect a scholar in the

egg, and prophesied Latinity from a boy that seemed only fit to be a cowherd.

(Ibid.: 8)

Whatever the merits and influences of the Kailyard tradition, the 'lad o'pairts' appears to have been a central image of late nineteenth- and early twentieth-century Scotland. However, the egalitarian element of the lad o'pairts had a precise meaning and specific sociological significance, for as Allan MacLaren has pointed out:

the egalitarianism so often portrayed is not that emerging from an economic, social or even political equality; it is equality of opportunity which is exemplified. All men are not equal. What is implied is that all men are given the opportunity to be equal. Whatever the values attached to such a belief, if expressed today, it would be termed elitist not egalitarian.

(MacLaren, 1976: 2)

Strictly, of course, MacLaren is correct that it is elitist, but the key point is that it is an instance of competitive equal opportunity. This 'opportunity' did not simply relate to equality of educational achievement or outcome for broad classes or collectivities. Instead it referred to a formal opportunity afforded to an able pupil to proceed through the parish school to university. In this regard, it drew upon a meritocratic tradition rather than an egalitarian one. The lad o'pairts' path was smoothed by the local dominie who would bully, cajole and persuade affluent members of the parish, as in the case of Drumsheugh, the local farmer, to give a bursary to support his lad o'pairts.

It is interesting to note that the lad had no gender equivalent in a 'lass o'pairts', although we cannot rule out the ubiquitous use of the male descriptor to cover males and females. Critics have pointed out that the egalitarian tradition in Scotland has hidden gender inequalities in education (Fewell and Paterson, 1990). A lass o'pairts, they argue, has no status at all in the Scottish educational tradition, and beliefs about the importance of domesticity have overwhelmed female education. It is important to note, however, that while opportunities were gendered, they were not absent for women. While teaching was highly segregated, teacher training offered significant social advancement for women (Corr, 1990; McPherson, 1992). One of the main problems we have with this debate about the lad o'pairts is that we have very little evidence as to whether or not it had an impact on ordinary people. In a fine piece of oral history of those who were schoolchildren in the early part of this century, Lynn Jamieson points out that while girls' and boys' experience of schooling has to be set in a gendered context, 'the reality for both boys and girls remained overwhelmingly one in which you left school as soon as possible' (1990: 37). Most pupils and their parents would have agreed with the character in William Alexander's novel set in the north-east in the late nineteenth century: 'there's little use for vreetin' [writing] aiven to loons; an' for lassies to hae ocht adee wi't's gaun clean oot o' reel' (quoted in Donaldson, 1986: 17).

In the context of eighteenth-century Scotland, however, the lad o'pairts system might work tolerably well, for a small, local elite was being catered for in a limited number of professions – education, law, the ministry and religion, and sometimes medicine. The failure of a talented lad to make it was rarely an indictment of the system itself because it seemed to rely on personal contacts and moral worth. Failure could result from a poorly connected dominie, or the imputed moral laxity of the candidate. Hence, the 'lad o'pairts' phenomenon seemed to have survived for much longer than it might otherwise have done, because, in Anderson's words: 'The myth of the lad of parts became part of the ideology of 19th century individualism or meritocracy, in which a limited equality of opportunity was held to justify the reinforcing of structural inequalities' (1985: 84).

In many respects, egalitarianism was a key element in a conservative ideology which congratulated itself on the openness of Scottish (essentially rural and small-town) society and its social institutions. What we have termed the 'idealist' version of egalitarianism was conservative, and in the 1960s was being mobilised to defend the existence of state fee-paying schools on the grounds that they, uniquely, afforded the lads o' pairts an educational and social opportunity not given in big city comprehensives. The lad o' pairts was an individual who escaped his working-class or peasant origins. Houston perceives the essentially conservative nature of the myth in his study of literacy. What is interesting to him is not simply the evidence for or against literacy in eighteenth-century Scotland, but why such an ideology should operate in the nineteenth century. He concludes: 'The myth of equality of opportunity in education which purports to describe the social system actually helps to reproduce it by guiding perceptions and actions' (Houston, 1985: 254).

Alongside the lad o' pairts stereotype sat a belief in the inherent democracy of Scottish society. In many ways these were connected because the Kirk, and its secular arm, the parish, lay at the heart of each. Presbyterianism was clearly a more democratic form of church government than Catholicism or Episcopalianism, and the doctrine of predestination, the essence of Calvinism, helped confirm the equality of this elect. Its association with national identity helped it retain its hold for longer than elsewhere. As Callum Brown points out: 'Scotland has been seen as one of a number of regions within European countries where the secularisation of religion has been held in check by the association of religion with a thwarted political nationalism' (1987: 9).

The more conservative side of Presbyterianism was able to translate its belief in character formation into a respect for modest money-making and enterprise. In his study of religion in nineteenth-century Aberdeen, Allan MacLaren showed how religion, education and economy were fused in the Presbyterian mindset: 'Religion is beyond all comparison the most important part of education . . . when properly taught it includes every moral and social duty; and among others, industry, temperance and economy' 1974: 148).

The egalitarian myth is 'old' because it is premised upon the existence of a hierarchical social order, not a classless society. It described ideal conditions in the typical pre-capitalist and pre-industrial community, often rural. Says MacLaren: 'There is some evidence to suggest that the "Scottish Myth" is a product of a former rural paternalism rather than an urban industrialism in which class identity and economic individualism overruled a declining concern for communal and parochial obligations' (1976: 9).

The image of social identity which is held up for praise is one of community, not class. The commitment is to the parish, secular and religious, made up of sturdy and self-sustaining individuals. The social hierarchy of the parish is not questioned, and differences of economic and social power are taken for granted, rather than resented. Material rewards may even bring social or psychological disbenefits, if the social duties and obligations which wealth brings are not carried out. The unalloyed pursuit of profit offends the moral economy of the community (as the anti-Kailyard novels at the turn of this century by George Douglas Brown, *The House with the Green Shutters* (1901), and by J. McDougall Hay, *Gillespie* (1914) set out to show. In this regard, they share the scepticism of Kailyard writers like Ian MacLaren with his suspicion of 'mercantile pursuits'). The political economy of the community inhabited by lads o' pairts is pre-capitalist. Money-making is judged to be too readily motivated by avarice and greed, rather than to be pursued in a rationalistic and emotionally neutral way. The locus of egalitarianism is the parish, in the country village or the small town. Such sentiments might well have chimed with the values of the Presbyterian bourgeoisie in the nineteenth century with its commitment to 'civic duty' (Walker and Gallagher, 1990: 4). In this respect, the cult of the lad o' pairts fitted in well. As Anderson points out:

> It suited the kind of stratified educational system thought appropriate for an industrial society, one in which a basic elementary education for the masses co-existed with a small secondary sector for the middle class; allowing a small number of talented children to cross the barrier satisfied the demand for merit to be rewarded, and was not incompatible with retaining a rather mediocre education for those who were not selected.
>
> (Anderson, 1985: 86)

We should not make the mistake of thinking that the lad o' pairts phenomenon simply belongs to history. The expansion of, first, secondary and then higher education in the twentieth century has provided new opportunities. With something approaching 50 per cent of young people in some form of higher education by the year 2000, access is of a quite different order than it was in the mid-twentieth century. While the middle classes continue to do well out of higher education, there is evidence that social class differences in terms of entry rates have narrowed. Lindsay Paterson has observed: 'whereas in 1981 the entry rates were 27% among school leavers with fathers in professional occupations and 4% among those with fathers in manual occupations (a ratio of nearly 7:1), in 1994 the proportions were 37% and 15% (a ratio of 2.5:1)' (Paterson, 1997a: 13). Lest we think that somehow social class differences are the exception as regards educational inequalities, he points out that young people from ethnic minorities – mainly Asians – have substantially better access rates to higher education than the majority population. In like manner, we have known for some time that Catholic schools have higher achievement rates than non-denominational schools, even though the Catholic population is mainly working class (Willms, 1992). This is not to deny that, largely as a result of parental choice legislation in the 1980s, in Glasgow, for example, there was greater segregation among schools in the final decades of the twentieth century (Adler *et al.*, 1989; Willms, 1995). Growing class inequalities throughout the 1980s and 1990s have also played their part in reinforcing polarisation among schools.

Much of diminishing class differentials in Scottish education derives from the success of comprehensive education. Examination pass rates as a proportion of the age group have steadily risen since such schooling was formally introduced in the 1960s, and with them higher rates of staying on into post-16 education and post-school education. Higher achievement rates for girls over boys are also in evidence (Paterson, 1997b). The Scottish population continues to value comprehensive education positively (Brown *et al.*, 1998), and there has not been the attrition to private education seen in England since the 1980s, reflecting the loss of faith in public education south of the border.

Much of the reason for the relative success of Scottish education lies in the fact that the progressive coalition has held together better than in England. Believers in economic efficiency made sufficient common cause with popular educators and humanists who argued for universal education, reinforced by a more widespread nationalistic belief that Scottish education was one of the defining characteristics of the nation. The role of the 'Scottish myth' has been to translate national distinctiveness into institutional characteristics, reinforced by relative success in improving access to cultural capital. That is reflected in significant improvements in staying on rates among the children of those who benefited from the expansion of comprehensive education in the 1960s and 1970s (Burnhill *et al.*, 1990). It also helps to explain why education and national identity are inextricably linked in Scotland (McCrone, 1999). Education, however, is not the only means of 'getting on'. So is 'getting out'.

Getting on and getting out

The frequently forgotten feature of the Kailyard school, which we will examine in greater depth in Chapter 6, is that this genre of literature was written largely for an overseas market, especially in North America (Donaldson, 1986). To the exiled Scot, the Scottish self-image of egalitarianism evoked a nostalgia for a homely, rural past of the forefathers which 'produced the full Kailyard and

"Canadian Boat Song" nostalgia, fixated on the auld hame, the wee hoose and the whaups crying on the moor' (Craig, 1961: 148). The role of émigré Scots in sustaining this idealisation of the homeland is crucial. Some two million people have left Scotland in the twentieth century (Lindsay, 1991), and at least similar numbers did so in the previous century. In their account of Scotland's population in the nineteenth century, Anderson and Morse have argued that:

> not far short of 2m people left Scotland for overseas destinations between 1830 and 1914. This probably places Scotland in second place after Ireland in a European league table of the proportion of the population involved in emigration overseas, and it implies a gross emigration rate of around one and a half times that of England and Wales.
>
> (Anderson and Morse, 1990: 15)

Much of this emigration in the nineteenth century was to Canada, Australia, New Zealand and South Africa, but otherwise the United States was the predominant destination. Anderson and Morse estimate that as many as half of all emigrating Scots went to the USA between 1853 and 1914. The propensity of Scots to 'get on' by 'getting out' in all probability underestimates the true rates of social mobility outlined above. We know, for example, that those who left were usually people of some means, as this comment from *Scottish Population History* makes plain:

> Of adult male emigrants from Scotland in 1912 and 1913, 47% described themselves as of skilled trades (compared with only 36% from England and Wales), a proportion which rose to 55% in the early 1920s. A further 21% in 1912–13 (15% in 1921–4) came from the middle class categories of 'commerce, finance, insurance, professional and students'. Only 29% were described as labourers, and of these 19% came from agriculture. The proportions changed little in the 1930s despite the vast reduction in the numbers emigrating.
>
> (Flinn, 1977: 453)

The social strata of skilled artisans and lower-middle class were probably those to whom the Scottish egalitarian myth appealed most, and as such they appear to be the main makers and sustainers of the myth. For such people, 'getting on' often meant 'getting out', migrating to better opportunities with a reasonable chance of success, and sending back optimistic messages as well as encouragement for others to join them. For many Scots, then, as Bob Morris has put it, 'family was not home-sweet-home but the ballads of parting and the attempts to maintain contact by letter' (1990: 2–3). Their accounts of life in the new country probably did much to promote ambitions of upward mobility, for the myths of being able to make it from a relatively humble background did not specify that you had to do it in Scotland, merely that you had to start from there. It was true, of course, that there was a considerable amount of return migration, and it is estimated that by the turn of the nineteenth/twentieth centuries as many as one-third of Scots emigrants came back (Devine, 1999: 477). This was not a sign of failure, for many, such as north-east stone masons who went to the United States every spring and returned in winter, were migrant workers for whom the industrialising world was their labour market.

It is hard for us even at the beginning of a highly mobile twenty-first century to appreciate the scale and meaning of emigration of the previous 150 years. Scots had several advantages over others. They were English-speaking and mainly Protestant, and hence fitted in easily with the culture and ethos of the settler societies, especially with shared experiences of education. They came from one of the world's most advanced economies, bringing with them professional and technical skills which were in great demand. They often brought with them or had access to substantial amounts of capital for reinvestment. In short, in a world and at a time of imperial opportunity which lasted one way or another until well after the Second World War, Scottish emigrants were simply continuing the centuries-old tradition of 'brizing yont' in search of greater opportunity. They took their skills, their capital and their values, which in turn helped to embed and embellish the same at home.

While Scots émigrés helped to sustain and embody the egalitarian myth, institutional and social arrangements within Scotland cannot be ignored in explaining why it prospered. We have seen how the educational system embodied and celebrated the myth, and provided some validity for the egalitarian view of Scottish culture and institutions. The influence of Presbyterianism on Scottish social institutions is important, for it provided the basis of a conception of 'civic duty' which emphasised communal values and social responsibility. Its attenuation into what Arthur Marwick called 'secular presbyterianism' (1986: 16) provided a civic doctrine which underpinned social relations long after the direct influence of the Kirk declined. Similarly, the emergence of the trade union movement reflected this strain of somewhat dour and puritanical egalitarianism which gave to the movement in Scotland a different set of traditions and perspectives than its southern counterpart (Harvie, 1990).

The myth of egalitarianism, then, is a highly flexible and ambivalent one. In its assumption of the primordial equality of Scots, it lends itself to radical and conservative interpretations. Certainly, the 'facts' about social inequality in contemporary Scotland offer support for the myth, and, as we have seen, the patterning of social mobility in Scotland is not all that different from that which operates in England and Wales. Essentially, the Scottish myth is not dependent on 'facts', because it represents a set of social, self-evident values, a social ethos, a celebration of sacred beliefs about what it is to be Scottish. It helped to underpin a social and cultural order which placed a premium on collective, cooperative and egalitarian commitments. It is an ideological device for marking off the Scots from the English, which seems to grow in importance the more the two societies grow similar, and it played a key role in accounting for political divergence between the two countries in the second half of the twentieth century, which will be the concern of the next chapter.

5 Power and politics in a cold country

It is rare for political trends in modern advanced societies to be as dramatic as they have been in Scotland in the last half of the twentieth century. What above all marks them out has been the growing divergence between electoral behaviour in Scotland and England, and the emergence of an alternative political agenda north of the border. These trends are both the effect of long-term change in different parts of the United Kingdom, as well as the catalyst for political change in their own right, most notably the establishment of a devolved Scottish parliament in 1999. Such major developments would probably have been unthinkable fifty years earlier when Scotland was so firmly bound into the unitary state that all possibilities of Home Rule seemed dead.

This chapter has as its main themes:

- the rise and fall of Scottish Conservatism, and the transformation of the relationship between capital and politics in Scotland;
- the politics of the 'national interest' and statism which underpinned Labour's mid-twentieth-century electoral success;
- social change and Scottish nationalism, and the emergence of the Scottish National Party as the second force in Scottish politics;
- the politics of Home Rule, which led to the establishment of the Scottish Parliament on the cusp of the century.

The argument in this chapter will be that in the last half of the twentieth century, electoral behaviour in Scotland diverged markedly from England, and that this divergence cannot simply be attributed to quite different social and economic forces impacting on Scotland, but rather their differential political impact north of the border. In most respects, Scotland has undergone quite similar social changes to the rest of the UK (and, indeed, to other advanced industrial countries). These changes are, however, refracted through diverging political agenda, and hence the political outcomes of these social changes tend to be different. It will be an important part of this argument that different forms of political behaviour do not necessarily require different sets of social changes to be in operation, merely their different expression in political culture.

The first task is to document political trends in Scotland as measured by electoral behaviour at general elections (Table 5.1). For the sake of completeness, all elections since 1832 have been included.

For much of the nineteenth century, Scotland was Liberal territory to an extent that even Labour failed to match in the twentieth century. Indeed, the Liberal Party won a majority of Scottish seats at every election between

Table 5.1 Votes and seats in Scotland at British general elections, 1832–1997: Percentage of vote; seats in brackets

Year	Labour	Conservative	Liberal	SNP	Other	Total no. of seats
1832	–	21.0 (10)	79.0 (43)	–	–	53
1835	–	37.3 (15)	62.8 (38)	–	–	53
1837	–	46.0 (20)	54.0 (33)	–	–	53
1841	–	38.3 (22)	60.8 (31)	–	0.9	53
1847	–	18.3 (20)	81.7 (33)	–	–	53
1852	–	27.4 (20)	72.6 (33)	–	–	53
1857	–	15.3 (14)	84.7 (39)	–	–	53
1859	–	33.6 (13)	66.4 (40)	–	–	53
1865	–	14.6 (11)	85.4 (42)	–	–	53
1868[1]	–	17.5 (7)	82.5 (51)	–	–	58
1874	–	31.6 (18)	68.4 (40)	–	–	58
1880	–	29.9 (6)	70.1 (52)	–	–	58
1885[2]	–	34.3 (8)	53.3 (51)	–	12.4 (11)	70
1886	–	46.4 (27)	53.6 (43)	–	–	70
1892	–	44.4 (19)	53.9 (51)	–	1.7	70
1895	–	47.4 (31)	51.7 (39)	–	0.9	70
1900	–	49.0 (36)	50.2 (34)	–	0.8	70
1906	2.3 (2)	38.2 (10)	56.4 (58)	–	3.1	70
1910 (Jan)	5.1 (2)	39.6 (9)	54.2 (58)	–	1.1 (1)	70
1910 (Dec)	3.6 (3)	42.6 (9)	53.6 (58)	–	0.2	70
1918[3]	22.9 (6)	32.8 (30)	34.1 (33)[4]	–	10.2 (2)	71
1922	32.2 (29)	25.1 (13)	39.2 (27)[5]	–	3.5 (2)	71
1923	35.9 (34)	31.6 (14)	28.4 (22)	–	4.1 (1)	71
1924	41.1 (26)	40.7 (36)	16.6 (8)	–	1.6 (1)	71
1929[6]	42.3 (36)	35.9 (20)	18.1 (13)	0.2	3.5 (2)	71
1931	32.6 (7)	49.5 (48)	13.5 (15)	1.0	3.4 (1)	71
1935	41.8 (24)[7]	42.0 (35)	13.4 (10)[8]	1.1	1.8 (2)	71
1945	49.4 (40)[9]	41.1 (27)	5.0	1.2	3.3 (4)	71
1950	46.2 (37)	44.8 (32)	6.6 (2)	0.4	2.0	71
1951	47.9 (35)	48.6 (35)	2.7 (1)	0.3	0.5	71
1955	46.7 (34)	50.1 (36)	1.9 (1)	0.5	0.8	71
1959	46.7 (38)	47.2 (31)	4.1 (1)	0.8	1.2	71
1964	48.7 (43)	40.6 (24)	7.6 (4)	2.4	0.7	71
1966	49.9 (46)	37.7 (20)	6.8 (5)	5.0	0.6	71
1970	44.5 (44)	38.0 (23)	5.5 (3)	11.4	0.6	71

Table 5.1 continued on next page

Table 5.1 continued

Year	Labour	Conservative	Liberal	SNP	Other	Total no. of seats
1974 (Feb)	36.6 (40)	32.9 (21)	8.0 (3)	21.9 (7)	0.6	71
1974 (Oct)	36.3 (41)	24.7 (16)	8.3 (3)	30.4 (11)	0.3	71
1979	41.5 (44)	31.4 (22)	9.0 (3)	17.3 (2)	0.8	71
1983	35.1 (41)	28.4 (21)	24.5 (8)	11.7 (2)	0.3	72
1987	42.4 (50)	24.0 (10)	19.2 (9)	14.0 (3)	0.3	72
1992	39.0 (49)	25.6 (11)	13.1 (9)	21.5 (3)	0.8	72
1997	45.6 (56)	17.5 (0)	13.0 (10)	22.1 (6)	1.9	72
Scottish parliamentary elections, May 1999						
1999 constituency	38.8 (53)	15.6 (0)	14.1 (12)	28.8 (7)	2.7 (1)	73
1999 list	35.4 (3)	16.1 (18)	13.0 (5)	28.7 (28)	6.8 (2)	56

Notes
1 Extension of franchise to all male householders and tenants.
2 Extension of franchise to all male occupiers.
3 Extension of franchise to all men over age 21, most women over age 30.
4 Comprising 19.1% (25) for coalition; and 15.0% (8) for non-coalition.
5 Comprising 17.7% (12) for National Liberals, and 21.5% (15) for Liberals.
6 Extension of franchise to all women over age 21.
7 Includes 5.0% (4) for ILP.
8 Includes 6.7% (7) for National Liberals.
9 Includes 1.8% (3) for ILP who joined Labour in 1947; Scottish Universities seat which was abolished in 1948 has been excluded.

1832 and 1910, except for 1900. Between the 1840s and 1880s, for example, the Liberals notched up huge majorities north of the border, especially in 1847 when 82 per cent of Scots voted Liberal compared with 57 per cent in England, and again in 1865 when the figures were 85 per cent and 59 per cent respectively. By the mid-1880s, however, largely reflecting the Liberal crisis over Irish Home Rule, the differential between Scotland and England in terms of the Liberal vote began to diminish. Between the Great War and the mid-1950s, the Conservative Party was the most popular party in Scotland, winning 37 per cent of all the Scottish seats contested at the eleven elections in that period. The Labour Party and its allies (the ILP) won 35 per cent of seats during this time. In the period after 1945, the deviations between the two countries in terms of voting for the three main British political parties were small, and major differences in voting behaviour north and south of the border only emerged in the 1960s. It is only since the 1950s that Labour has been the dominant party in Scotland, and it has been challenged for the anti-Tory vote by the Liberals who made a modest comeback in this period, and above all, by the rise of the Scottish National Party.

In many respects, Scotland has been less politically radical than other parts of the UK, notably Wales, which returned Liberal or Labour MPs for 70 per cent of seats fought between 1868 and 1983, while Scotland returned 58 per cent. Wales and the north of England have averaged, since 1945, a higher percentage of 'left' seats than Scotland, and Labour's success north of the border has come belatedly since the late 1950s, and that only partially. If anything, polarisation between England and the rest of Britain was more pronounced before 1914 (Conservative versus Liberal) than in the modern period between Tories and Labour. Further, there was little evidence up until 1983 that the Tory south of England, despite its population, imposed its political will on the 'Celtic' periphery (Punnett, 1985: 32). Nevertheless, since 1979 Britain has become politically divided not simply between England and the Celtic countries, but also between north and south Britain in which a marked north–south political gradient developed.

In Scotland, however, there are two broad and interrelated trends in post-war electoral behaviour: the rise of the Scottish National Party, and the growing divergence in the electoral performance of the Conservative and Labour parties north and south of the border. Both of these trends are separate but inter-connected in so far as they reflect social change in Scotland over the past three decades. Much of the focus of political attention has been on the rise of the SNP since the late 1960s, although the party's advance up until 1970 was concentrated on fighting more seats in Scotland rather than on increasing its share of the vote (Table 5.2).

Table 5.2 Trends in SNP voting: share of total vote in seats fought at British general elections, 1945–1997

Year	Seats fought	Vote in seats fought (%)	Total vote (%)
1945	8	7.6	1.2
1950	3	7.4	0.4
1951	2	12.2	0.3
1955	2	14.5	0.5
1959	5	11.4	0.8
1964	15	10.7	2.4
1966	23	14.1	5.0
1970	65	12.2	11.4
1974 (Feb)	70	22.1	21.9
1974 (Oct)	71	30.4	30.4
1979	71	17.3	17.3
1983	72	11.6	11.6
1987	71	14.2	14.0
1992	72	21.5	21.5
1997	72	22.1	22.1

Source: Craig, 1989; Brown *et al.*, 1998.

These data show that, while the SNP's rising electoral support began in the 1950s rather than the 1960s, it was not until the 1970 election that it could be considered a national party fighting virtually all Scottish seats. The electoral appeal of the Nationalists will be examined later in this chapter, but it is necessary to outline the second major trend in Scottish politics: namely the growing divergence between Scotland and England in terms of support for the Conservative and Labour parties (Table 5.3). These data reveal the extent to which the fortunes of the major parties have diverged in these two nations of the United Kingdom. Whereas in England the Conservative vote held up, in Scotland it was more than halved between 1955 and 1987, and by 1997 it was barely one-third of what it had been.

While the only marked improvement in the Conservative vote in Scotland came between October 1974 and 1979, being a partial recovery of the vote in February 1974, Labour's share of the vote in Scotland and England provides no such clear-cut contrast. The trends in Labour support are close between 1945 and 1955, and again between 1964 and February 1974. Labour was vulnerable to the SNP in the 1970s, but since 1979 when the Nationalist threat receded, it has been much more successful than its southern counterpart, although it has not regained the level of its post-war support.

The systematic swing away from the Conservatives and towards Labour in Scotland, excepting the period of SNP success between 1966 and 1974, can

Table 5.3 Conservative and Labour shares of the vote in Scotland and England at British general elections, 1945–1997

Year	Conservative[1]		Labour	
	England (%)	Scotland (%)	England (%)	Scotland (%)
1945	40.2	41.1	48.5	47.6
1950	43.8	44.8	46.2	46.2
1951	48.8	48.6	48.8	47.9
1955	50.4	50.1	46.8	46.7
1959	49.9	47.2	43.6	46.7
1964	44.1	40.6	43.5	48.7
1966	42.7	37.7	48.0	49.9
1970	48.3	38.0	43.4	44.5
1974 (Feb)	40.2	32.9	37.6	36.6
1974 (Oct)	38.9	24.7	40.1	36.3
1979	47.2	31.4	36.7	41.6
1983	46.0	28.4	26.9	35.1
1987	46.2	24.0	29.5	42.4
1992	46.7	25.6	34.7	39.0
1997	33.7	17.5	43.6	45.6

Note
[1] 'Conservative' includes 'National' and 'National Liberal' between 1945 and 1966.
Source: Craig, 1989; Brown *et al.*, 1998.

best be gauged by focusing on the 'combined gap' between Labour and Conservative voting in Scotland and England. Such a measure is simply constructed by adding the Labour gap – the Labour share in Scotland minus the Labour share in England – to the Conservative gap – the Conservative share in England minus the Conservative share in Scotland (Table 5.4).

The general election of 1987 marked the high point of Scottish–English divergence, while the apparent convergence in the 1990s is largely the result of a swing to Labour in England. In general terms, the overall impression is of a systematic swing since 1945 away from the Conservatives and towards Labour in Scotland, excepting the period of the SNP upsurge – from 1966 through to the mid-1970s. Despite Liberal successes in the north and south of Scotland, the party has done less well in Scotland than in England in the past fifty years. Only at the 1951 election did the Liberals perform marginally better in Scotland than in England. When the SNP was at its peak in the two 1974 elections, the Liberals were taking only around 8 per cent of the vote compared with over 20 per cent in England. By the 1980s, the gap in Liberal performance in the two countries had fallen to a few percentage points (1.8 in 1983, and 3.2 in 1987).

The move away from the Conservatives has been much more pronounced and more consistent than the swing to Labour, and the non-Conservative parties have at different times been the beneficiaries – first Labour in the mid-1960s, then the SNP in 1970 and 1974, and, since 1979, Labour again. To be precise, much of the growing divergence between Scotland and England is the result of a long-run decline in support for the Conservative Party in

Table 5.4 Differences in Labour and Conservative performance in Scotland and England at British general elections, 1945–1997

Year	Labour advantage in Scotland	Conservative shortfall in Scotland	Combined gap
1945	−0.9	−0.9	−1.8
1950	0.0	−1.0	−1.0
1951	−0.9	0.2	−0.7
1955	−0.1	0.3	0.2
1959	3.1	2.7	5.8
1964	5.2	3.5	8.7
1966	1.9	5.0	6.9
1970	1.1	10.3	11.4
1974 (Feb)	−1.0	7.3	6.3
1974 (Oct)	−3.8	14.2	10.4
1979	4.9	15.8	20.7
1983	8.2	17.6	25.8
1987	12.9	22.2	35.1
1992	4.3	21.1	25.4
1997	2.0	16.2	18.2

Scotland, rather than sustained electoral popularity for Labour. Further, the decline in the Conservative vote has occurred since the mid-1950s, for in the decade after the war the 'combined gap' in Labour and Conservative performances in Scotland and England was negligible. The first task in constructing a political sociology of modern Scotland, then, is to explain the rise and fall of support for the Conservative Party north of the border.

The rise and fall of Scottish Conservatism

'Unionism' – that brand of Scottish Conservatism which flourished in the first half of the twentieth century – had a particular appeal to local Scottish capital. At the end of the nineteenth century, the owners of both land and capital in Scotland were powerful and self-confident, and as a result 'Scotland became endowed with great commercial and industrial families, taking their place alongside the landed nobility, and to some extent linked together by marriage' (Checkland and Checkland, 1984: 175). The new commercial dynasties were often assimilated into the older landed ones in this way. The alliance was also political. The lairds had provided leadership for the Conservative Party in Scotland, and indeed had helped to give it its somewhat reactionary image right down to the 1890s. In the intake of MPs following the 1895 election, nine Conservative MPs were landowners, seven were businessmen and one came from the professions. This was in contrast to the Liberal-Unionists who had broken away from the Liberal Party over Irish Home Rule in the 1880s. Nine Liberal-Unionists were businessmen, two were professionals, and only three described themselves as landowners. Such was the power of this Unionism that, unlike the English case, it was able to absorb the ideologically weaker Conservatism. It drew its strength from the burgeoning, imperialist-inclined capitalist class concentrated in west-central Scotland. As Michael Fry pointed out, 'It was Unionist because imperialist; it was imperialist because its prosperity was bound up with Empire' (1987: 110).

The cousins and brothers of these industrialists entered the professions, to become the lawyers, doctors and churchmen of Edwardian Scotland. Crucially, the professions were Scottish, educated at fee-paying and Merchant Company schools in Edinburgh and Glasgow, in local academies in rural areas and small towns, and at Scottish universities. The traditional bourgeoisie, big as well as small, was nothing if not Scottish. Since the Treaty of Union in 1707, it had dominated Scottish civil society, its institutions and its mores. This was not some pliant agent of southern power, but a class with its roots deep in Scottish culture and tradition. Not only did it speak with a Scottish accent, it immersed itself in the folklore and literature of its native land. It spoke the poetry of Burns, it knew the novels of Scott, and it took pride in the folk memories of Wallace, Bruce and the Covenant. Its Kirk had long seen itself as one of the few institutions left to speak for Scotland, although its capacity to do so had been fatally weakened in the disruption of 1843. It celebrated its distinctive values of thrift, hard work and personal achievement. 'Getting on' was an unspoken but vital aim in life, as well as a moral duty.

Scottish Unionism had deep roots in Scotland, and the Conservatives are by far the oldest political party north of the border. At a relatively low ebb for much of the nineteenth century, the party polled between fifteen and twenty fewer percentage points in Scotland than in England, much as it was to do in the late twentieth century. The party's political strength among the landed classes kept it penned into the rural areas, until the Liberals began to fragment over the issue of Irish Home Rule after 1886. That year, the Liberal Unionists broke away from the Liberal Party, and strengthened the connection between Protestantism and Conservatism.

This Unionism was assertive and resilient, and carried all before it the general election of 1900, making a clean sweep of Glasgow's seats, and although its fortunes ebbed in 1906 and 1910, it retained the capacity to mobilise its coalition of bourgeoisie and Protestant workers alike. As a result of this burgeoning power, Toryism, hitherto regarded, in Hutchison's words, as the creed of 'lairds and law agents' (1986: 200), had to accommodate to this new Unionism. Gradually, Conservatism moved from its reactionary position in the 1890s to a degree of commitment to progressive reform. Above all, how-ever, as the Checklands observe, the Liberal-Unionists acted as 'a bridge over which middle class man could pass from Liberalism to Toryism without suffer-ing any sense of betrayal' (1984: 85).

By 1900, the Liberals for the first time did not win a majority of Scottish seats, their 34 being beaten by a combination of 19 Tories and 17 Liberal Unionists. In that election, the Liberals took 15 of the 31 burgh seats in Scotland, while the Conservatives and Liberal Unionists took the other 16. Similarly, there was little difference between the two political blocks in so far as both took the same proportion of burgh and county seats. The right-wing grouping took all seven of the Glasgow burgh seats, while the Edinburgh seats were shared, with the Liberals winning the two Aberdeen and the two Dundee seats. The rural predominance of Liberal voting did not occur until after the First World War (and the debacle over Irish Independence).

The rise of Labour, the extension of the franchise, and the granting of Home Rule in Ireland in 1922 allowed the bulk of the Scottish Catholic working class to support Labour. Partly as a response, the middle-class vote swung increas-ingly behind the 'Unionists'. As James Kellas pointed out: 'The Conservative Party in Scotland has until recently derived its strength in the industrial west from the remnants of this Liberal-Unionist vote' (1973: 109). By the 1920s, the Conservatives and their allies had overtaken the Liberals in Scotland, and while they never managed to perform as well as their counterparts in England, they were – culminating in 1955 – the most successful party in electoral terms north of the border.

What made this achievement all the greater was the fact that, in terms of social structural factors, Scotland was not fertile soil for Conservatism. The party's performance after 1945 is surprising when one considers that in terms of social class and housing tenure, variables traditionally linked to political behaviour, the Conservatives were at a disadvantage, since both manual workers and council tenants were more likely to vote Labour. Since Scotland had more of each social category, the performance of the Conservatives in matching Labour was unusual. Miller's assessment of the 'normal' Scottish–English difference in terms of social class alone (involving the Tories doing 4 per cent worse in Scotland and Labour doing 4 per cent better) implies that in the 1950s when there was actually rough parity in voting, the Tories were doing 8 per cent better than they should have done (Miller, 1981). In this regard, then, the question becomes: Why was the Conservative Party doing so much better in the 1950s than it should have done (in terms of the social structure of Scotland at the time)?

The success of the Conservatives nationally was all the more remarkable given that they did not operate at the level of local politics for much of the twentieth century. They had put up candidates at municipal elections in the early part of the century, but by the 1930s they had all but disappeared, to be replaced by a coalition of Tories, Liberals and Independents gathered in the major cities under 'non-political' labels such as 'Progressives' or 'Moderates'. These fairly loose coalitions kept alive the belief that local government was essentially a 'non-political' business in which individuals were elected on their merits. The appeal of the Progressives and Moderates was particularly to small local businessmen, who believed in apolitical administration by knowledgeable, essentially local, people like themselves.

At the same time as these new coalitions were put together, militant Protestantism became a feature of local politics in the large cities. In Edinburgh, Protestant Action operated an informal electoral pact with the right-wing Progressive Association in the 1930s, and was a presence on the city streets right through until the 1950s. In Glasgow, there is irony in the fact that the intervention of the Scottish Protestant League in 1933 gave Labour control of the city for the first time (Gallagher, 1987b).

Although Conservatism as such did not intervene in Scottish local politics in modern times until the late 1960s, they were able to mobilise, at the national level, a similar set of social and religious beliefs. Religion has always mattered in Scottish politics, and it dominated the nineteenth century and structured its cleavages to a significant extent. These influences were carried into this century in a potent form. While direct and systematic evidence on the middle years of this century is hard to come by, survey data from the 1950s and 1960s suggest that strong religious connotations were continuing to be played out in Scottish politics. National and local surveys show that 'one important influence – religion – does seem to carry a different and stronger weight among Scottish electors when they are compared to English electors' (Budge and Urwin, 1966: 71). On the basis of a survey carried out in Dundee in 1968, Bochel and Denver (1970) found that, if anything, there was a continuing link between religion and voting. Of Church of Scotland manual workers, 40 per cent voted Conservative compared with only 6 per cent of Roman

Catholic manual workers. As late as 1986, 45 per cent of Kirk members claimed to vote Tory and only 17 per cent Labour, although by this time there were far fewer church-goers to matter (Brown, 1990: 82).

These surveys were carried out when many of the social mechanisms under-lying Catholic–Labour and Conservative–Protestant voting associations were losing their force, but they do testify to the power of Unionism to mobilise an older – and essentially Protestant – sense of what it meant to be Scottish. This identity consisted of a complex of interrelated elements of Protestantism and Unionism welded together by a strong sense of British national and imperial identity, and symbolised by the Union Flag (an enduring emblem of Glasgow Rangers Football Club). This version of Scottishness chimed with Conservative rhetoric about British national and imperial identity, and drew upon the powerful strand of militarism which ran through Scottish society in the late nineteenth and early twentieth centuries. The mobilisation of men for war during the later imperial period and on through two world wars helped to fit together Scottish and British identities, a connection reinforced by the religious factor, which in turn received emotional resonance and respectability from the national and imperial elements of the complex.

This ideological complex underpinned the relative success of the Con-servatives in Scotland in the mid-twentieth century, and helps to explain Conservative success in terms of some of the most powerful and deep-rooted strands of Scottish popular consciousness. It is important to point out, however, that this version of Toryism also laid stress on civic duty and social responsibility rather than on the reductionist individualism which emerged in the 1970s in the form of the political ideology of neo-liberal Thatcherism.

By the 1970s and 1980s, alternative versions of political Scottishness, asso-ciated with the SNP and nationalist elements in the Labour Party, sought to emphasise the gulf between Scottish and British national consciousness, rather than their continuity. The ending of empire, of military conscription, together with fifty years without a major war, coupled with the extensive secularisation of Scotland and Britain, combined to erode and enfeeble the con-nection between Conservatism, Protestantism and British national identity. As the native leaders of Scottish capital, the local businessmen and great Clydeside dynasties found their influence slipping away, Conservatism fell once more into the hands of 'lairds and law agents'. By 1964, the 'Unionist' label was dropped in favour of the Anglicised 'Conservative' one. The native social base of Scottish Unionism continued to erode, and with it its power to mobilise the Scottish Protestant working class. By the second half of the twentieth century, this particular version of Scottish identity, centred on religion and patriotism, was being relegated to history.

By the 1970s, wider social changes were sweeping through Scottish society and politics. Rapid rates of social change, coupled with increased rates of social and geographical mobility, were detaching many from their traditional allegiances. As we shall see later in this chapter, the Scottish National Party became one of the main recipients of these changes, appealing to the young and socially semi-detached in particular. The capacity of the SNP to destabilise party politics in Scotland in large part reflected an increasingly volatile electorate. Scottish Conservatism, on the other hand, had lost its traditional social leadership among Scotland's bourgeoisie at a time when national differences between Scotland and England became more salient. In short, there simply was not a sufficient social base left in Scotland in which to domesticate the Conservative message, and political opponents found it relatively straightforward to label the Tories an 'English' party. The long hegemony of the Right at Westminster was built firmly on English, not Scottish (nor Welsh) votes. Instead, new versions of Scottish national consciousness began to emerge in the 1960s to open up a new political divide.

Nationalism, identity and the state

In the post-war world, nationalism was central to the endeavours of the modern state. Most analyses of nationalism, including the Scottish variety, tend to explain the phenomenon in internal terms, that is, in terms of the specificities and peculiarities of the society in question. Such a view tends to ignore the fact that virtually all modern societies are nationalist, although nationalism, practised successfully, often remains implicit. 'It is as if a really secure nationalism, already in possession of its own nation-state, can fail to see itself as "nationalist" at all' (Williams, 1983: 183).

Modern societies, however, are indubitably, if implicitly, nationalist. Ernest Gellner argued that the size, scale and complexity of these societies require an explicit sense of loyalty and identification on the part of the population, an explicit binding of citizenship to the state. This requirement becomes all the more imperative because of the elaborate division of labour, coupled with rapid rates of social change. The modern social system makes an assumption – in his words, 'a kind of null hypothesis' – of social equality based on equality of citizenship, and the modern industrial economy stimulates this aspiration to equality. This is not to deny the extent or salience of economic inequality in capitalist society, but to argue that it does create problems of legitimacy. So one of the key reasons why nationalism is a feature of modern societies is because equality of status and a shared culture are preconditions for the functioning of complex industrial societies. These societies do not tolerate cultural fissures within them which can become correlates of inequality and 'which thereby become frozen, aggravated, visible and offensive' (Gellner, 1978: 108).

In the modern state, therefore, national identification becomes a *sine qua non* of citizenship. Social inequality in modern industrial societies is a precarious phenomenon. The assumption of equality of citizenship laid down by the state makes conspicuous inequality a more problematic issue; it has to be justified. Similarly, citizens have to be bound legally and culturally to the modern state in a way that was not required of its pre-industrial counterpart. As Poggi says: 'The modern state is not bestowed upon a people as a gift of God, its own

Geist or blind historical forces; it is a "made" historical reality' (Poggi, 1978: 95). Because it is a 'purposively constructed, functionally specific machine' (ibid.: 101), the modern state has to mobilise commitment to it through 'national' ideology. The modern state is continuously faced with legitimating itself before its citizens. The importance of citizenship, the guaranteeing by the state of civil, political and social rights (Marshall, 1963), ultimately makes nationalism more, not less, important. Nationalism appeals to the 'national interest'; it is applied as an ideological balm to societies with many centripetal tendencies.

After the Second World War, the search for legitimacy became a problem for states, for they had been drawn more and more into full participation in the economic and social life of societies. A 'corporate bias' was introduced into Britain as early as the second decade of this century, and it flourished after 1945 before falling into disrepute in the 1970s (Middlemas, 1979, 1986). 'Corporatism', despite its association with fascism, was a system in implicit use after the war, partly because, in Western societies, the conditions of war had led to a considerable degree of central control. The need to coordinate production efforts and to resolve differences of interest between employers and employees laid many of the foundations for corporatist structures. The state, through its civil servants, mobilised groups on the basis of 'the national interest'. Middlemas pointed out that 'those who aspire to and are able to compete at the "altruistic" level of the national interest enter the environs of the state' (1986: 10). Those who remained outside the invisible boundary were defined as self-interested lobbies or pressure groups.

The focus on the 'national interest' provided the political legitimacy for corporatism. Nationalism is one of the central elements of corporatism, as Winckler observed in a seminal article in 1976:

> It is a collectivist system, not an individualist one. The collectivity on which concern focuses is the nation, not the class, the family, religion, caste or ethnic group. The aim is national economic well-being, not personal affluence or mobility. The general welfare has moral primacy over individual preferences or rights. 'Individualism' is a label for stigmatising recalcitrance, not eulogising freedom.
>
> (Winckler, 1976: 107)

Winckler has been criticised for simplifying and stereotyping corporatism, but he was correct to identify nationalism as one of the central foci of corporatism.

Almost regardless of political ideology, the state in the post-war period intervened in economic processes, and played a more central role in directing economic resources. It was seen as the appropriate instrument for guaranteeing the individual life-chances of its citizens, and ironing out social inequalities. In the post-war period, the state endeavoured to hitch its star to the quest for economic growth. As Poggi commented:

The state found a new and different response to the legitimacy problems; increasingly it treated industrial growth per se as possessing intrinsic and commanding political significance, as constituting a necessary and sufficient standard of each state's performance, and thus as justifying further displacement of the state/society line.

(Poggi, 1978: 133)

Britain was not an exception to this rule in the post-war years. Throughout the 1950s and 1960s, there existed an agenda and a set of rules for the political game shared by both the main British political parties, sometimes referred to as 'Butskellism', or 'consensus politics'. The government took explicit responsibility for employment, prices, the balance of payments and economic growth. The Second World War, and the inception of the Welfare State (a counter to Hitler's 'Warfare State' (Marwick, 1986: 49)), ushered in a new social contract between the state and its citizens, a post-war settlement which was underpinned by the long economic boom of the post-war period.

The relative economic decline of Britain in the post-war years has thrown these problems into harsh relief. Successive governments have sought to appropriate 'the national interest' to justify their actions and policies. Appeals to nationalism and patriotism, the stock in trade of parties and governments in all countries, are made by the parties of the Right as well as the Left. Politics, in other words, became the struggle for the 'national soul'. Nevertheless, this nationalism remained largely implicit, and politics were defined as about the delivery of economic benefits by means of economic management of the national economy. However, nationalism has become more, not less necessary in societies characterised by 'mobile privatisation'. 'National statism' helped to preserve a coherent domestic social order, to regulate and contain what would otherwise be intolerable divisions and confusions.

In Britain, the failure of policies to promote economic growth at a fast enough rate destabilised the political arrangements of the United Kingdom. The attack by the Left on corporatism was less incisive than that by the Right in the 1970s, led by the radical Right and Mrs Thatcher. Even centrist academics like Anthony King, writing a tract in 1976 called 'The problem of overload', concluded: Governments have tried to play God. They have failed. But they go on trying. How can they be made to stop? Perhaps over the next few years they should be more concerned with how the number of tasks that government has come to perform can be reduced' (1976: 29). The thesis of 'state overload' chimed nicely with the separate critiques from both Left and Right. Nevertheless, the radical successor to 'consensus politics' – Thatcherism – involved the re-mobilisation of nationalism. A different piper played a new variation on an old tune.

What does this have to do with Scotland? The disintegration of the post-war settlement occurred at a crucial conjuncture in Scotland's history. Briefly put, Scotland underwent its own version of economic planning. The lessons of Keynesian economic management had been applied to Scotland by the Scottish

Office, that 'semi-state' which had acquired more and more administrative power from Whitehall since 1886 when it was founded (Kellas, 1989: 32–3). Given the collapse of indigenous industry after the war, the Scottish Office had played a more directive role in restructuring the economy by means of direct employment, and by offering inducements to foreign capital to locate in Scotland. Like other declining industrial regions of the UK, it relied more heavily on public initiative than on private enterprise. In its desire to act as the midwife of economic regeneration, the state devolved a significant part of its administrative resources to Scotland. In the absence of devolved government, the Scottish Office provided a powerful administrative apparatus, or 'negotiated order', in the phrase of Moore and Booth. In their words: 'We are not arguing that Scotland can be seen as a separate political system, but that there is a degree of decision-making and administrative autonomy in certain sectors, and over certain issues a Scottish interest emerges' (1989: 15). The point was reinforced by their research which suggested that, while in strict terms Scotland cannot be called a 'corporatist state', if only because it is not a separate political system, it does contain a 'pattern of policy networks' in which the values and culture of decision-making elites sustain a distinctive set of institutions and relationships which influence bargaining and policy outcomes. Scotland, said Moore and Booth, is a 'close-knit community where a high level of individual contact is possible' (ibid.: 29). Central to this policy network were bodies such as the CBI in Scotland, the Scottish Trades Union Congress (STUC), the Scottish Council (Development and Industry), and the Scottish Development Agency/Scottish Enterprise. The authors argued that Scotland represented a 'negotiated order' operating somewhere between corporatism and free-market pluralism, that the 'Scottish policy community' mediated through the Scottish Office represented a 'meso-level of the British state' (ibid.: 150).

In certain fields of administration, most notably education, there is an identifiable 'policy community' made up of a 'community of individuals who mattered; it was also the forum in which the interests of groups were represented, reconciled or rebuffed' (McPherson and Raab, 1988: 433). There operates in Scotland a set of 'policy communities', in which the values and culture of decision-making elites help to sustain a distinctive set of institutions and relationships which influence bargaining and policy outcomes. Such a 'community' stretches across government and outside groups who are involved in the implementation of policy, and while there is no single 'policy community' covering Scotland, the scale and administrative history of the country has made this form of governance particularly apt. It also helps to explain why the Thatcherite strategy of cutting down the state and asserting the primacy of the market proved to be less than popular among the governing classes of Scotland, as well as among the population more generally.

The late 1950s and early 1960s saw the transmission of the idea of Scotland as a unit of economic management to the mass electorate, via the Labour Party in Scotland, and especially via the Scottish media, and television in particular.

Labour's strategy in this period was, according to Keating and Bleiman, largely pragmatic: Labour's attitude to the Scottish question was based upon the assumptions that the basis of any discontent was economic, and that the electorate was more concerned about the economic goods it received than about the constitutional mechanism by which these goods were delivered (1979: 151).

The perception of Scotland as a separate unit of political and economic management coincided with the arrival of North Sea Oil, which opened up the political possibility of an alternative Scottish future, and which the SNP was to exploit brilliantly. The post-war belief in 'equal citizenship' was mobilised as equal citizenship for Scots within the UK in such a way that the (British) nationalist assumptions built into the Welfare State could be transferred easily in the rhetorical form of Scottish nationalism. Certainly, the ability to transfer from one form of nationalism (British) to another (Scottish) occurred at the right moment for the Nationalist Party, as well as for many Scots.

The SNP was in the right place at the right time, making explicit, as well as problematic, the 'national' dimension of the post-war consensus, and providing a political alternative when the British settlement began to fail. Both the Conservative and Labour Parties paid the electoral price, the former more profoundly than the latter. Labour's early success was based on a view of the state as a generator of economic growth. As Labour was seen to fail to deliver the economic goods in the 1970s, the SNP increasingly became the beneficiary. Ironically, when the next major ideological battle occurred later in the decade – between the radical Right with its anti-state project, and the defenders of the post-war settlement – Labour in Scotland was in a much better position than the SNP to switch the terms of the struggle on to a Left/Right dimension, while taking on some of the nationalist mantle. Nevertheless, the SNP acted as a key electoral catalyst for change, and provided a political home for the socially mobile and the young, in search of a new political identity in a rapidly changing Scotland. It is in the systematic swing away from the Conservatives, however, that we have the most coherent manifestation of the emerging Scottish political system, a system increasingly incompatible with the ideology of that party's role as the British or English national party.

Social change and Scottish nationalism

What was the social base of nationalism? In the early phase of its electoral success, commented James Kellas:

> At all times, it seems to have attracted defectors equally from all parties, although this varies from constituency to constituency. Up to 1974 it seems to have appealed to first-time voters or previous abstainers. Its declining support after 1978 was particularly marked among young voters and New Town voters, many of whom had consistently supported the party since the late 1960s.

(Kellas, 1989: 141)

The appeal of the party to such social groups was reflected in the volatility and unexpectedness of its successes and failures. Its first major by-election victory in modern times was at Hamilton in 1967 when Winnie Ewing took the seat with 49 per cent of the vote. In the local government elections of the following year, it held its support at 30 per cent nationally, allowing it to maintain the balance of power in Glasgow. However, at the Glasgow Gorbals by-election in 1969, it could muster only 25 per cent. The volatile appeal of the SNP to the young, the socially and geographically mobile was reinforced by the absence of a significant class base. Hence it performed uniformly across all social classes. The October 1974 election in which the SNP took 30 per cent of electoral support in Scotland proved to be the party's best performance to date in a British general election. In that election the SNP did well across all classes, but especially among skilled manual and routine non-manual workers, those groups who had become electorally detached from traditional social bases. Further evidence suggests that the party's appeal was stronger among the 'new' working class – technicians and craftsmen – than it was among 'traditional' manual workers – steelworkers and miners (Davis, 1969). The Scottish Election Survey for October 1974 indicated the 'classless' appeal of the SNP, which proved to be both its strength and its weakness (Table 5.5).

In contrast to its broad-based class appeal, the SNP attracted the young in high proportions. The age structure of SNP support was virtually the mirror image of Conservative strength. Thus, whereas the SNP captured 42 per cent of electors aged 18 to 24 (Conservatives took 10 per cent of this age group), they managed only 16 per cent of those aged 65 and over (Conservatives, 38 per cent). The SNP also did proportionately well among those who were upwardly socially mobile from manual working-class origins. For example, 32 per cent of SNP voters in non-manual jobs had fathers who were manual workers, compared with 24 per cent of SNP non-manual

Table 5.5 Percentage of each socio-economic group voting SNP in October 1974 general election

Group	%
Employers and managers	27
Professionals	30
Intermediate	40
Junior non-manual	26
Foremen & supervisors	18
Skilled manual	35
Semi-skilled manual	23
Unskilled manual	23

Source: Scottish Election Survey, October 1974.

voters who had non-manual fathers. Hence, non-manual workers who had been upwardly socially mobile from the working class were especially susceptible to the appeal of the SNP, as were younger workers, and those buying a house with a mortgage. Since then, of course, a new generation of voters has appeared, notably the children of those who were socially mobile in the 1960s. The fact that there is now a substantial thirty-year history of SNP voting provided a solid platform for later electoral success, although it remains Scotland's second-place party after Labour.

The SNP benefited from key social changes in Scotland in the 1960s and 1970s: rising affluence, full employment and upward social mobility. Groups who became less reliant on the support of kin as well as being more home-centred – Scotland's analogues of the classic 'affluent workers' studied in England – found themselves drawn to the Nationalists less for reasons of political ideology than because of their social detachment from their class of origin. This social base paid electoral dividends where Labour was historically weak. For example, Peterhead, a town where the SNP made an early and last-ing impact, and which Alex Salmond, who went on to lead the party, won in 1987 as part of the Banff and Buchan constituency, pointed to this important Nationalist social base. The researchers observed: 'The SNP was most successful in winning affiliations from the upwardly aspirant who were renouncing the class of their homes while not yet entering the middle class' (Bealey and Sewel, 1981: 160).

It appears that the lack of class connotations in the SNP was perhaps the key appeal to this socially mobile group in the 1970s. Such people were susceptible to alternative frameworks of perception, for their traditional forms of social and political identities were weakening. This was also a generation which learned much of its politics via television and the media. It served a mobile and privatised way of life because it provided a more appropriate frame of political and social reference.

It is important to stress that Scotland differed little from the rest of the UK with regard to these social and cultural changes, but from the late 1960s, 'Scotland' was a frame of cultural reference in terms of which the political world could increasingly be interpreted. Crucially, the SNP was a political party which could more easily capture this 'Scottish' label, because it was a taken-for-granted reference in much the same way as the Conservative Party had implicitly assumed a 'national' identity in England. In another important respect, the SNP was a 'media' party, well suited to an increasingly volatile electorate, and one which did not need to make the long march through the political undergrowth as the Labour Party had to do at the turn of the century. Just as the SNP came to rapid prominence through the media, so it fell from electoral grace at a later stage. The party was in the right place at the right time, making an appeal to the right people. In many ways, its Scottishness was almost incidental, yet vital.

The SNP captured the generation entering the electorate in the 1960s and 1970s which in England tended towards the Conservatives or the Liberals. Having been captured for the Scottish frame of reference, the collapse of the SNP in the late 1970s left the bulk of its support nowhere to go but to Labour. By the late 1970s, the Scottish stage was set for a new – yet more traditional – battle over the role of the state, between Labour and Conservative, which the latter were singularly ill equipped to fight. This is the final key element in the process of political divergence between Scotland and England. As we have seen, the slippage in Conservative support began well before 1979 and the election of the first Thatcher government, but as the data also make plain, the 1980s drove a considerable wedge between the electoral performances of the two nations. Mrs Thatcher may not have created the divergence, but she gave it a flavour all of her own.

Thatcherism in a cold climate

As long as the Scottish political dimension remained latent, it was perfectly possible for generalised Conservative rhetoric about the nation to coexist with the everyday reality of Scottishness, and, of course, for much of the twentieth century the presence of an ideological affinity between Conservatism, Unionism and Protestantism was useful to the party. Latterly, however, alternative dimensions of Scottishness emerged, making Scotland as an ideological category incompatible with Conservative Anglo-British rhetoric. Nothing did more to make explicit this Conservative nationalism than the election of Mrs Thatcher in 1979.

A large part of Thatcher's success south of the border derived from harnessing conservative motifs. Much of the explanation for the rise of Thatcherism focused on neo-liberal ideas of extending market power, but alongside these lay a powerful stream of ideas which were quite distinct. Its neo-conservative motif was authority not freedom, the desire to re-establish and extend the power of the state over many aspects of social, political and even personal life. If the notion of the 'citizen' derived from liberal ideas of the state, then the conservative idea of the 'subject' was drawn from an allegiance to the nation. Earlier in this chapter, we argued that in post-war societies, politics operated by claiming the legitimacy of the 'national interest'. Clearly, Thatcherism represented a radical break with this consensual, corporatist style of government. Nevertheless, nationalism – a key element in this discredited system – was remobilised by the radical Right in the new cause. What Britain saw after 1979 was the reassertion of nationalism under a new set of political and economic ideas, and it was a nationalism which was distinctly at odds with the new alternative variety north of the border. While the older Unionist one was quite compatible with Anglo-British nationalism, the newer post-1979 version was not. Thatcher's unpopularity in Scotland was the down-side of her electoral support in England. In Gamble's words:

Thatcherism has reinvigorated it [the old Tory state-authority], and restored the confidence of the party in its basic appeal to the English. This is not Unionism. The Scots, Welsh and Irish are increasingly detached; but then so too are the former colonies of Greater Britain. There can be no return to the dreams of Empire.

(Gamble, 1988: 172)

In Scotland, the attack on state institutions – the nationalised industries, the education system, local government, the public sector generally, even the Church, institutions which carried much of Scotland's identity – was easily perceived as an attack on 'Scotland' itself. Essential to current Conservative appeal south of the border was an appeal to 'the nation' on whose behalf politicians and the state act, but Scots had a nation of their own, and the vision of re-creating bourgeois England was out of kilter not only with Scottish material interests, but with this alternative sense of national identity.

Modern Conservatism spoke overwhelmingly with a southern English voice. The populist, nationalist, anti-state appeal which sustained Thatcher in England for the whole of the 1980s had distinctively negative resonances north of the border. It is hard to envisage a political message more at odds with what had gone before, and one which so ran counter to the grain of Scottish civil society.

The failure of the Conservative Party in Scotland was not the result of an unfavourable class structure. Even among the middle classes, there was a distinct anti-Conservative differential, as Table 5.6 demonstrates. Across all social classes there is an anti-Tory differential in Scotland. Among manual workers, the Conservative vote in Scotland is 50 per cent or under what it is in the rest of Britain, while among professional and managerial classes it ranges from a high of 78 per cent of the similar class vote south of the border in 1979 to a low of 62 per cent in 1997 when all seats in Scotland were lost. That defeat ushered in the most fundamental transformation of Scottish governance in almost 300 years.

Table 5.6 Conservative vote in general elections by social class, Scotland (rest of Britain in brackets)

Social class	1974 (%)	1979 (%)	1992 (%)	1997 (%)
Professional and managerial	36 (51)	46 (59)	35 (53)	23 (37)
Skilled non-manual	29 (43)	46 (53)	33 (56)	17 (37)
Skilled manual	14 (25)	17 (36)	18 (40)	7 (22)
Semi/unskilled manual	12 (23)	21 (33)	15 (31)	3 (22)

Source: British Election Studies, 1974, 1979, 1992 and 1997.

The politics of a Scottish parliament

The first elections for the Scottish Parliament were held in May 1999, with Labour winning 56 of the 129 seats, the SNP 35, The Conservatives 18, Liberal Democrats 17, and others 3 (1 Independent, 1 Scottish Socialist Party and 1 Scottish Green Party). How are we to assess the sociological significance of the Scottish Parliament? Much was made in the 1990s of the threat or promise of constitutional change. Unionists opposed it on the grounds that it was the slippery slope which would lead to the breakup of the United Kingdom. Nationalists saw it as the thin end of the wedge which would sunder the Union. The middle, devolutionist ground spoke of the 'settled will of the Scottish people', in the expectation, or perhaps the hope, that it would form a consensus. Plainly, all cannot be correct. At the time of writing it is too soon to draw any firm conclusions, and, in what has become something of a political cliché, setting up the Scottish Parliament is not so much an event, more of a process. Nevertheless, we have a number of surveys at key moments which offer some guidance to possible outcomes: the general election of May 1997, the referendum of September 1997, and the first parliamentary elections held in May 1999 (Brown *et al.*, 1998, 1999; Paterson *et al.*, in press).

Throughout the 1990s it was often asserted that constitutional change, in the form of either devolution or independence, came well down the priority list of the electorate. Those either lukewarm or opposed to change argued that what they termed 'bread and butter' politics such as education, housing and health were far more important in determining how people voted than constitutional change. Behind such an assertion lay the assumption that one could rank these in some kind of league table, that whether or not one wanted a parliament was a matter of 'expressive' rather than 'instrumental' politics. We are able to show from quite detailed studies of electoral opinion that in many ways juxtaposing constitutional politics against 'bread and butter' politics is a false dichotomy. For example, whether or not people voted for a parliament could not be explained in terms of social location or social identity. In other words, the influence of social class, educational level, housing tenure, age and gender did not in and of themselves determine votes. Similarly, feeling strongly Scottish rather than British did not explain why the electorate voted yes. Rather, as one might expect, people with a strong sense of Scottish identity did vote in large numbers for a parliament, just as SNP voters did likewise. However, those who did give priority to being British, while less keen, did vote yes. In other words, identity matters, but does not explain the whole picture.

What does seem of greater significance was that, put simply, a Scottish parliament was seen as a means to an end, and that end was better government and an expected improvement in social and public welfare. This emphasis on 'instrumental' factors derived from a concern with improving welfare for Scotland as a whole, rather than a highly individualistic perspective of 'pocket-book' voting. We know this because, while most people expected taxes to rise, they were willing to pay the price in order to raise the standard of social and economic welfare in Scotland generally. On the other hand, those voting no were those who also expected taxes to rise, but thought that welfare would not improve on a range of social issues, and these voters tended to be Conservatives. Indeed, Tory voters, who were minded to support a Home Rule parliament, found themselves caught in something of a dilemma, and seem to have resolved it by voting yes, contrary to party policy. One might say, then, that the Conservatives lost the argument with even their own electorate, and were deemed by the wider one as not having Scotland's interests at heart. The Tories found themselves marginalised not only in the general election of 1997, but also in the referendum four months later, and only the system of proportional representation, which they had strongly opposed, gave them a presence of eighteen seats (all list seats) in the 1999 Scottish election for the first Parliament.

In short, the Scottish electorate was willing to back those parties, Labour, Liberal Democrat and SNP, who were enthusiastic about using the Parliament to improve welfare in the widest sense of the term. This was reflected in the greater propensity to perceive these parties as being trusted to act in Scotland's interests. The differential between Labour and the SNP on the one hand, and the Conservatives on the other – with the Liberal Democrats seeing a rise in their trustworthiness after they entered the coalition with Labour – was a marked feature of each of the three survey points. What seemed to underpin this trust was the degree to which political parties were able to articulate key social values and policy preferences of the electorate. For example, if we measure Scottish opinion *vis-à-vis* that in the rest of Britain, we find that Scots are somewhat more likely to be more 'socialist' (as opposed to pro-market), more 'liberal' (as opposed to socially conservative), and less 'British national' (as opposed to Scottish). Similarly, there was little regional variation within Scotland on these matters, though people in west-central Scotland were more likely to be found at the socialist/social democratic end of the spectrum. In a similar way, Labour voters in Scotland were significantly more left-wing than their English counterparts, and less 'British' in national orientation. There was clear association between 'Scottish' and having social democratic values which had been building up during the previous twenty years, and which helps to explain why the Conservative Party came to be identified as an 'English' party (reinforced, of course, by its hostility to Home Rule). It is important to point out that British public opinion as a whole remained 'social democratic' for much of the Thatcher years, electing a series of Conservative governments in spite of, rather than because of, its neo-liberal views, a curiosity having more to with the perceived division and incompetence of Labour in those years. However, in a social democratic Britain, Scotland remains significantly more left-of-centre as regards private education, educational selection, redistribution of income and wealth, as well as attitudes to poverty, the EU social chapter and the minimum wage. Even comparing like with like, in the case of public sector professionals north and south of the border, reveals that such Scots are more leftist and liberal than their English counterparts.

As far as party competition within Scotland is concerned, Labour and SNP voters are virtually identical with regard to social values and policy preferences, and only on attitudes to Independence do they differ significantly. Analysis of the Scottish Parliamentary Election Study (SPES) suggests that SNP voters are, if anything, marginally more left-wing than Labour voters, while Liberal Democrats are more centrist but tending towards the two main parties, with the Conservatives occupying something of an ideological ghetto on the Right. It seems that they had lost the argument with the electorate in terms of translating social values into political choices, and that only the electoral system which they had resolutely opposed, gave them a presence in the Parliament.

The key battleground in Scottish politics lies between Labour and the SNP, Scotland's two major parties. Both are trusted to work in Scotland's interests, and both tap into similar left-of-centre policy preferences. The parties do, of course, differ with regard to constitutional preferences, devolution versus Independence, but both have expressed enthusiasm for constitutional change, and a significant minority of supporters in each party prefer the constitutional preference of the other. Further, around two-thirds of the supporters of each give the other party as their second choice, reinforcing the competitive nature of Scottish politics around a similar battleground.

How will this unfold in the Scottish Parliament with regard to the devolutionary status quo versus Independence? Much will depend on which party is able to capture Scotland's trust from the other, which best expresses the prevailing social democratic mood of the electorate, and how well each is able to translate its constitutional preference into the political common sense of the times. For example, support for Independence at the start of the new century stands at between 25 and 30 per cent, in second place to devolution, behind which most non-SNP opinion has swung, Conservative included. Nevertheless, as many as six out of ten Scots expect Independence to occur within a twenty-year period, suggesting that while it is not their current preference, there is no mental obstacle to imagining Scotland as such. Similarly, around 60 per cent think that the devolved Parliament should have more powers. It is important to note that Scottish opinion differs from that elsewhere in Britain with regard to issues such as economic redistribution, poverty, and other matters of macro-economic policy which are powers currently reserved to Westminster. If, through time, the Scottish Parliament is deemed a success by the electorate, there might well be pressure to devolve further matters, notably relating to fiscal autonomy. If, on the other hand, the Parliament is judged to be stymied by Westminster, there is likely to be pressure in a similar direction to devolve further.

There is additional evidence that the Scottish Parliament has become the prime focus of welfare politics in Scotland in so far as it is deemed to be the more important institution than Westminster, even in its short life, and that people expect this to develop in the longer term. There is a whole range of social issues – education, health, welfare and so on – in which the distinctions between devolved and reserved matters does not resonate with the electorate in Scotland. Labour, the largest party in Scotland at the first Scottish election, appears to be losing support, on its Left to the SNP and the Scottish Socialist Party (SSP), and on its Right also to the SNP, but also the Liberal Democrats, and the Greens, but not to the Tories (Paterson et al., forthcoming).

Is Independence, then, inevitable? Nothing is so in politics, and much will depend on the outcome of party competition, structured as it is around a social democratic/Scottish agenda. While support for Independence is in the minority, there is a more even split between those who see it as 'good' and 'bad', suggesting that there is no systematic barrier to imagining an Independent Scotland.

Conclusion

This chapter has analysed political trends in Scotland, and has argued that in the second half of the twentieth century, distinctive political agenda emerged north of the border. Important social changes, notably the decline of an indigeneous class of Scottish capitalists, and new opportunities for social and geographical mobility, compounded the problems for the Conservative Party in Scotland, wedded as it has been to an attack on the state and to an Anglo-British national identity. The Scottish National Party found itself the recipient of a cohort of new electors in the late 1960s and early 1970s who, south of the border, would have tended towards the Conservatives.

The emerging Scottish frame of reference fixed a new dimension in politics, and when the SNP began to falter in the late 1970s the Labour Party inherited the new electoral cohort, and with it the neo-Nationalist mantle. Faced with a hostile Conservative government, Labour found itself playing the Nationalist card in the defence of Scottish interests. At the time of writing, the Conservative Party in Scotland has no Westminster MPs, and its performance at the next British election in Scotland is almost irrelevant. In an important sense, Scotland's politicians are all Nationalists now. Scotland's political system resembles those of other European countries much more than that of its southern neighbour. There is, for example, a Conservative right-of-centre party; a centre party, the Liberal Democrats; a social democratic party, Labour, as well as a small overtly socialist party, the SSP; a Green Party; and a nationalist party, the SNP. In this regard, the Scottish political system also resembles that of Wales, whose assembly elections produced almost identical results to those in Scotland.

The emergence of a national(ist) frame of reference raises the question of how politics and culture engage. It seems, however, that the emergence of a nationalist agenda has brought into focus the problematic character of Scottish culture. Oddly and unusually, there was no simple correspondence between cultural and political nationalism. Politics and culture appear to have grown apart. We will explore this conundrum in the next chapter.

6 Scottish culture

Images and icons

'He's dreaming now,' said Tweedledee, 'and what do you think he's dreaming about? Why, about you! And if he left off dreaming about you, where do you suppose you'd be?'

'Where I am now, of course,' said Alice.

'Not you!' Tweedledum retorted contemptuously. 'You'd be nowhere. Why, you're only a sort of thing in his dream!'

'If that there king was to wake,' added Tweedledum, 'you'd go out – bang – just like a candle!'

'I shouldn't!' Alice exclaimed indignantly. 'Besides, if I'm only a sort of thing in his dream, what are you, I should like to know?'

(Lewis Carroll, *Through the Looking Glass*)

Scotland as dream-time; a 'land out of time'; an 'enchanted fortress in a disenchanted world' (Rojek, 1993: 181): what if Scotland only exists in the imagination? – if its potent imagery has overpowered a puny reality? After all, for almost 300 years it had no parliament, no formal political reality of its own; yet its iconography is virtually universal: tartan, kilts, heather, haggis, misty landscapes. There is a story told by the film historian Forsyth Hardy about the making of a Hollywood production of the escapist romance *Brigadoon* in the 1950s. While film correspondent of *The Scotsman* newspaper, he was visited by its producer who was looking for a suitable site for the movie, preferably a village in the Highlands which would look unchanged after a hundred years. Hardy took him to Culross in Fife, Dunkeld and Comrie in Perthshire, and Braemar and Inveraray in the Highlands. The producer returned to Hollywood, deeply disappointed: 'I went to Scotland,' he said, 'but I could find nothing that looked like Scotland' (Hardy, 1990: 1).

We may mock the naivety of the Hollywood producer, or accord him a connection with a 'reality' all too recognisable in a discussion of Scottish culture, namely the overwhelming and distorted iconography of what passes for Scotland in the movie and tourist industries. Perhaps he appreciated that the imaginary Scotland was far more powerful than reality. The box-office success of *Braveheart* in the mid-1990s was merely testament to the power of image, however much historians might scoff at the mixed-up masquerade which passed for historical events. No amount of cold fact could douse the flame of cultural passion. Even the Scottish National Party, which usually takes a civic rather than an ethnic view of national identity, was moved to ride the band-wagon by issuing a leaflet. 'Today it's not just bravehearts who choose indepen-dence – it's also wise heads – and they use the ballot box. You've seen the movie – now face reality.' *Braveheart* may have been bad history but it made good politics, at least for a time. However, there is a reluctance among many Scottish nationalists today to mobilise simply around the signs and motifs bequeathed from the Scottish past. This tendency within Scottish nationalism to look sideways rather than backwards has much to do with a wider character-isation of this Scottish past. It is deemed to be dominated by negative motifs; it is deformed and distorted.

The 'Scottish story' seems to be full of fragmented narrative. It has been a fairly standard complaint that not much Scottish history was taught in schools, and that it seemed to have little point to it. The novelist William McIlvanney commented:

> Not only was our history largely suppressed but those parts of it which were acknowledged were often taught in such a way that they seemed to appear suddenly out of nowhere. A sense of continuity was difficult to grasp. This was the pop-up picture school of history. Oh, look. There's Bonnie Prince Charlie. Where did he come from? And that's Mary Queen of Scots. Somebody cut her head off. Wasn't it the English?
>
> Moments of history isolated in this way from the qualifying details of context can be made to mean whatever we want them to mean. Our rela-tionship to them tends to be impulsive and emotional rather than rational, since there is little for rationality to feed on. We see our past as a series of gestures rather than a sequence of actions. It's like looking in a massively cracked mirror. We identify our Scottishness in wilful fragments.
>
> (*Herald*, 6 March 1999)

There seems to be too much history in Scotland rather than too little, or perhaps too much of the wrong sort. McIlvanney's own explanation is as follows: 'when a country loses the dynamic of its own history, the ability to develop on its own terms, its sense of its past can fragment and freeze into caricature. For a long time this was Scotland's fate.' In other words, there is a clear connection between Scotland's cultural and political development. It was as if, following the Union of 1707, Scotland was left with a deficit of politics, and a surfeit of culture. Marinell Ash, in her seminal book *The Strange Death of Scottish History*, thought that one followed the other, that the Scots suffered a failure of nerve following the Union of 1707 and took refuge in the 'emotional trappings of the Scottish past' (1980: 10). She observed: 'Modern perceptions of Scotland's past are like foggy landscape; small peaks and islands of memory rising out of an occluded background. The name of some of these peaks are Bruce, Wallace, Bannockburn, Mary Queen of Scots, Bonnie Prince Charlie and the Clearances' (n.d.: 1).

A glance at the 'Scottish' shelves in any major bookshop reveals that much of Scotland seems to be 'over', for they are weighed down with accounts of the country's past. The conventional wisdom has been that since Scotland lost its formal political independence in 1707, it could not have a 'national culture' worthy of the name. After all, it lacked distinctiveness as regards language and religion, being both English-speaking and Protestant, and it had chosen to throw in its political lot with its richer and more powerful southern neighbour. If proof were needed of that, the argument goes, most of its inhabitants had supported the suppression of the Gaelic-speaking and largely Catholic Highlanders after their defeat at Culloden in 1746. Further, they became enthusiastic Unionists and imperialists in the context of the British Empire, compared with the Irish and even the Welsh. The failure of political nationalism to emerge in the nineteenth century when it was the rage of Europe seemed to confirm that whatever form cultural identity and nationalism was taking at that time, it was not being mobilised in the cause of regaining statehood. Scottish history, the argument went, ceased to be important because it could not be reworked into a political programme for a separate state. Colin Kidd (1993) has argued that Scottish Whig historians looked to England for a progressive and liberating vision of society, and hence the absence of a nationalist historiography in the nineteenth century was because there was no real demand for one. Liberation and progress were to be achieved through the medium of the Anglo–British state, not via opposition to it in a struggle for national liberation. The absence of such a struggle was not, in Kidd's view, because there was insufficient material in Scottish history to construct a myth of national origins, but rather because the 'future' lay with the Anglo–British state. Later in this chapter we will see that this is a contentious viewpoint, but for the moment it helps to establish what became a conventional wisdom about Scottish culture, namely that it became separated from a nationalist political project, and as a result became 'deformed' and fragmented.

The strain of cultural pessimism runs deep among Scottish intellectuals. The perceived absence of a 'rounded' culture, reflecting the Scottish/British split, mapping as it does on to the culture/politics split, has long had an appeal. Edwin Muir, for example, writing in the 1930s, spoke of a Scotland 'gradually being emptied of its population, its spirit, its wealth, industry, art, intellect, and innate character' (*Scottish Journey*, 1935 (reprinted 1980: 3)). George Davie's *The Democratic Intellect* (1961), a powerful indictment of what he saw as the Anglicisation of Scottish culture and education in the nineteenth century, is one of the most influential books of the late twentieth century.

The most powerful and dominant analysis of Scottish culture remains Tom Nairn's *The Break-Up of Britain* first published in 1977. His later book *After Britain* (2000) returns to some of these themes over twenty years later, albeit in a revised form. Scottish culture is characterised as split, divided, deformed. This is a not unfamiliar view of Scottish culture, epitomised by Walter Scott, that Scotland is divided between the 'heart' (representing the past, romance, 'civil society') and the 'head' (the present and future, reason, and, by dint of that, the British state). There is the 'Caledonian Antisyzygy', a term borrowed by Hugh MacDiarmid from Gregory Smith's (1919) characterisation of Scottish literature as containing an antithesis of the real and the fantastic.

The image of Scotland as a divided and unhealthy society is a common one in Scottish literature which has acted as a key carrier of Scottish identity. In Douglas Gifford's words:

> Through recurrent patterns of a relationship such as father versus son, brother versus brother, or variants, a recurrent and shared symbolism states overwhelmingly the same theme; that in lowland Scotland, aridity of repressive orthodoxy, religious and behavioural, tied to an exaggerated work ethic and distorted notions of social responsibility, have stifled and repressed vital creative processes of imaginative and emotional expression, to the point where it too often has become, individually and collectively, self-indulgent, morbid and unbalanced.
>
> (Gifford, 1988: 244)

Nairn's view of Scotland is similar. It suffers, he claimed in *The Break-Up of Britain*, from 'sub-national deformation', 'neurosis' (and psychiatric disorders seem to be a Scottish speciality), and 'cultural sub-nationalism':

> It was cultural because of course it could not be political; on the other hand, this culture could not be straightforwardly nationalist either – a direct substitute for political action, like, for example, so much Polish literature of the 19th century. It could only be 'sub-nationalist' in the sense of venting its national content in various crooked ways – neurotically, so to speak, rather than directly.
>
> (Nairn, 1977: 156)

This 'sub-nationalism' is, according to Nairn, a poor, shilpit thing. While Scottish civil society survived in the bosom of the British state, the Scottish 'heart' was split from the British 'head'; the 'national', with its overemphasis on the past, was separated from the 'practical', with its emphasis on the present and future. This came about because, by the late eighteenth and early nineteenth centuries, the intelligentsia was 'deprived of its historic nationalist' role. Says Nairn, 'there was no call for its usual services' (1977: 154) of leading the nation to the threshold of political independence. Intellectuals after the Union migrated, if not in body at least in spirit, to the bigger, more rounded culture of Anglo-Britain, leaving, he thought, a stunted residue of intellectual life in Scotland. In this context, then, it is easy to explain the Scottish Enlightenment of the late eighteenth century, an otherwise awkward phenomenon to arise in a 'deformed' culture. In essence, says Nairn, it wasn't Scottish at all, or rather it represented the belated intellectual fruits of the Union. Operating on a much bigger stage before a larger and more sophisticated audience, it was 'strikingly non-nationalist – so detached from the People, so intellectual and universalising in its assumptions, so Olympian in its attitudes' (Nairn, 1977: 140).

Smith, Hume, the Mills, Robertson, Adam and its other luminaries, Nairn argues, may have been Scots by birth and education, but they were universal men, and certainly, if anything, 'British' in orientation. The cultural void in Scotland was created largely by the migration of Scots intellectuals to the richer pastures of England. Macauley, Carlyle, Ruskin, Gladstone and many more were not even thought of as Scots at all. England, says Nairn, was a 'mature, all-round thought-world': 'It was an organic or "rooted" national-romantic culture in which literature – from Coleridge and Carlyle up to F. R. Leavis and E. P. Thompson – has consistently played a major role' (1977: 156–7).

Dominant discourses

The purpose of this chapter is to set out the ways in which dominant discourses about Scotland have handled it, not to establish what Scottish culture 'is'. The cultural sociologist Raymond Williams spoke of 'cultural formations' as 'effective movements and tendencies, in intellectual and artistic life, which have significant and sometimes decisive influence on the active development of a culture, and which have a variable and often oblique relation to formal institutions' (1977: 117). Such cultural formations help to set the framework within which matters are discussed. We might group discussion about Scottish culture into the following broad formations: tartanry and the 'Kailyard'.

This chapter examines the view that Scottish culture has been dominated by these mythic structures (Craig, 1983) to such an extent that they seem to offer only negative representations of Scotland, reflecting the political and cultural developments since the Union of 1707. This view has been so predominant among Scottish intellectuals that their contribution to the development of neo-nationalism in Scotland has been negative and critical, that their analysis itself represents a dominant discourse which itself has to be examined critically. The argument here is not that Scottish culture is necessarily deformed – that Scottish culture contains nothing but distorted motifs, for that would be to accept what is highly problematic. It is not the case that Scottish culture consists of tartanry and Kailyard and nothing else, but that these have remained important discourses on Scottish culture. There is, of course, more to Scottish culture than these sets of images, but the search for a distinctive culture has been so dominated by them that they cannot be avoided. The argument of this chapter will be that they are far less dominant than is made out, and that their influence is not quite as unproblematic and pernicious as has been claimed. Indeed, it will be argued that the variety and eclecticism of Scottish culture today corresponds to world conditions in the late twentieth century rather than the distorting legacy of these 'mythic structures'.

To describe tartanry and Kailyard as mythic structures is not to imply that they are false, to be driven out of Scottish culture by wholesome reality. Deconstructing myths in an anthropological sense is to identify the social and cultural forces which keep them alive, for they often serve key legitimatory purposes, as we saw in relation to education myths in Chapter 4. If myths and legends are kept alive and embellished, even invented, it is not enough to show that this is so; it is necessary to ask why some are retained and others disappear. As Tom Nairn pointed out in his study of the British monarchy (1988), it is easy to show up the discontinuities and inventions in this supposed unbroken lineage; seeking to show why it retains its 'glamour' (a word he uses in its Scottish sense – its magic, its enchantment) in the late twentieth century is quite another matter.

The fall and rise of tartanry

Tartanry is a cultural formation which has involved the appropriation of Highland symbolism by Lowland Scotland. Tom Nairn has called it the 'Tartan Monster' (note the motif of fear, nightmare, neurosis here – sub-Freud – Scotland as a psychiatric condition). Tartanry is never treated as seriously as the Kailyard by Scottish intellectuals; perhaps it is too unspeakable to be worthy of their analysis, although they are often linked conceptually together, as in this comment by Christopher Harvie: 'Tartanry attained its fullest extent in the shrewd marketing of the Kailyard authors in the 1890s' (1988: 27).

Tartanry was not a literary movement at all, but a set of garish symbols appropriated by Lowland Scotland at a safe distance from 1745, and turned into a music-hall joke (Harry Lauder represented the fusion of both tartanry and Kailyard – the jokes and mores from the latter, the wrapping from the former). The appropriation of Highland motifs by Lowland Scotland has been described elsewhere (Chapman, 1978; McCrone *et al.*, 1982), but tartanry has come to stand for tourist knick-knackery, sporting kit for football and rugby supporters, and the Edinburgh Tattoo. There are few systematic analyses of tartanry, the set of symbols and images, by Scottish intellectuals, although there are a number of studies of the history of tartan (Telfer-Dunbar, 1962, 1981; Hesketh, 1972; Stewart and Thompson, 1980; Cheape, 1995). The most notorious account is that of the English historian Hugh Trevor-Roper (Lord Dacre) in his chapter in Hobsbawm and Ranger's collection *The Invention of Tradition*, in which he attempts a demolition job on tartanry. Not only does it have no basis in history, it was invented, he claims, by *an Englishman* who did Highlanders a favour. He asserts:

> The kilt is a purely modern costume, first designed and first worn by an English Quaker industrialist, and that it was bestowed by him on the Highlanders in order not to preserve their traditional way of life but to ease their transformation: to bring them out of the heather and into the factory.
>
> (Trevor-Roper, 1984: 22)

It has to be said that Trevor-Roper's interpretation is thoroughly contentious, and Telfer-Dunbar, the major historian of tartan, dismissed similar views (1981: 69–70). He concluded: 'One cannot help wondering if any of this argument would have arisen if it had been claimed that the kilt was invented in the early 18th century by a Highlander' (ibid.: 72).

Other parts of the tartan story are fairly well known, and less contentious. The Proscription Act of 1747 forbade the wearing of tartan until 1782. The Act enacted

> That from and after the first day of August . . . one thousand seven hundred and forty seven no man or boy within that part of Great Britain called Scotland, *other than shall be employed as Officers and Soldiers in his Majesty's Forces,* [my emphasis] shall on any pretext whatsoever, wear or put on the clothes commonly called Highland clothes (that is to say) the Plaid, Philabeg or little Kilt, Trowse, Shoulderbelts, or any part whatsoever of what peculiarly belongs to Highland garb.

This Act helps to question the myth that tartan was invented by Rawlinson, the English Quaker industrialist referred to by Trevor-Roper. If a lone Englishman could effect such a change in Highland fashion, why was it deemed necessary for such an Act of Parliament to be passed, given that it brought seven years' transportation to the wearer? Why this legal sledge-hammer to crack such a puny nut?

Sumptuary laws to curb extravagances in dress had, in fact, been passed in many European countries for centuries, while the English King Henry VIII had passed a proscription act in Ireland in 1539. Henry seemed to have understood the political and ethnic symbolism of dress. Once the Scottish Proscription Act was passed in 1747, the kilt and tartan were appropriated by the British army in its colonial wars – quite literally stealing the enemy's clothes – and it set about with gusto inventing new tartans, notably darker shades of green, browns, blues and blacks more suited as camouflage in its wars on the North American continent. The Proscription Act itself was not repealed until 1782, under lobbying from the London Highland Society which had such establishment members as General Fraser of Lovat, Lord Chief Baron MacDonald, the Earl of Seaforth, Colonel Macpherson of Cluny, and MP John Graham, Duke of Montrose. It was a measure of the incorporation of Highland landed aristocracy into the British elite that they were able to effect such a change. In this respect, Trevor-Roper is correct in saying that the development of (modern) tartans originated 'more often in the officers' mess than in the straths and glens of Scotland' (1984: 29).

The 'gentrification' of tartan was aided considerably by Walter Scott, who, as impresario, persuaded George IV, a large man by all accounts and with a poor command of English, to visit Edinburgh in 1822, and worse, to wear a kilt set off fetchingly by pink tights. Despite, or perhaps because of this, tartan became an instant fashion, and members of polite society clamoured to have their own version. The weaving company William Wilson of Bannockburn duly obliged, and was not averse to allocating the same tartan to more than one clan label. Wilson seems to have developed his list of tartans in an opportunistic way without worrying overmuch about the authenticity of the design, as we can see from this selection from a 1794 list of patterns:

> black and red tartan
> red and white tartan
> 42nd sett
> red and white drumluthy sett
> blanket tartan green ground plaids
> McDonalds sett
> common kilt
> Bruce sett
> blue and green
> blue and green with red stripes
> Gordon
> Gordon with silk

By 1800, Wilson had, according to Telfer-Dunbar, doubled his repertoire of patterns to eighty, including 'the Aberdeen sett, the Atholl pattern, the Perth sett, and the Caledonian'. The colonial market was booming, and slave owners in the West Indies and the southern States had found it a useful uniform for identifying their human property in a crowd.

Queen Victoria's acquisition of her Deeside estate at Balmoral in 1848 gave the royal seal of approval to the tartan enterprise, and she and Albert had one of their very own designed. The royal association, begun by 'German Geordie', helped to guarantee commercial success. Behind all this was a considerable 'heritage' industry bent on authenticating the ancient designs for an anxious world eager to believe. The picture was completed by the Allen Brothers, John and Charles, who so fell in love with the mythology of tartan that they changed their names to the Sobieski Stuarts, claiming to be the grandsons of the Young Pretender (and to have a Polish connection to boot). There is little doubt that they fabricated their most famous work, the *Vestiarium Scoticum*, published in 1842 in Edinburgh, supposedly from a manuscript of 1721, compiled in 1571. This was soon to be denounced as a forgery (Stewart and Thompson, 1980), but seemed to do nothing to dampen the desire to accept the authenticity of tartan. Trevor-Roper describes the Sobieski Stuarts' *The Costume of the Clans* of 1844 as 'shot through with fantasy and bare-faced forgery'. Telfer-Dunbar is more relaxed in his assessment: '[It] is, without doubt, one of the foundation stones on which any history of Highland dress is built. It cannot be ignored, and it is surprising how little it has been consulted by writers on the subject. We can think what we like about the ancestral claims of the Stuart brothers, but this does not reduce the value of their monumental books' (1962: 111).

What are we to make of the claims and counter-claims as to the authenticity of tartan? Its survival and development occurred because a number of factors came together at an opportune time: the Romantic search for the 'noble savage', and the 'discovery' of the Ossian poems by Macpherson in the 1760s; the raising of Highland regiments after Culloden, a master-stroke by the British state in incorporating the symbols of its enemies into its own identity. By the nineteenth century, the climate was right for Walter Scott's romantic tales to become bestsellers, the King effectively acting as literary agent by visiting Edinburgh in 1822, accoutred in the way Scott wanted. The self-styled Sobieski Stuarts simply took the whole thing to its logical extremes. Wilsons of Bannockburn added the commercial element, and gave material expression to this fantasy. The whole enterprise was rounded off by the royal seal of approval, first by George IV, and then by Queen Victoria in 1848.

This, in brief, is the tartan story. A form of dress and design which had undoubtedly real but haphazard significance in the Highlands of Scotland was taken over by elements of lowland society anxious to claim some distinctive aspect of culture at a time when the economic, social and cultural identity was ebbing away in the late nineteenth century. This was the point in history when Scotland as a whole could safely appropriate Highland images, when the threat to the British state and to Protestantism had safely receded.

The appropriation of tartan has also helped to translate Highland images and identities into Scotland as a whole. Presenting Scotland as 'Celtic' took some-what longer, for it was not until the second half of the nineteenth century that a discursive separation between 'Saxon' and 'Celt' took place (McArthur, 1994). This distinction became part of an ethnological fiction and system of symbolic appropriation whereby Gaelic culture, life and language became the focus of associations required by the external discourse of wider English and European cultures (Chapman, 1992). 'Celtic' became a term for non-Anglo-Saxon, an identity constructed around the requirements of modern geo-politics. So, Chapman argues, Scotland 'has, on the whole, settled for a Celtic and Gaelic definition, in pursuit of difference from England. This accounts for the extra-ordinary efflorescence of Highland and Gaelic imagery in the self-presentation and assumed genealogy of modern Scotland' (ibid.: 92). There are also deeper ideological antinomies being employed in the use of this vocabulary:

the Anglo-Saxon . . . appears a brutal soulless figure, disfigured by every wart and sore that industry, cities, pollution, capitalism and greed can cast upon the countenance. The Celt, by contrast, is a magical figure, bard, warrior and enchanter, beyond the reach of this world, and an object of love and yearning for those doomed to wander among material things in the cold light of reason.

(Ibid.: 253)

Nor should we think that this characterisation has been wished upon a reluctant Scotland from the outside. The social anthropologist Sharon Macdonald (1999) has pointed out that within the country itself there is a deep ambivalence between the contrasting tropes of 'improvement/modernity' and 'remaining true to oneself', especially through appropriating Gaelic and Highland culture to convey the essence of a people. She argues that in fact it was only in the second half of the twentieth century that the language of Gaelic came to be seen as central to Scottish identity, and this in the context of continuing decline in the number of Gaelic speakers in Scotland.

The Kailyard culture

In his collection of essays entitled *Out of History: Narrative Paradigms in Scottish and British Culture*, Cairns Craig touches a nerve: '*Parochial*: the word has haunted discussion of Scottish culture; it damns up before we start because we must leap in desperation to join "the world"; condemns us when we finish with having been no more than ourselves' (1996: 11). Perhaps no other accusation bites so deeply into Scottish consciousness than being 'parochial'. Tom Nairn in *After Britain* refers to 'pickle-jar parochialism' (2000: 240), with its own psychic condition of self-colonisation.

This is no casual slight, for it appears to connect with the second cultural formation, Kailyardism. The Kailyard, or 'cabbage-patch' tradition flourished, with its petty obsessions and mean-minded parochial jealousies. Kailyardism is usually described as a popular literary style celebrating Scottish rural quaintness, at its height from about 1880 until 1914. It helped, as we saw in Chapter 4, to give cultural expression to the 'lad o' pairts', the boy of academic talent but little financial means, which became an ideal type in Scottish educational ideology. The term 'Kailyard' is usually attributed to the critic George Blake, who described its essential elements as domesticity, rusticity, humour, humility, modesty, decency, piety and poverty (Shepherd, 1988). Its key writers were 'Ian MacLaren' [John Watson] (1850–1907), S. R. Crockett (1860–1914) and J. M. Barrie (1860–1937). Shepherd points out that not all late nineteenth- and early twentieth-century writers belonged to the Kailyard School (R. L. Stevenson, G. D. Brown and W. Alexander were obvious exceptions), nor did all Kailyard works conform to the 'formula' which involved an omniscient narrator, a rural setting, imprecise chronology and episodic format, and key roles for the minister and the schoolmaster.

Scotland in the late nineteenth century was an industrialised society, occupying a place in the sun of Victorian prosperity. In social and political terms, the latter decades of the century brought special anxieties. The mid-century destruction of the unity of the Kirk, the removal of the last vestiges of the old Scottish administration, betrayed anxieties about national identity. Mass migration into towns and cities from the Highlands and the Lowlands, and from Ireland, reflected unprecedented social change. In rural areas, as Ian Carter (1979) points out, the penetration of peasant agriculture by agrarian capitalism was undercutting the social and economic organisation which had supported peasant culture and values. In this respect, the Kailyard with its homely celebration of, and panegyric for, the virtues of independence, hard work and 'getting on', became a celebration of a doomed culture and way of life. The parish, the community, was no longer the typical locus of social existence; the industrialised and anonymous city was now dominant. In this environment, the lad o'pairts was no longer an appropriate social model.

Although the Kailyard School probably failed to survive the Great War, its influence on Scottish culture has been adjudged to be long-lasting and malevolent. Nairn argues that much of the Kailyard's output was produced by Scottish émigrés with rosy, romantic memories of the simple Scotland they had left behind for richer pickings in the south. Their pawky simplicities had a ready market in Scotland, and while kitsch was in no way unique to Scotland, it took on the character of a national-popular tradition. The implication is that Scottish culture became overwhelmingly the Kailyard, and as a result, a proper 'mature, all-round thought-world' (as in England) could not be Scottish.

In recent years, however, the notion that the Kailyard dominated literary and cultural representations of Scotland has begun to be questioned. T. D. Knowles (1983) was critical of the view which explains the Kailyard entirely within a Scottish historical context and literary tradition. The output of writers like MacLaren, Crockett and Barrie, he argued, was geared to a wider British, and even American, market with its vogue for religious fiction and sentimental retrospection. The editor of the Nonconformist *British Weekly*, W. R. Nicoll, encouraged such writers to address this growing political-religious market in the UK, as well as the demand for 'local-colour' writing in the USA (where the Scottish-American audience was sufficiently large and influential to adopt highly coloured tales from home). The key role of the émigré both as producer and consumer was vital. Knowles points out that MacLaren was Essex-born, and based in Liverpool, while he describes Barrie as the 'classic émigré' (1983: 22). All in all, the Kailyard writers had significance furth of Scotland: 'Their work contained British Victorian elements as well as Scottish; they were regionalists, and there is influence from the gothic novel, the fairy tale, 18th century sentimentalism, and the Victorian penchant for dying and death' (ibid.: 64).

Such a revisionist view of the Kailyard is not only echoed but developed by Willie Donaldson (1986), who argues for a clear distinction between book-publishing (which carried the Kailyard novels) and the popular Scottish press in the late nineteenth century. It was, he points out, the weekly press (at the end of the century there were over 200 weekly titles all over Scotland) which had much greater impact than the London-centred book trade. This press was much more willing to use vernacular Scots, and to address major issues of social change in both urban and rural Scotland. He concludes:

> On the whole, popular fiction in Victorian Scotland is not overwhelmingly backward-looking; it is not obsessed by rural themes; it does not shrink

from urbanisation or its problems; it is not idyllic in its approach; it does not treat the common people as comic or quaint. The second half of the 19th century is not a period of creative trauma or linguistic decline; it is one of the richest and most vital episodes in the history of Scottish popular culture.

(Donaldson, 1986: 149)

Writers like William Alexander, Donaldson argues, had a realistic appreciation of social change and its impact in north-east Scotland, quite distinct from the narrow and distorting imagery and 'pietistic fiction' of bourgeois Kailyard writers addressing the British and American bourgeois book markets.

These revisionist accounts by Knowles and Donaldson help to undermine the view that Scottish culture was overly dependent on Kailyard themes and values, which in turn were deemed largely responsible in the twentieth century for a deformed and distorted sense of Scottishness. If Scotland was 'parochial', it was a view held of the old country by those who had left it, and who required to have their stereotypes confirmed for their own purposes. In this regard, the role of the diaspora in preserving the homeland in aspic is especially important, and is a feature of other societies, notably Ireland, which have seen massive emigration in the past 150 years.

This sense of separation, of fragmentation, runs throughout much intellectual analysis of Scotland. The historian, Chris Harvie (1975), for example, argued that this schizophrenia – Scotland's split personality again – has taken a social form: between the 'red' Scots – those who leave in search of new opportunities, the outward-bound strain of 'Scot on the make', unspeakable or otherwise – and the 'black' Scots – those who stay to nourish the home culture, the Kailyard and Tartan Monsters. It seems that only if one has lived in the 'wider' culture – the 'mature, all-round thought-world' of England perhaps – the 'real world', is one immune from the insidious psychological effects of Scottish culture. Indeed, at its extreme, this strain of criticism seems to imply that even to *think* about Scotland is proof of 'neurosis', thereby seeming to lock us into a pessimistic catch-22. Indeed, to be 'normal' (un-neurotic) you would be advised not to think of Scotland at all. The language of this critique is certainly sub-Freud. It is replete with 'monsters', with 'neuroses', with 'split personalities', and, after all, it was a Scotsman, Robert Louis Stevenson, who invented Dr Jekyll and Mr Hyde.

Much of the discussion in the final decades of the twentieth century has focused around deconstructing the 'Scotch myths' of tartanry/Kailyard (see, for instance, 'The politics of tartanry', in *Bulletin of Scottish Politics*, 1981). The exhibition mounted by Barbara and Murray Grigor at the 1981 Edinburgh Festival was also a key event. This exhibition had gathered together representations of Scotland, from postcards to orange box labels from California to media representations of Scotland in film and television, and aimed to generate discussion of Scotland's 'deformed' culture. In 1982, the Edinburgh Film Festival held a showing of *Scotch Reels*, the film of the exhibition, as it were, together with a three-day discussion event around a collection of essays (McArthur, 1982). The remit was clear. In McArthur's own words: 'Clearly the traditions of Kailyard and Tartanry have to be exposed and deconstructed, and more politically progressive representations constructed, circulated and discussed' (1981: 25)

Much of the evidence was based on graphic representations in film, television and the 'sign media' generally. The semiotics of Scotland, it was argued, are regressive in cultural terms, and in their political manifestations lock us into subordination and dependency. Tartanry/Kailyard helped to maintain cultural hegemony over Scotland's sense of itself. In the words of McArthur: 'a limited number of discourses have been deployed in the cinema to construct Scotland and the Scots, and to give an impression that no other constructions are possible' (1982: 69). These 'pathological discourses' can be traced through how Scotland is represented, notably in the visual arts. By the twentieth century, modern cultural media were reproducing the stereotypes, and in film it was the decade and a half after the Second World War which laid down 'the definitive modern statements of tartanry and Kailyard in the cinema' in Scotland (McArthur, 1983: 45). Films such as *Bonnie Prince Charlie* (1948), *Rob Roy, The Highland Rogue* (1953), *Kidnapped* (1960), *Greyfriars Bobby* (1961) and the doyen of them all, *Brigadoon* (1954), were all Hollywood creations and representations of Scotland. McArthur comments on the latter: 'at one level it takes the Romantic representation of Scotland as a given, but at another level . . . this representation is revealed as the dream par excellence, as a fiction created to escape from the urban horrors of the twentieth century' (1983: 47).

Other discourses were judged to be healthier, and indigeneous to Scotland. 'Clydesidism' was seen as 'extremely refreshing in the Scottish context', says McArthur; it is not a 'pernicious discourse'. What Clydesidism had in its favour is that it is constructed from 'real' images of working-class life, from the discourse of class, and from naturalism. Says John Caughie, the tradition is 'based on working class experiences which, since the twenties, have seemed to offer the only real and consistent basis for *a Scottish national culture*' (1982: 121; my emphasis).

And that is it. The search is for a national culture which will speak to people in their own terms, an integrated discourse which will connect with political and social realities in Scotland. The problem, however, with Clydesidism as a discourse was not that it was resonant of socialist realism (heroic workers and all: 'Stakhanovite political iconography', says McArthur (1983: 3)) and, as Cairns Craig (1983) pointed out, it was becoming a 'historic discourse' even in its heartland of west-central Scotland by the late twentieth century. Its language is redolent of early twentieth-century Clydeside, with its appeal to the 'industrial masses' and to skilled masculine culture, and, as Eleanor Gordon and Esther Breitenbach observe, 'skill' is a social construct which is 'saturated with male bias' (1990: 6). It is fine, says Cairns Craig, to break out of the mental traps of the historic myths of tartanry and Kailyard, to imagine a future, even a revolutionary future, through which to overcome the static quality of the dominant myths, but we risk embracing another myth based on a fast-disappearing working-class culture. Craig observes: 'What is worrying in the contemporary situation is the way that the death throes of industrial West-Central Scotland have become the touchstone of authenticity for our culture.' He continues: 'if we make the victims of that decline the carriers of our essential identity, we merely perpetuate the cultural alienation in which we negate the on-going struggle of our experience by freezing its real meaning in a particular defeat' (1983: 9).

Ten years later, McArthur was still expressing pessimism about a newer genre of film. Movies such as *Local Hero* were in his view still being written within dominant Scottish narratives of an 'elegaic discourse', in which 'we tend to be written by the dominant Scottish narratives rather than ourselves writing stories about Scotland' (1993: 102). Such discourses were not inevitable however: 'it has to be understood that the historically dominant narratives about Scotland can impede political advance and must therefore be confronted, deconstructed and replaced with new narratives' (ibid.: 104). The problem, as McArthur saw it, was that the discourses continue, in his words, 'to lurk, iceberg-like, in the Scottish discursive unconscious'. Here we confront a now-familiar theme of the deformed nature of culture in Scotland, which is, of course, a powerful discourse in its own right, and one which has dominated discussions about Scottish culture for much of the last fifty years.

The eclipse of Scottish culture?

One familiar answer, presented in its starkest form by Beveridge and Turnbull (1989, 1997), is to argue that Scottish culture has undergone an eclipse as a result of its cultural subordination to England. Drawing on notions of dependency, and its cultural correlate, 'inferiorism' (derived from a Third World context by Franz Fanon), they argue that, so overwhelming has been the application of 'metropolitan ways' that it is believed that Scotland has ceased to produce important thinkers. These authors argue that it is the power of the *belief* that causes intellectuals to devalue their own culture, and there is good evidence, particularly in the fields of philosophy and theology, that Scotland has in fact produced important and original thinkers. They argue that 'the inferiorist view is as false as it is powerful' (1989: 3).

Their starting point, then, is quite similar to that expressed in this chapter, namely that a narrow set of discourses – crucially tartanry and Kailyardism – has been employed in the cultural analysis of Scotland, and the end result is a fairly pessimistic and misleading account of Scottish culture. This analysis has political overtones: suspicious of concepts like 'tradition' and 'identity', many tough-minded left-wing nationalists were even prepared to abandon the cultural argument entirely. Scottish nationalism's cultural-intellectual base was therefore altogether too narrow for the nationalist challenge to be sustained over any extended period (ibid.: 4).

Beveridge and Turnbull, on the other hand, promote as the central task of cultural nationalism 'the recovery of Scottish cultural practices', which have to be rescued from the metropolitan-influenced analysis of Scotland. Intellectuals like Tom Nairn are accused of a 'deep aversion to everything native and local' (ibid.: 58), which in turn derives from long-standing processes of 'cultural colonisation'. Such processes inflict a Manichean view on Scottish culture. 'In Nairn's description, there are no shades or contours; everything stands condemned' (ibid.). Fundamentally, they continue, Nairn is essentially a unionist, not a nationalist at all; the nationalist project is suborned to the cause of socialism: 'Restated, the meaning of Scottish nationalism for Nairn is as a moment in the development of British socialism. His commitment to nationalism is pragmatic and conditional rather than principled' (ibid.: 60).

Beveridge and Turnbull argue that Nairn was converted to nationalism as a way out of the crisis of the British Left in the late 1970s, and that, fundamentally, he 'exemplifies the adoption by Scottish intellectuals of metropolitan perspectives' (ibid.: 61). In contrast, Beveridge and Turnbull set themselves the task of identifying and promoting Scottish cultural traditions, untainted by the 'anglicised traditions' of the universities in Scotland (not, of course, in their view, 'Scottish universities'). This is a theme developed by George Davie in *The Democratic Intellect* (1961) in which he argued that Scottish higher education underwent an unprecedented and fatal Anglicisation in the late nineteenth century, a thesis described by Lindsay Paterson as persuasive and usually undisputed, but quite wrong in its interpretation of events and processes (1994: 66).

As regards the analysis of Scottish culture, Beveridge and Turnbull make the valid point that those who argue that tartanry and Kailyardism are hegemonic in their effects fail to acknowledge that cultural meanings are never passively consumed, but always subject to selection and adjustment to other discourses. Consumers' responses to tartanry, therefore, are 'not uncritical assimilation, but a complex negotiation dependent on the beliefs and values which are bound up with those of other concerns' (1989: 14). Much of the attack on tartanry and Kailyard has depended on an uncritical assumption that their impact has been comprehensive and undifferentiated.

The essence of Beveridge and Turnbull's argument is that there is an unwarranted focus on the 'deformity' of Scottish culture among intellectuals, and that this focus arises from 'inferiorism', a form of cultural dependency on the metropolitan, English, power. They draw on the powerful paradigm of dependency which illuminates much research on Scottish social structure, discussed in previous chapters. They present us with its cultural correlate; cultural dependency is the result of employing limited discourses. In crucial respects, however, they make one central assumption: that Scottish national culture exists, and remains to be uncovered and rescued from intellectual pessimism. Thus,

> If a *national culture* is to remain alive, its history too must live in some distinctive way and must be perceived as integral to the lives of those

who share it. This helps to define their sense of collective identity, gives them their confidence, lets them know where they are.

(Beveridge and Turnbull, 1989: 16, my emphasis)

The search for Scottish culture

We might, however, ask an altogether more radical set of questions: Why should there be an obsessive search to find a 'national identity'? Why is the question even framed in this way? Where does it come from? The answer is that it derives from an older, essentially 'nationalist' assumption that all societies worthy of the name should have a distinctive culture. Despite the fairly critical stances taken against political nationalism by Scottish intellectuals, this perspective seems to echo its assumption that Scotland has (or had) a 'national' culture waiting to be discovered. This is essentially an idea traceable back to the eighteenth-century Enlightenment notion of sovereignty, embodied in the culture of a nation waiting to be brought to its political realisation.

The role of intellectuals, generally, has been to identify the 'essential character' of a people, and to give it political expression. Such a modernist project involved distilling the essence of national culture, and presenting it as distinctive and self-contained. This process required that the contradictions and paradoxes be smoothed out so that national identities were clear-cut and paramount. Above all, these identities were gendered, relegating women to walk-on parts, and to their role as keepers of the moral and family values of the nation (Boden, 2000). It is, then, no coincidence that those identities diagnosed as archetypically Scottish by friend and foe alike – the Kailyard, tartanry and Clydesidism – have little place for women. There is no analogous 'lass o'pairts'; the image of tartanry is a male-military image (and kilts were not a female form of dress); and the Clydeside icon was a skilled, male worker who was man enough to care for his womenfolk. Even the opponents of these identities took them over as their own images of social life.

Similarly, those who wish to inject a class-based national identity into the contemporary Scottish context run the risk of adopting the 'big man' myth. More radically, we might argue that the search for a single carrier of national identity is doomed to ignore the pluralism and complexity of identities of modern life. The search for such a single identity in contemporary nationalism seems increasingly time-bound and anachronistic. How does this perspective connect with the analysis put forward by critics of tartanry/Kailyard? In some fundamental ways the critique of this 'mythic structure' as a discourse is not radical enough. It is premised upon the previous existence or at least the future possibility of a rounded, mature national culture. As Cairns Craig pointed out, the problem of identity is precisely the one we should not be trying to solve, because 'the "identity" we construct will be an essentialising, an idealising, a reduction to paradigmatic features, of Scotland as *home*, a

counterbalance to the "home counties" as core of English/British culture'
(1983: 8).

So, applying tartanry/Kailyard as the essentials of our national culture, albeit
negative ones, is to simplify and freeze them. This process will also predispose us
to look for what we have lost, to reduce culture to a series of tragic failures.
Once the issue is set up in this negative way, we can find any number of
contradictory 'explanations' for the national condition. Thus it results from
too little independence, or too much (insufficient incorporation into British
civil society); it results from too little industrial capitalism (failure to have a
thoroughgoing capitalist revolution), or too much; from too little Calvinism
(the Catholic legacy) or too much. All seem plausible if we define the problem
as a failure of a 'Scottish national culture' to develop. The point here is that
once we frame the problem in this way, we imply the uniqueness of the Scottish
problem; we look inside for the explanation. The assumption that certain forms
of Kitsch are uniquely Scottish cannot be true in a comparative context, and
Scotland did not invent the soap opera.

A considerable amount of effort has gone in to discovering the 'real' Scottish
culture, especially in the pre-industrial past. Lying behind the deformed images
is a sense of the 'golden age', pre-Independence, when society and the state
were one, when it was possible to argue that this 'Scottish culture' was a
communal culture, reflected in the sturdy vernacular literature of the Makars,
of Henryson, Dunbar, Barbour, then Ramsay, Fergusson and Robert Burns
(Wittig, 1958; Craig, 1961). This search for a truly 'Scottish' culture is
frequently retrospective and romantic, a celebration of the past, the golden
age, and helps to explain Scottish history's obsession with what has ended, as
Marinell Ash's trenchant critique makes plain.

So the search into the past for a distinctive and un-neurotic Scottish culture is
doomed to reproduce a new set of myths about what Scotland was like. Instead,
it is argued here that we have to look not simply into the future, but at what is
going on in other societies. The quest for Scottish cultural independence from a
culturally suffocating and homogeneous Anglo-British one ignores the fact that,
as Cairns Craig has pointed out, the latter has fragmented. The post-1918
period saw the collapse of the English cultural imperium, and subsequently,
'English culture' could no longer be equated with 'the culture of England'.
In most English-speaking countries, there was a burgeoning of indigenous
literature – in Canada, Australia, South Africa, New Zealand, the United
States and Ireland.

The Scottish literary renaissance of the 1920s expressed itself in the work of
MacDiarmid, Grassic Gibbon, Linklater, MacColla, Muir, Bridie, as well as
Violet Jacob and Naomi Mitchison (Harvie, 1981). These socio-cultural developments were rooted in a pluralistic cultural system in Scotland – in Gaelic
(Sorley MacLean), in Scots (notably, MacDiarmid and Gibbon) and even in
standard English (Muriel Spark). These traditions have survived and prospered,
and have ceased to be simply literary forms. Spoken language through radio and
television has also contributed to a multi-varied culture which cannot in any

serious way be reduced to the discourses of tartanry and Kailyard. The point is that only rarely do they seek to address the Scottish condition as such, although it is the implicit starting point for much of it. The aim, it seems, is not to identify the unique Scottish experience, but to address the universal condition through day-to-day (Scottish) reality. The search for new images which express these experiences is no longer simply literary but artistic and cultural in the widest sense. The folk music revival which has become a key carrier of Scottish culture is cross-fertilised in terms of styles, tunes and instruments. The search for what is 'traditional' can no longer be taken as pre-dating the nineteenth century, or confined to oral conventions (Munro, 1996).

These ways of expressing Scottish culture are inclusive rather than exclusive, building on the erstwhile alternative ways of being 'Scottish' – Lowland and Highland, Protestant and Catholic, male and female, black and white. This involves borrowing and adapting what is available. In Cairns Craig's words:

> The fragmentation and division which made Scotland seem abnormal to an earlier part of the 20th century came to be the norm for much of the world's population. Bilingualism, biculturalism and the inheritance of a diversity of fragmented traditions were to be the source of creativity rather than its inhibition in the second half of the 20th, and Scotland ceased to have to measure itself against the false 'norm', psychological as well as cultural, of the unified national tradition.
>
> (Craig, 1990: 7)

In his later analysis of Scottish culture, *Out of History* (1996), Craig points out that Scotland at no time in its history could be described as an 'organic' or 'unified' culture, being a country of considerable internal cultural diversity. Borrowing the phrase 'being between' from the poet Sorley MacLean with reference to the mediums of Gaelic and English, Craig comments that: 'Culture is not an organism, nor a totality, nor a unity: it is the site of a dialogue, it is a dialectic, a dialect. It is being between' (1996: 206). What this condition signifies is not a divided, but a diverse culture, which Scotland had to be from its earliest forms of statehood. It was neither feasible nor desirable to impose a single, uniform sense of culture. The sheer geo-cultural diversity of Scotland made this inevitable. In Christopher Smout's words:

> If coherent government was to survive in the medieval and early modern past, it had, in a country that comprised gaelic-speaking Highlanders and Scots-speaking Lowlanders, already linguistically and ethnically diverse, to appeal beyond kin and ethnicity – to loyalty to the person of the monarch, then to the integrity of the territory over which the monarch ruled. The critical fact allowed the Scots ultimately to absorb all kinds of immigrants with relatively little fuss, including, most importantly, the Irish in the 19th century.
>
> (Smout, 1994: 107)

If this made sense in the Middle Ages and the nineteenth century, how much more relevant it is in modern times. These cultural developments are seeking to make sense of shared social, economic and political experiences – of urban living, of working or not working, of living in a capitalist society, a society in which our own ability to control even limited political power is severely constrained. Identities as well as societies can coexist. If Scots were 'Scottish' for certain purposes and 'British' for other purposes, as John Mackintosh pointed out, they were simply recognising the complex pluralities of modern life. 'This sense of a dual consciousness or loyalty is true of most periods and most people in Scottish life. Again, to say so is neither to praise, to blame nor to recommend, it is simply a fact' (1982: 148).

Similarly, being black, Glaswegian and female can all characterise one person's cultural and social inheritance without one aspect of that identity being paramount (except in terms of self-identification). What is on offer in the late twentieth century is much more of a 'pick-'n'-mix' identity, in which we wear our identities lightly and interchangeably, and feel we can change them according to circumstances. Those who would argue for the paramountcy or even the exclusivity of a single identity have a hard time of it. The question to ask is not how best do cultural forms reflect an essential national identity, but how do cultural forms actually help to construct and shape identity, or rather, identities – for there is less need to reconcile or prioritise these. Hence, national identity need not take precedence over class or gender identities (or, indeed, vice versa) except in so far as people prioritise it. These identities themselves, in turn, cannot be defined except with reference to the cultural forms which give them shape and meaning. We will explore these themes in the next chapter.

The argument in this chapter has been that the critique of tartanry/Kailyard as the hegemonic discourse in Scottish culture arises from an essentially 'internalist' account of Scotland, that it ignores major cultural and social changes in the world generally. It arises because it sets out to address the issue of Scottish national culture, the hunting of a Scottish snark. The search for a distinct identity is likely to degenerate into a pessimistic conclusion that none is possible because we are prevented from seeing it by the power of the regressive 'Scotch Myths', rather than because in modern, pluralistic societies it is increasingly the case that no single 'national' culture is there to be found. In other words, the argument has been that we cannot find it precisely because the myths are hegemonic, when the real answer should be that the search itself is increasingly becoming invalid.

To argue that in modern societies, Scotland included, social identities are much more diverse and complex than hitherto, is not to imply that such societies are normless. To point out that 'traditions' are social – invented – constructions which people have evolved to make sense of their lives, and which are malleable according to their needs, is not to argue that they do not have a shared system of values. It is interesting that critics are unwilling to give up the view that the Scottish 'self' is especially prone to ambiguity and disarray.

For example, in their most recent book, Beveridge and Turnbull take this author to task for his view that 'pick-'n'-mix' identities are a feature of the modern world. This might actually represent, they say, a 'self in a state of profound disorder', that modern societies seem especially prone to the condition diagnosed by the early twentieth-century French sociologist, Emile Durkheim, as 'anomie' (Beveridge and Turnbull, 1997: 169). My view is that there is little evidence that Scotland is anomic in this regard, and that, on the contrary, one can identify a coherent body of social and political values which makes Scotland a cohesive society, as well as one with a complex array of social identities (Brown *et al.*, 1999: Ch. 4; Paterson *et al.*, forthcoming: Ch. 8).

It is also interesting that in his latest book *After Britain*, Tom Nairn continues to invoke psychiatric models to explain the Scottish condition. In an important essay 'The unmaking of Scotland', he argues that the loss of Independence in 1707 led to a process of 'self-colonisation', 'for subjection, marginalization and inferiorization to be self-imposed' (2000: 227). Again, '"self-colonization" is like "self-censorship": a chosen and pre-emptive suppression, undertaken to avoid something worse' (ibid.: 231). To summarise Nairn's argument, the lack of statehood led both to an over-concern with civil societal institutionalism for the middle classes, and to 'display identity' as a substitute form of culture. The new parliament arrives with considerable baggage: 'It does so weighed down by the detritus of its inbred institutionalism, and also by the partly aberrant identity code of fake Celticism. These are like the Siamese twins of an abnegated polity' (ibid.: 252). It is interesting that the model of Scotland as not so much a country, more a psychiatric condition, is remarkably resilient in social and political analysis at the beginning of the twenty-first century.

A sociology of Scottish culture

Why, one might ask, should we invoke such psychoanalytic models to explain Scotland? It is an irony that in spite of the supposed deformation of Scottish culture, Scottish political behaviour has never in post-war politics been so divergent from its southern counterpart. It is true that there has been a significant revival in Scotland of cultural matters – literature, music, theatre, popular culture and so on – but by and large one could not conclude that culture has been the main driving force behind the political developments of the past twenty years. Here, it seems, is a political manifestation which is not tied in any neat way to a specific *cultural* divergence. Instead, it seems to be much more of a 'political' manifestation, a concern with the practicalities of decision-making and control, although in so far as it celebrates and mobilises certain values (such as the Scottish Myth), it is in that sense cultural.

We know from recent studies of the Scottish electorate, at the general election of 1997, the referendum of the same year, as well as the first Scottish parliamentary election in 1999, that public opinion is on the Left and liberal ends of the spectrum of social and political values. To be Scottish is to be left-of-centre, which helps to explain, as we saw in the previous chapter, why the Conservatives did so badly north of the border in the final decades of the twentieth century. The corollary – that being left-of-centre is to be Scottish – is manifestly untrue, for, with a few exceptions, people in England share many of these values. What makes this especially relevant for our discussion of Scottish culture is that one can identify a suite of social and political values which is an integral part of that culture (and is counter to the view that Scotland is an 'anomic' society), and is perceived as a key element of national identity (Paterson *et al.*, forthcoming). The most recent survey following the Scottish parliamentary election in 1999 also indicated a strong pride in being Scottish (as many as 90 per cent said they were very or somewhat proud of being Scottish). Further, there was precious little evidence to support a view that the main icons of Scotland – tartan, Scottish music, William Wallace, Gaelic, the Scottish landscape – were held in low esteem, that people saw them as tainted in some way. For example, the percentage saying they were very or somewhat proud of each of these was as follows:

Scottish landscape: 97%   Scottish music: 82%
Tartan: 79%   William Wallace: 76%

with the Gaelic language at 43 per cent, the lowest, but undoubtedly reflecting the low percentage of Scots who can speak or understand it. There was also strong pride in 'Scottish community spirit' (82 per cent), an item which correlates strongly with attachment to left-of-centre social and political values. What these data suggest is that people in Scotland connect their perceptions of cultural, social and political matters in an integrated way. There is little to sustain an argument that 'Scottish culture' in this broad sense is viewed suspiciously by a population deeply at odds over its social identity. Scotland, in other words, looks remarkably normal. It does not carry a heavy baggage of language, religion or cultural identity which has to be defended at all costs against a hostile world. Its nationalism has a strongly 'political' rather than a simply 'cultural' message. People, as it were, are not ashamed of their culture, they do not express ambivalence at the dominant icons, but prefer to pursue a parliament as a means to social and political – rather than narrowly cultural – ends.

In fact, one might claim that Scottish culture is actually much healthier and more progressive than many critics have claimed. Rather than it being subject to fragmentation and division, to split personality, cultural identity reflects the socio-political condition of 'being between' full, formal independence and incorporation into greater England. As Lindsay Paterson has put it, there was not 'duplicity or even ambivalence, but merely cultural subtlety to accompany the unavoidability of shared sovereignty' (1994: 26). Indeed, as he points out in *The Autonomy of Modern Scotland* (1994), Scotland had greater de facto autonomy over its civil institutions than many independent states, and that only in the late twentieth century did the marriage of convenience which was the British state seem to the Scots in need of reform, but not – as yet at least –

replacement by formal independence. Lest we think that this is a particularly modern condition, Graeme Morton has argued that we might be better to construe the condition of Scotland as early as the nineteenth century as one in which 'civic nationalism' ruled. 'What if', he asks, 'Scotland's nationalism had embraced the types of national identity which are taken as the norm in the late 20th century?' (1999: 160). This is to put a quite different construction on the conventional wisdom that Scotland was and continues to be a deeply psychically damaged society. What if, instead of being some deviant case of arrested political and cultural development, Scotland was neither fragmented nor colonised, but remarkably well adapted to being a small northern European country nested, at least for the moment, within a multinational British Union, as well as a broader pan-European one?

It is as if, in the journey into the new century, the Scots looked to see what was on offer, and have decided to travel light. No cultural icons need to be genuflected at, no correct representation needs to be observed in this journey into the future. It is almost, but not quite, a cultureless, post-industrial journey into the unknown. In this respect, it seems to conform to a kind of 'post-materialist' politics (Inglehart, 1977), not in the sense that it is unconcerned with economic issues, but that it seems to have left behind the kind of nationalist/culturalist agenda bequeathed from nineteenth- and early-twentieth century politics. Scotland, like other societies, may be entering a post-national, but not a post-nationalist, age.

7   Roots and routes

Seeking Scottish identity

> For that is the mark of the Scot of all classes: that he stands in an attitude towards
> the past unthinkable to Englishmen, and remembers and cherishes the memory
> of his forebears, good and bad; and there burns alive in him a sense of identity
> with the dead even to the twentieth generation.
>
> (Robert Louis Stevenson, *Weir of Hermiston*)

Knowing who you are has long seemed something which has distinguished the Scots, certainly from their neighbours south of the border. A sense of identity, of distinctiveness, seems at times to have been held against all the odds, and, critics might say, much of the evidence. After all, the distinctive markers of national identity, such as language and religion, have been largely absent, certainly in comparison to other inhabitants of these islands, notably the Irish and the Welsh. The Scots have long spoken a variant of English, and from the middle of the sixteenth century marked themselves out as Protestant, to such an extent that they took to being British without much trouble, and, indeed, considerable success, in the eighteenth century. Assertions of difference might appear to amplify minor differences in a world growing increasingly homogeneous.

In like manner, this argument goes, being Scottish is simply a device for not being English, at a time when the vagaries of the British electoral system foisted an 'alien' government on the Scots. Eric Hobsbawm's view of these things used to be that the proxies had got mixed up, that being 'English' and 'Conservative' had somehow become entangled, and that good sense and proper balance would be restored once the Scots got a London government they had voted for. However, the election of Labour north and south of the border in 1997 has not seen Scottishness recede. It cannot be explained away by the vagaries of electoral politics, simply by a tactical need to oppose the ruling party on national rather than social grounds.

Rediscovering identity

Such an argument, however, does allow a glimpse into the complexities of what has come to be called 'identity politics' in the modern age. As recently as the late

1970s, the political scientist Bill Mackenzie, himself a Scot by birth, was sounding the death-knell of 'identity' as a political concept (Mackenzie, 1978). Like the prophet Ezechiel, he doubted where the dry bones of identity could any longer live. A mere twenty-five years later, identity politics seem to be everywhere, and the eagerness to talk about identity is symptomatic of what many take to be the post-modern predicament of the social and political condition. The sociologist Zygmunt Bauman has commented:

> if the modern 'problem of identity' was how to construct an identity and keep it solid and stable, the postmodern 'problem of identity' is primarily how to avoid fixation and keep the options open. In the case of identity . . . the catchword of modern was creation; the catchword of postmodernity is recycling.
>
> (Bauman, 1996: 18)

Bauman's view is that identity has become a fashionable concept because people are no longer sure who they are. Identity becomes the name for escape from uncertainty, especially with regard to the moorings of modern social and political life. Stuart Hall's perspective on these matters is that the key social identities of the modern world, long formed in the process known as modernisation, have become detached. In Hall's metaphor, identity 'sutures' the subject into relevant social structures, giving social interaction a degree of predictability and unity. It is taken to be a feature of the 'post-modern' condition that self and identity have become more fragmented, and the generic process of identification more problematic and contentious. According to this formulation, no 'master-identity' is possible, such that people defined their social interests in terms of social class, the classical mode of emancipatory politics in modern society. As Hall points out: 'Class cannot serve as a discursive device or mobilising category through which all the diverse social interests and identities of people can be reconciled and represented' (1992: 280). The emergent 'politics of difference' is defined by new social movements engaging with issues of gender, ethnicity and nationalism.

The other set of social forces which has helped to re-centre identity issues is the reassertion of individualism, notably around people's identities as consumers. After all, saying, as Mrs Thatcher did, that there is no such thing as society is to assert that individuals are free to construct their identities as they please. 'I buy therefore I am' is the economic expression of consumer supremacy. Bauman observes:

> it is the consumer attitude which makes my life into my individual affair; and it is the consumer activity which makes me into the individual. . . . It seems in the end as if I were made up of the many things I buy and own; tell me what you buy and in what shops you buy it, and I'll tell you who you are. It seems that with the help of carefully selected

purchases, I can make of myself anything I may wish, anything I believe it is worth becoming. Just as dealing with my personal problems is my duty and my responsibility, so the shaping of my personal identity, my self-assertion, making myself into a concrete someone, is my task and my task alone.

(Bauman, 1992: 205)

The apparent demise of overarching, meta-identities seems to have allowed a plurality of new ones to emerge from beneath the corpse. These are not simply expressions of supreme individualism, but reflect greater opportunities to play out who one wants to be, selecting from an array of choices and with greater control over the messages and signs given off. The 'politics' which drive this process are indeed 'personal', in so far as they appear to give the individual greater leeway and choice. Although one may be critical of the assumption that identities are chosen freely and without constraint, they do highlight a new set of assumptions that people make identity a very personal matter, rather than having it foisted upon them in a mechanical fashion. However, as the Scottish novelist Willie McIlvanney commented: 'Identity, personal or national, isn't merely something you have like a passport. It is also something you rediscover daily, like a strange country. Its core isn't something solid, like a mountain. It is something molten, like magna' (*Herald*, 13 March 1999).

How does this help us to understand what it means to be Scottish in the twenty-first century? While it would be a foolish claim to make that such an identity, with a history of almost a millennium behind it, is on offer for the first time, it is proper to view the growing salience through a modern perspective. After all, how are we to know that being Scottish in the fourteenth century means the same thing in the twenty-first century? Of course we cannot, but there are sufficient continuities in our institutional arrangements, in the commitment to the public character of education which dates at least from 1560, for example, to link past and present. What it does highlight, however, is that competing issues of 'national' identity, or strictly, territorial identity, are on offer. In this chapter we will explore where conceptions of being Scottish have come from, how they are generated and reproduced, how they compete with one another, and the extent to which they are engines of social and cultural change in modern Scotland.

The title of this chapter – roots and routes – is meant to emphasise that we should see identities as maps for the future as well as trails from the past. As Stuart Hall has observed:

Though they seem to invoke an origin in a historical past with which they continue to correspond, actually identities are about using the resources of history, language and culture in the process of becoming rather than being; not 'who we are' or 'where we have come from' so much as what we might become, how we have been represented and how that bears on how we might represent ourselves. Identities are therefore constituted within, not outside representation.

(Hall, 1996: 4)

Here, Hall is touching on a fundamental and contentious issue in understanding identity. To what extent do people simply play out their allotted identities, at least within the tight frames laid down by these representations, and/or how much freedom do they have to interpret and mobilise them in ways they want to? Elsewhere, Hall stresses that we work within cultural representations whether we know it or want it. Thus, 'we only know what it is to be "English" because of the way "Englishness" has come to be represented, as a set of meanings, by English national culture' (1992: 292). In other words, we may think that we are making it up as we go along, but we are in fact dancing to a tune laid down by others. We can do it our way, but, like karaoke, it must bear a passing resemblance to its representation to be treated as tolerably recognisable and authentic by the audience. We cannot, in other words, make it up as we go along if others are to take our performance and our presentation seriously.

Terms like 'performance' and 'presentation' evoke a quite different approach to identity, which places the onus on the performer, not the song-sheet. This derives from a symbolic interactionist stance on social life associated with Erving Goffman (1973), whose interest in the 'presentation' of self implied that identity was basically a badge with little real substance. Goffman, of course, was following a line of thought out of symbolic interactionism in which identity was a tactical construction designed to maximise player advantage. To return to our karaoke metaphor, performance is what matters, and the audience judges this rather than how true it is to the original song.

Although Goffman was writing mainly in the late 1950s and early 1960s, he was an important precursor of what ultimately became a post-modern conception of identity in which constant and rapid social change makes a fixed and immutable sense of self largely redundant. The result of this discontinuity is that social life is increasingly open, offering opportunities and choices for individuals in a rapidly changing world. In this formulation, life-style choice becomes more important in the constitution of identity, and as a result, a new kind of life-style politics emerges out of the shadow of 'emancipatory politics' (Giddens, 1991).

Whether or not people have as much freedom as implied, such a perspective highlights the complexity and choice which 'being someone' involves. When we deal with 'nationality', however, we may think we have little choice in the matter. We may treat it as a matter of birth – in common parlance, an 'accident' of birth – or an issue of citizenship for which the state holds all the important cards. Anyone who has tried to change their citizenship knows how difficult that can be unless one gives up the former one and meets the conditions of the new. Yet nationality and citizenship are not the same thing (McCrone and Kiely, 2000). One can, for example, receive state benefits and protection as a citizen, and yet feel oneself a member of a national grouping outwith that state, as many do in central Europe. Rogers Brubaker (1996) has written of the different types of 'nationalism' in which people there can participate: notably state or 'nationalising' nationalism reflecting the state one lives in; and 'homeland' nationalism, the ethnic group to which one feels one belongs.

As challenges to existing states have grown more common, processes of state reformation have problematised national identities. Quite suddenly, identity politics are back on the agenda, for, in Mercer's words, 'identity only becomes an issue when it is in crisis, when something assumed to be fixed, coherent and stable is displaced by the experience of doubt and uncertainty' (1990: 43). This problematising process makes it much easier to see how people are involved in 'personalising' national identity. Anthony Cohen's useful concept of personal nationalism asserts the primacy of the actor as a 'thinking self' (1994: 167). His argument is that 'people construct the nation through the medium of their own experience, and in ways which are heavily influenced by their own circumstances. The nation is mediated through the self' (Cohen, 2000: 146). This interest in the 'micro', the small-scale, personalised and negotiated nature of national identity is at the centre of Michael Billig's concept of 'banal nationalism', a term indicating fundamental or basic, not unimportant. Thus, national flags 'melt into the background as "our" particular world is experienced as *the* world' (Billig, 1995: 50). Something similar was meant by Ernest Renan's famous late nineteenth-century dictum of national identity as a daily plebiscite which requires each individual to assert in action (hence, 'daily') their national identity.

The idea that national identity is not fixed, like a badge which is attached to one at birth, can be gauged from research on people who migrate from one society to another, even when this happens within the same state. Our research on landed and arts elites in Scotland (McCrone *et al.*, 1998; Bechhofer *et al.*, 1999) has shown that actors have considerable capacity to construct and negotiate national identities, especially in contexts where they have leverage. Presenting oneself as Scottish, English, British or whatever is a matter of meaning and mobilisation which involves actors and their audiences, as well as the ability to read off signs of identity. There is a complex matrix involving how actors define themselves, how they attribute identity to others, and how, in turn, they think others attribute identity to them. Such an approach helps us to move beyond the more commonly held view that national identity is handed down in the form of a relatively fixed repertoire by power systems, and enables us to focus on how actors negotiate and mobilise identities which are open to them. In talking about 'national identity', however, there is a tendency to focus on the 'national' rather than on 'identity'. In his book, *On Nationality*, David Miller, for example, comments that 'to understand what we mean when we talk of someone having a national identity, we must first get clear about what nations are' (1995: 17). In other words, the weight of the question is conventionally placed on the existence or otherwise of the 'nation' rather than on the mechanisms where actors themselves do the defining and constructing.

What implication does this have for studying Scottish identity? It means we have to be cautious in assuming that Scottishness denotes the same thing through both time and place. The debate about the 'reality' of Scotland evokes the dictum of W. I. Thomas, that something is 'real' when people treat it as such. Anthony Cohen has explored this question in his valuable essay on the 'problem of the objective correlative' in which he concludes, like Billig, that 'the nation does not need to be made explicit, possibly cannot be made explicit, but survives rather by being taken for granted and continuously expressed implicitly' (2000: 151). One might add that there has to be something to be expressed, and that this something is sustained by social discourse around the idea of Scotland.

When was Scotland?

This useful, if slightly odd, question was raised in inimitable fashion by the Welsh historian, the late Gwyn Alf Williams, to locate Wales, less in place than in time. Williams wanted us to take note of the fact that nation was not simply a matter of geography but of history, that nations could come and go.

Let us apply this to Scotland. There is dispute as to whether 'Scotland' in a meaningful sense existed before the wars with England at the end of the thirteenth century. However, as Dauvit Broun observed: 'To insist that Scotland was not a meaningful concept, or that Scotland did not exist before the end of the 13th century, would surely be to allow our modern idea of Scotland to take precedence over the view of contemporaries' (1994: 38). Part of the problem lies in our implicit assumption that 'Scotland' has the same meaning through history. Broun argues that by the eleventh century, 'Scotia' strictly meant the Scoto-Pictish kingdom north of the Forth, south of the Spey, and east of the central Highlands. Thus, from the beginning, one had to distinguish 'Scotland proper' – over which the King's remit ruled with some ease – from 'greater Scotland' – including Moray and Nairn, Argyll and the Isles, and Galloway, where much of the time it did not. By the mid-thirteenth century, however, '"Scotia" came to denote the kingdom of Scotland, *regnum Scotiae*, and covered not only the country north of the Forth but south of it as well, including Lothian, Strathclyde and Galloway' (Ferguson, 1998: 27).

This preference for referring to the 'kingdom of the Scots', and to their ruler as *rex Scottorum* – king of Scots – reflected the ethnic diversity of the territory. Sandy Grant has argued that by the twelfth century, 'Scotland was very much a hybrid kingdom – in stark contrast to Wales and Ireland, where concepts of racial purity were more strongly maintained' (1994: 76). This meant, not only that there was a linguistic split between Gaelic, English and French, but that these were '*gens*' within the '*natio*' of Scotland, that English speakers were not considered 'English' but Scots. Here is Geoffrey Barrow's observation:

The kingdom of Scotland, the territory which the king ruled, on which his writs and laws were current, from which he levied his taxes and services . . . was . . . a unifying concept, not only geographically, bringing together east and west, Lowlands and Highlands . . . but also culturally and racially, for the sense of *regnum Scotie* was identical for the native population and the Anglo-Continental incomers alike.

(Cited in Stringer and Grant, 1995: 96)

The unification of the territory around kingship reflected its ethnic diversity, and the fact that it was held together by rulership rather than race. Without the concentration of political power, it would not have been possible to hold the territory together, and, indeed, it took some centuries before the north-western territories were subdued within the authority of the crown. James Hunter (1999) has argued that conquest of the Highlands by first the Scottish, and then, after 1745, by the British state was not an unthinking overuse of military power but a careful reflection of the real threat to the respective states. However much we might deplore the oppression of these territories, it seemed to have been the judgement in those days that only this ensured they would not threaten the state. Christopher Smout has also made the valuable point that:

If coherent government was to survive in the medieval and early modern past, it had, in a country that comprised Gaelic-speaking Highlanders and Scots-speaking Lowlanders, already linguistically and ethnically diverse, to appeal beyond kin or ethnicity – to loyalty to the person of the monarch, then to the integrity of the territory over which the monarch ruled.

(Smout, 1994: 107)

Smout's point is that modern Scottish identity is firmly embedded in a 'sense of place' rather than a 'sense of tribe', and that this actually derives from medieval *realpolitik* rather than moral superiority on the part of the Scots. In other words, no narrowly 'ethnic' definition was going to hold the state together, a feature reflected in adopting St Andrew as Scotland's patron saint. St Andrew had the benefit of being indubitably a foreigner, and hence avoided benefiting or slighting Scotland's many regional contenders for the title (Ash, n.d.). Lest we think that medieval Scots were somewhat too deferential to regal authority, the Declaration of Arbroath which sought papal approval for Scottish Independence from England prefaced the famous comment 'for as long a hundred of us remain alive, we will never on any conditions be subjected to the lordship of the English', with this warning constraint on kingly power: 'Yet if he [the King] give up what he has begun, seeking to make us or our kingdom subject to the king of England or to the English, we would strive at once to drive him out as an enemy and a subverter of his own right and ours and we would make some other man who was able to defend us our king.' There is not much evidence there of regal deference.

How, one might ask, can we be sure that people in the twelfth and thirteenth centuries actually thought of themselves as 'Scots'? Surely this is to impose modern conceptions on a past we cannot know? The first thing to be said is that in modern Scotland we live quite happily with multiple meanings of what it means to be a Scot: by birth, descent and residence, and we know from analysis of the 1999 Scottish election that each of these is sufficiently distinct from each other, but are also valid in their own right. Broun's point (1998: 11) about the thirteenth century that 'Scotland and the Scots are, first and foremost, images which have been adapted and recreated according to the experiences and aspirations of the society to which they related' applies just as validly to the twenty-first century. Although it is a much more difficult task to know what the thirteenth-century peasant made of being Scottish, the historical consensus does seem to be that at least the 'middling folk' and foot soldiers of Scotland at that time certainly made something of it (Stringer and Grant, 1995; Broun, 1998; Ferguson, 1998). The concept of the 'community of the realm' – *communitas regni* – appears to have been a sufficiently understood concept to rally the nation against the English foe, just as there is support for the existence of 'national' consciousness in England in the Middle Ages (Greenfeld, 1993). In short, the conditions for generating national awareness contra the 'other' were surely there for Scotland and England in the context of each other, as Grant observes: 'in the two medieval kingdoms of the British Isles, the people were involved along with their elites in their countries' wars; in France, they were not' (1994: 95), which is why 'making Frenchman' took so much longer (Weber, 1977). The point is also made by Adrian Hastings (1997) in his analysis of the development of national consciousness in these islands. It was the designs of the English state on its neighbours, particularly Scotland, which helped to mould diverse peoples into a single nation in the face of this common threat.

This is not to say, of course, that the Scots and English settled down quite happily to be the appropriate 'other'. Bill Ferguson's monumental study *The Identity of the Scottish Nation* (1998) shows that the ideological battle raged as fiercely as the military one, and for longer. To twenty-first-century eyes, debates about the ancient origins of peoples seem arcane, even mildly racist. The myths, however, were deadly serious, because whether or not peoples had a right to exist depended on winning the ideological battle of origins. Much rested on who the founding peoples were judged to be. Geoffrey of Monmouth's twelfth- century English history was long accepted as the standard history of that realm, and helped to promote feelings of Englishness to the considerable advantage of the state. It was, in turn, judged by the Scots to be unacceptable because it appeared to reinforce English claims to the feudal over-lordship of Scotland. The medieval English appropriated the Brutus legend, that the Trojan was the founder of the early kings of Britain. In Geoffrey's account, the descendants of Brutus carried sway over the entire island, the Picts were dismissed as latecomers, and the Scots were simply a mongrel race begat by Picts and Hibernians. The Scots, in turn, mobilised their own origin-myth based on Gaidel Glas who was either the husband or son of Scota, daughter of the Pharaoh of Egypt, and who had come to Hibernia via Spain. The point of all this is the claim that the Scots, and the Irish, were deemed to have Greek, not Trojan, roots, and as a consequence could not possibly be of the same root-stock as the English.

This claim to roots was deeply serious. It helped to shape claim and counter-claim among historians, and much focused on whether the founding peoples were the Scots (from Ireland) or the Picts. In the fourteenth century, John of Fordun minimised Pictish roots in favour of the Scots so as to counter English claims that Picts were 'really' Teutons, and hence Britons. Hector Boece, born in the second half of the fifteenth century, took the claim further forward by alledging that it was the 'Scots' who resisted the Romans, who had conquered the Picts, and held out against the Norse and the English. Boece also subscribed to the 'forty kings' theory which purported to trace the lineage of Scottish monarchs, and his view was shared by the Protestant reformer and historian George Buchanan in the sixteenth century who argued that the Scots had come from Ireland. On the other hand, the Catholic priest and Jacobite Thomas Innes took a contrary view in the late seventeenth century, and preferred the Pictish view of origins. By the late eighteenth and early nineteenth centuries, Pictomania had come to serve the views of those such as John Pinkerton that the true aboriginals were the Picts, Teutons, and thus like the English. James Macpherson, who claimed to have discovered the Gaelic poems of Ossian, fell foul of anti-Scottish feeling in the eighteenth century which had a direct political purpose in denying a distinct origin-myth to the Scots as they entered the British Union. Lest we think that this sort of historiography was well and truly over, Ferguson reminds us that the English historian Trevor-Roper was still employing Celtophobic arguments in the 1970s to undermine the claims to Scottish autonomy. Ferguson, on the other hand, says that 'there can be little doubt . . . that the national identity of the Scots sprang from an early Gaelic tribal root that first flourished in Ireland' (1998: 306).

The point of all this historiography is that it is almost impossible to escape it being subordinated to one political claim or the other. Ferguson, for his part, concludes: 'Scottishness was never exclusive, but, on the contrary, has always been highly absorptive, a quality that it retains even in the vastly different circumstances of today' (1998: 305). There are distinct echoes here of William McIlvanney's claim that Scots are a 'mongrel nation', drawn from many roots, but primarily concerned with the future rather than the past; routes rather than roots again. Those who wish to argue that an ethnically diverse Scotland is the morally correct one are able to mobilise history to considerable effect.

Scottish and British

In spite of popular opposition to the Union in the early years of the eighteenth century, it proved, in the nineteenth century, relatively easy to refashion the

Scots into British. The Jacobite legacy always had the power to be a potent nationalist myth, but, as Richard Finlay (1994) has observed, that was a step too far. In the first place, Jacobite ideology could not be moulded into the Scottish Presbyterian spirit: it was too Catholic and Episcopalian for that. In the second, Jacobite adherence to the divine right of kings could not be worked into meritocratic and liberal ideology. Finally, it contradicted the notion of a bloodless Union. While Jacobitism has always had complex potential as an alternative Scottishness – although Christopher Smout is critical of some historians, and judges that 'it is a sad misconstruction of Scottish history to see in the Jacobite movement some appeal to an archaic, anti-capitalist, anti-improvement, green past' (1994: 110) – it was too far removed from the experiences of most Scots for the connection to be made.

Rather, Scottishness in the nineteenth century was refashioned around the three identity pillars of Church, state and empire. Protestantism, as Linda Colley observed, helped to 'forge' the business of being British. Most people in Wales, Scotland and England, she observed, 'defined themselves as Protestants struggling for survival against the foremost Catholic power. They defined themselves against the French as they imagined them to be, super- stitious, militarist, decadent and unfree' (1992: 5). That, in essence, is why most people in Ireland could not consider themselves as British, nor were they permitted to be. Scottish Protestantism proved to be an important seed- bed for the three dominant political creeds: Liberalism, Unionism, and latterly, Labourism.

Scottish military culture had a long pedigree in a country which relied on fighting other people's wars for a living (Wood, 1987). The Union, first after Culloden in 1746, and later in the imperial wars of the following century, offered new and improved opportunities for soldiering as a living, and through- out the following centuries Scots had disproportionately been found to make a living, and a dying, in the ranks of the military (Smout, 1994: 106). It was no coincidence that Cliff Hanley's song 'Scotland the Brave' became an unofficial embodiment of the national character, to be succeeded in turn by another hymn to war, 'Flower of Scotland'.

The empire provided the battleground, both military and ecclesiastical, for what Graeme Morton (1999) has called 'unionist-nationalism'. In the nine- teenth century, graduates from Scottish universities saw new opportunities in empire. In short, they believed that they had a mission to spread Scottish liberalism and Scottish Protestantism, and that only the Union could have given them the political influence to do that. The missionary movement, in places like southern Africa and India – associated especially with David Livingston and Mary Slessor – provided a powerful justification for empire, union and Presbyterianism. Tom Devine has commented: 'By underwriting the empire as a moral undertaking, religion helped to strengthen the union with England but also assumed greater significance as an important factor reinforcing Scottish identity' (1999: 367).

Scottish Unionists in particular were able to draw together these strands of the Protestant ethic, and to infuse ideas of civic responsibility in the nineteenth century to their considerable political advantage, as we saw in Chapter 5, and it was not until the final quarter of the twentieth century that such an ideology came to lose its electoral power. However, even by the 1920s, the Reformed tradition had begun to deteriorate into a 'preoccupation with the moral senti-ment of patriotism and the preservation of a mythical Presbyterian racial identity' (Storrar, 1990: 47).

Post-1945, the pillars, first of Protestantism, then Imperialism, and finally Unionism, began to crumble, and a new edifice and a different sense of 'being Scottish' emerged. On the one hand, growing secularisation, but above all, the moral economy of the welfare state had transformed people's depen-dence on the Church. On the other hand, demobilisation and the end of empire released the need for a standing army, and a military attachment to the state. Finally, and not until the 1970s and 1980s, political Unionism lost its appeal to Scotland's middle classes, while there was less reason for workers to be thirled to the Conservative Party.

Who do we think we are?

The focus in the final quarter of the twentieth century was on the assertion of Scottishness, but in many ways the key story has been in what has happened to being British. David Marquand has pointed out that the British state was, in essence, a global state, and so the 'British' were defined as a global people. The New Zealand historian, J. G. A. Pocock, has been credited with discover-ing British (as opposed to English) history, as reflected in the relationship of the people of these islands and their kith and kin in far-flung places. Marquand concludes: 'Shorn of empire, "Britain" had no meaning' (1995: 288). That may seem over-strong for some, and tends to ignore new ways of being British reinvented by black Britons in the second half of the century, but it does mark the end of an older, white imperial construction.

To be sure, Scots even in the heyday of empire never ceased to recognise and assert their national (Scottish) identity even while remaining proud of being British, their state identity. Here is Robert Louis Stevenson writing in 1894:

> The fact remains: in spite of the difference of blood and language, the Lowlander feels himself the sentimental countryman of the Highlander. When they meet abroad they fall upon each other's neck in spirit; even at home there is a kind of clannish intimacy in their talk. But from his com-patriot in the south the Lowlander stands consciously apart. He has had a different training; he obeys different laws; he makes his will in other terms, is otherwise divorced and married; his eyes are not at home in an English landscape or with English houses; his ear continues to remark

the English speech; and even though his tongue acquire the Southern knack, he will still have a strong Scots accent of the mind.

(Quoted in Ferguson, 1998: 315)

Issues of identity are essentially comparative ones, strongly influenced by context. Thus, the question here is how people in Scotland balance national (Scottish) and state (British) identity, if they do so at all. These are, of course, not mutually exclusive categories, and we know from historical work that for much of the history of the Union they were nested, one within the other (Smout, 1994; Morton, 1999). The election studies of the past twenty-five years have been asking questions about the relative balance between these two identities, and we have constructed a useful time-series. Asking people how they see themselves produces the patterns shown in Table 7.1.

Since the mid-1980s we have built up a body of survey data using a fairly simple five-point Likert scale which has been used fairly regularly in surveys and opinion polls. The Spanish sociologist Luis Moreno adapted and applied it to Scotland in 1986, and for shorthand we will refer to it as the Moreno question. It is a straightforward question: 'Which of these best describes how you see yourself? Scottish not British; more Scottish than British; equally Scottish and British; more British than Scottish; and British not Scottish.' We can of course criticise it on methodological grounds: Can we be sure that respondents interpret the categories in the same way? What if one feels differently in different circumstances? What we can say, however, is that the measure has a robustness to it. It correlates well and consistently with social variables such as social class, age, gender and educational achievement. The key to it, of course, is that most people in Scotland (and Wales for that matter) seem to grasp what the question is getting at: the relationship between national identity (Scottish) and state identity (British). English people appear to find the distinction

Table 7.1 National identity, by year

			Survey		
National identity	1979	1992	1997 General election	1997 Referendum	1999
	(%)	(%)	(%)	(%)	(%)
Scottish[1]	56	72	72	85	77
British[1]	38	25	24	15	17
Sample sizes (= 100%)	661	957	882	676	1482

Note
1 Figures shown are % of respondents choosing 'best' identity, either Scottish or British.

Source: Scottish Election Surveys, 1979, 1992 and 1997; Scottish Referendum Survey, 1997; Scottish Parliamentary Survey, 1999.

more puzzling. This was put especially well by Anthony Barnett in his book
This Time: Our Constitutional Revolution:

> What is the difference between being English and being British? If you ask
> a Scot or a Welsh person about their Britishness, the question makes sense
> to them. They might say that they feel Scots first and British second. Or
> that they enjoy a dual identity as Welsh-British, with both parts being
> equal. Or they might say 'I'm definitely British first'. What they have in
> common is an understanding that there is a space between their nation
> and Britain, and they can assess the relationship between the two. The
> English, however, are more often baffled when asked how they relate
> their Englishness and Britishness to each other. They often fail to under-
> stand how the two can be contrasted at all. It seems like one of those
> puzzles that others can undo but you can't; Englishness and Britishness
> seem inseparable. They might prefer to be called one thing rather than
> the other – and today young people increasingly prefer English to British
> – but, like two sides of a coin, neither term has an independent existence
> from the other.
>
> (Barnett, 1997: 292–3)

Let us look at some data on nationality. These come from the British and
Scottish Election Studies of 1997, and the subsequent Scottish Referendum
Study later that year (Surridge *et al.*, 1999) (Table 7.2). They provide the
most up–to–date data we have, and allow us in the first instance to compare
national/state identities on this island of ours. These findings are broadly consistent with previous ones. We can see that more than seven times more people
living in Scotland give priority to being Scottish (either Scottish not British, or
more Scottish than British) than to being British. The ratio for Wales is just
under two to one; and in England, 'English' and 'British' are comparable at

Table 7.2 National identity, by country

National identity	Scotland (%)	Wales (%)	England (%)
X not British	23	13	8
More X than British	38	29	16
Equally X and British	27	26	46
More British than X	4	10	15
British not X	4	15	9
None of these	4	7	6
Sample sizes	*882*	*182*	*2551*

Notes
X = Scottish/Welsh/English.

Source: British and Scottish Election Studies, 1997.

Table 7.3 National identity in Scotland, Catalunya and Quebec

National identity	Scotland (%)	Catalunya (%)	Quebec (%)
X only	23	20	12
More X than Y	38	16	31
Equally X and Y	27	35	32
More Y than X	4	5	17
Y only	4	23	5

Notes
X = National identity, i.e. Scottish, Quebecois or Catalan.
Y = State identity, i.e. British, Canadian or Spanish.
Source: Scottish Election Survey, 1997; CIRES (Catalunya), 1998; CROP (Quebec), 1998.

around 25 per cent each. (Barnett's health warning about the meaningfulness of the categories applies, of course.)

If we shift our point of comparison beyond these islands, we find that national identity is proportionately stronger in Scotland than in Quebec and Catalunya, two other 'stateless nations' (Table 7.3). These results partly reflect the fact that in-migration into Quebec and Catalunya has been higher than in Scotland where around 10 per cent of the resident population have been born elsewhere. Nevertheless, such findings help to confirm the strength of Scottishness in comparative terms.

If people in Scotland currently forefront their nationality over their citizenship, how has this altered, if at all, over time? The broad trends are given in Table 7.4. There are a number of conclusions we can draw from these data:

- That people living in Scotland give much higher priority to being Scottish (categories 1 and 2) over being British (categories 4 and 5) (ratios are between 7:1 and 10:1).
- That nevertheless most people claim dual identity, and that Scots still remain 'British' in significant numbers.
- That over time the results are fairly consistent, and that one cannot conclude that there has been a shift towards or away from Scottish identity in any simple sense.
- That both the referendum and the first Scottish parliamentary election saw a firming up of 'Scottish only' identity.

Let us remind ourselves that identities should be seen as claims which people make in particular contexts. One of the most significant is the political-cultural context. Forefronting Scottishness over Britishness has to be judged in the heightened political environment in Scotland since the 1980s, in which national identity has been a key resource. That is possibly why the priority 'Scottish' responses were so strong in the 1980s and early 1990s, and faced

Table 7.4 National identity in Scotland

National identity	July 1986 (%)	September 1991 (%)	1992 (%)	1997 (%)	1997 Referendum (%)	1999 (%)
Scottish not British	39	40	19	23	32	32
More Scottish than British	30	29	40	38	32	34
Equally Scottish and British	19	21	33	27	28	23
More British than Scottish	4	3	3	4	3	3
British not Scottish	6	4	3	4	3	4
None of these	2	3	1	2	2	4
Sample sizes (= 100%)	1021	1042	957	882	676	1482

Source: July 1986: Moreno, 1988; September 1991: *The Scotsman*; Scottish Election Surveys, 1992 and 1997; Scottish Referendum Study, 1997; Scottish Parliamentary Election Study, 1999.

Table 7.5 National identity by vote in 1997 general election

National identity	Conservative (%)	Labour (%)	Lib-Dem (%)	SNP (%)	All (%)
Scottish not British	10	25	13	32	23
Scottish more than British	26	39	42	44	38
Equally Scottish and British	45	26	28	18	27
British more than Scottish	7	4	6	2	4
British not Scottish	7	3	5	2	4
Sample sizes (= 100%)	96	363	96	132	882

Source: Scottish Election Survey, 1997

with a 'democratic deficit' north of the border in which opposition to 'English' government might evoke a 'national(ist)' reaction. Politics, then, is a key. Let us examine identity by vote (Table 7.5). There are a number of important features here:

- Although Conservative voters are less likely than most to give precedence to being Scottish, they define themselves in clear Scottish terms. Only 14 per cent give priority to being British.
- While SNP voters are more likely than supporters of other parties to claim to be Scottish, only around one-third deny they are British, a feature we will explore further.

- Almost two-thirds of Labour supporters give preference to being Scottish, and only 7 per cent to being British.

The relationship between identity and preferred constitutional option is also complex (Table 7.6). While one might expect a stronger relationship between these variables such that those supporting Independence are self-proclaimed Scots and not British, and those opposed to constitutional change – the Unionists – are British first, we actually find that (a) only a minority (40 per cent) who are in favour of Independence say they are Scottish and not British; and (b) only 12 per cent of those wanting no constitutional change are 'British' first.

Let us review the relationship between vote, constitutional preference and identity. We might expect that those who vote SNP are in favour of Independence, and define themselves as Scottish not British. In fact, the relationship is much more complex (Bond, 2000). Almost half (43 per cent) of SNP voters at the 1997 general election did not support Independence, a substantial minority preferring Home Rule. Similarly, two-thirds of those in favour of Independence did not vote SNP, and were mainly Labour voters. Again, of those defining themselves as Scottish not British, only 44 per cent voted SNP. The lack of alignment between identity, vote and constitutional preference is partly explained by the presence of significant 'cross-over' voters, namely SNP supporters of Home Rule, and Labour supporters in favour of Independence. It is also explained by the fact that the modal SNP voter defines her/himself as Scottish rather than British (as opposed to simply Scottish), and that those in favour of Independence are evenly split between these two identity categories.

What are the implications of these findings? They suggest that national identity is not in itself a strong predictor of vote or constitutional preference. This does not imply that identity is unimportant or that it is weak, for this is not borne out at all when we compare Scotland with other nations such as

Table 7.6 National identity by preferred constitutional option

National identity	Independence (%)	Home Rule (%)	No change (%)	All (%)
Scottish not British	40	18	12	23
More Scottish than British	40	43	23	38
Equally Scottish and British	14	27	47	27
More British than Scottish	2	5	7	4
British not Scottish	2	4	5	4
Sample sizes (= 100%)	*231*	*449*	*150*	*882*

Souce: Scottish Election Survey, 1997

Wales, Quebec and Catalunya. Rather, it confirms the distinction between 'upper-case' and 'lower-case' nationalism in Scotland (Nairn, 1997), that cultural identity and political identity are sufficiently distinct. It is quite compatible, for example, to define oneself as Scottish, and yet be opposed to either Independence or Home Rule. Further, being a Conservative and claiming to be Scottish has a long pedigree, and in the words of the former Tory Secretary of State for Scotland, Ian Lang: 'we don't need a separate Scotland to prove that we are Scottish' (quoted in Penrose 1993: 37).

In Chapter 5 we examined what determined voters' views of the Scottish Parliament. Let us further explore this complex relationship between national identity and political behaviour. In the 1997 Scottish Election Study, we asked people to indicate how they intended to vote in a possible referendum on a Scottish parliament, and related their response to whether they saw the best description of their identity as Scottish, British, English, European and so on. All four groups gave a majority for a yes-yes vote. Further, in a logistic regression analysing intended referendum vote, Scottish, English and European identities had no independent effect (Brown *et al.*, 1999: 126). While British identity was associated with being somewhat less likely to vote yes, it was a fairly weak predictor.

We were also able to explore the effect of national identity on actual referendum vote in the Scottish Referendum Study, and found that while almost eight out of ten people who gave priority to being Scottish had voted yes-yes, those giving priority to being British were more likely (around five in ten) to vote no-no, although the numbers in the category were very small. Further analysis confirms that national identity *per se* was a weak predictor of referendum vote (Surridge and McCrone, 1999: 51). In other words, as we saw in Chapter 5, wanting a parliament had much more to do with people's policy expectations than as an affective expression of nationhood. We should be careful in interpreting what this means. Being Scottish is certainly important, but it does not determine whether Scots are in favour of a parliament or not. Those who thought of themselves as English or British were also in favour of a parliament. It is likely, none the less, that having a parliament will reinforce national identity, for 'standing up for Scotland's interests' seems to be the touchstone of political success.

What this analysis does is to remind us that national identity cannot be treated as some isolated variable fed into an equation. It is refracted through the political and policy process, which is why, in models of voting in Scotland, either at elections or in the referendum for a Scottish parliament, it has a weak independent effect. It also confirms the view that Scottishness falls at the 'civic' rather than the 'ethnic' end of nation-ness, and is threaded through the spectrum of Scottish politics and culture, a feature we will explore more fully in the final chapter. That is why most Conservatives think of themselves as Scots, why Labour voters see no contradiction in being in favour of Independence, and SNP voters think of themselves as British as well as Scottish. These are not contradictions or inconsistencies, the result of a failure of cultural or political will, but a recognition of the complexities and nuances of modern Scottish life. It is the fact that Scottishness is part of the taken-for-granted of life that helps to define a distinctively Scottish agenda.

Social class and national identity

Let us now explore some of the ways in which national identity permeates social life in Scotland, starting with social class. If we explore this relationship, we find a social class gradient as regards national identity such that there is a stronger sense of being Scottish among the working class (Table 7.7). We should not, however, lose sight of the fact that the middle classes define themselves as Scottish rather than British (a ratio of 3:1 in terms of Table 7.7), while manual workers are more likely to stress their Scottishness (by a ratio of almost 15:1). We know that middle-class people in Scotland, especially those who are upwardly mobile, are much more likely than their counterparts in England to describe themselves as 'working class'. In terms of national identity, self-defined middle-class as well as working-class people in Scotland describe themselves as Scottish, whereas in England both classes opt for describing themselves as equally English and British (Table 7.8).

Similarly, in terms of national identity and vote, there is almost no relationship between voting behaviour and national identity in England, reflecting the non-politicised nature of identity south of the border. In Scotland, on the other hand, the Conservatives do very badly among those who emphasise their Scottish over their British identity, with the SNP doing particularly well in this group, but having to share them with Labour (Brown *et al.*, 1999: 65).

The relationship between social class and national identity in Scotland is further complicated by the interactions between them. For example, there has been a shift over time towards identification with nation rather than

Table 7.7 National identity by social class (Registrar-General's categories)

National identity	I and II (%)	IIIn–m (%)	IIIm (%)	IV and V (%)	All (%)
Scottish not British	13	19	32	31	23
More Scottish than British	36	41	40	37	38
Equally Scottish and British	33	26	21	26	27
More British than Scottish	7	4	4	3	3
British not Scottish	8	4	1	1	3
Sample sizes (= 100%)	222	206	172	223	882

Source: Scottish Election Survey, 1997.

Table 7.8 National identity by self-ascribed social class

National identity	Scotland		England	
	Middle class (%)	Working class (%)	Middle class (%)	Working class (%)
Scottish/English not British	17	26	7	8
Scottish/English more than British	33	42	20	17
Scottish/English equal to British	34	26	45	52
British more than Scottish/English	10	2	19	13
British not Scottish/English	6	3	10	9
Sample sizes (= 100%)	205	590	852	1358

Source: British Election Survey, 1997.

social class. The assertion by some politicians that Scots identify more with people in the same class in England rather than those of a different class in Scotland is not borne out by the data (Table 7.9). This relative shift from class to national identification which appears to have happened during the 1980s is broadly shared across all social classes in Scotland (Table 7.10). What this suggests is that national identification is becoming more powerful than social class identification in cross-border terms, a change which the Labour Party in particular, with its UK focus, is having to address, especially in the context of the Scottish Parliament and the Welsh Assembly. These devolved institutions are likely to have their own momentum towards firming up national agendas in Scotland and Wales to the detriment of British ones, presenting Labour with particular difficulties in each country.

Table 7.9 Whom do you identify with most?

Identity group	1979 (%)	1992 (%)	1997 (%)	1997 Referendum (%)	1999 (%)
Same class, English	44	27	23	25	24
Opposite class, Scots	38	45	46	38	43
Sample sizes (= 100%)	483	957	882	676	1415

Source: Scottish Election Surveys, 1979, 1992, 1997; Scottish Referendum Survey, 1997; Scottish Parliamentary Election Survey, 1999.

Table 7.10 Class and national identification

Identity group	All	Salariat[1]	Manual working class[1]	Middle class[2]	Working class[2]
	(%)	*(%)*	*(%)*	*(%)*	*(%)*
Same class, English	24	27	19	24	22
Opposite class, Scots	43	41	47	45	43
Sample sizes (= 100%)	*1415*	*394*	*433*	*389*	*1026*

Notes
1 Social class by employment.
2 Self-ascribed social class.

Source: Scottish Election Parliamentary Survey, 1999.

Gender and national identity

It has long been assumed that in Scotland gender attitudes and behaviour are more conservative than in England and the rest of Europe. The myth of the 'macho Scotsman', as John MacInnes has called it, has rarely been subject to systematic scrutiny. Rather, as Alex Howson observed, debates about Scottishness and national identity are linked to a discourse of sexuality:

> Within debates concerning Scottish identity, either those which assert that Scotland is framed as inferiorist or those which allude to the positive images which may be provided by a reclamation of working class history, women are marginalised and femininity is selectively deployed as a symbolic category.
>
> (Howson, 1993: 48)

This fusion of discourses has led to a general assumption that women have a different relationship to national identity from men, that the iconography of Scottishness is so overwhelmingly masculine – war, work, football, tartan and so on – that being Scottish is not open to them. Analysis of the survey data does not support this (Table 7.11). In each case, more women than men opt for Scottish identity if asked to choose. Using the 'Moreno' question gives similar results for the 1997 Referendum Survey and the 1999 Scottish Parliamentary Election Survey.

Similarly, John MacInnes' analysis of international survey data suggests that attitudes to gender in Scotland are not conservative in comparison to the rest of the UK or to Europe as a whole (MacInnes, 1998). They are, if anything, slightly more egalitarian as regards shared roles between the genders. Again,

Table 7.11 National identity by gender

National identity	1979 (%)		1992 (%)		1997 (%)		1997 Referendum (%)		1999 (%)	
	M	F	M	F	M	F	M	F	M	F
British[1]	43	34	28	22	25	22	21	10	20	14
Scottish[1]	53	60	69	74	71	73	79	89	73	80
Sample size	325	336	445	512	410	472	309	363	712	770

Note
1 Forced-choice 'best' identity.

Source: General Election Surveys, 1979, 1992, 1997; Scottish Referendum Survey, 1997; Scottish Parliamentary Election Survey, 1999.

attitudes of men and women in Scotland are very similar with regard to views on marriage, divorce, children and reproductive rights. MacInnes concludes: 'The macho Scotsman, like his counterparts across Europe, is not yet a dying breed, but he is trapped in the quicksand of social and economic change' (1998: 121). We should, of course, be careful, as he suggests, not to translate shifts in attitudes to assumptions that patterns of behaviour automatically follow, but it does seem that it is no longer possible to present Scotland as a crudely misogynistic society.

Religion and identity

It has long been claimed that religion in Scotland has had a particular impact on Scottish life and politics. In Chapter 5, we explored the historic connection between Protestantism and Unionism, and it has frequently been claimed that Catholics were either excluded from thinking of themselves as Scottish, or did not wish to do so, stressing instead their Irish origins. Whatever the relationship between politics and religion – and the hostility of Catholics to Conservatism is its most important feature – there is little evidence that Catholics do not think of themselves as Scottish. Indeed, they mirror the population as a whole (Table 7.12).

While the sample sizes are small for Catholics, there is every reason to believe from other surveys such as the 1992 Election Survey, the 1997 Referendum Survey and the 1999 Scottish Parliamentary Election Survey that these results accurately reflect the assimilation of Catholics into Scottish society (Rosie and McCrone, 2000). This process has been helped by the breaking up of the old nexus between Unionism, Protestantism and Imperialism, and has allowed a more pluralistic notion of Scottishness to emerge which we will examine later.

Table 7.12 National identity by religion

National identity	Catholic (%)	Protestant (%)	Other/none (%)	All (%)
Scottish not British	23	19	28	23
Scottish more than British	38	41	35	38
Equally Scottish and British	26	31	23	27
British more than Scottish	5	4	4	4
British not Scottish	5	3	4	4
None of these	3	2	6	4
Sample size	*125*	*395*	*362*	*882*

Source: Scottish Election Survey, 1997.

Ethnicity and identity

The issue of religion and identity has frequently been a proxy for matters of ethnicity rather than religious belief *per se*. For example, it was the fact that most Catholics in Scotland had Irish roots that raised the issue of their national identity. Scotland is, of course, a country of emigrants rather than immigrants, for only around 10 per cent of the population were born elsewhere, whereas there are almost three-quarters of a million Scots-born living in England. Of the 10 per cent of the Scottish population not born in Scotland, the largest component, around 7 per cent, were born in England. In the early 1990s, fringe nationalist groupings such as Settler Watch and Scottish Watch ran public campaigns against what they saw as the 'Englishing' of Scotland, that key posts were being taken by English incomers. Press and media attention – including television documentaries with titles such as the 'Englishing of Scotland' – continued long after these groupings disappeared from political view. In the context of the demand for Home Rule, a number of newspapers from south of the border ran stories about anti-English feeling and discrimination, while the role of English incomers into rural communities, the so-called 'white settler' phenomenon, helped to raise the profile.

In the event, the evidence was that English-born immigrants to Scotland tended to 'go native', and to adopt political and social attitudes much more similar to native Scots than to the English population they had left behind (Dickson, 1994). Further research on members of arts and landed elites – two groups particularly highlighted by the press – confirmed that they were very sensitive to such accusations, and had developed sophisticated arguments to discount place of birth in favour of emphasising choice and commitment to Scotland (McCrone *et al.*, 1998; Bechhofer *et al.*, 1999). Such research has also helped to show that identity involves a complex process of claim, attribution and perception by others, and that individuals have considerable capacity to negotiate and mobilise identity for themselves. Anthropological research on the so-called 'white settler' phenomenon also confirms that defining 'insiders' and 'outsiders' is a much more complex and negotiated matter than either the media or protest groups imply (Jedrej and Nuttall, 1996).

It is, of course, the case that groups who are relatively privileged in socio-economic terms such as English-born residents in Scotland would, by and large, not consider themselves to be 'ethnic' at all. They would, in Michael Banton's phrase, see themselves as 'minus-one ethnics'. He comments: 'Members of that group perceive themselves not as ethnic but as setting the standard by which others are to be judged' (Banton, 1983: 65). There is a growing interest in the UK generally in how ethnicity, nationality and citizenship are interacting (McCrone and Kiely, 2000). The growing debate about Englishness has highlighted the identity politics of people of Afro-Caribbean and Asian origin, and whether they feel English and/or British, or are permitted to do so (Modood, 1997).

How do these issues play in Scotland? There is relatively little research, partly a reflection of the disproportionately small numbers who migrated to Scotland in the post-war period, and partly because race and ethnicity has not become a political issue compared with south of the border (Dunlop, 1993). 'Ethnic minorities' comprise only 1.3 per cent of Scotland's population, with the Pakistani community accounting for around one-third (51 per cent in Glasgow), 41 per cent of whom were born in Scotland, and a further 13 per cent in England (Census 1991 Report for Scotland). The black population, those of Afro-Caribbean or African origin, accounts for only 10 per cent of the ethnic minority population, and 0.13 per cent of Scotland's population as a whole (Saeed *et al.*, 1999). In a study of sixty-three school pupils in Glasgow from Pakistani backgrounds aged 14 to 17, Saeed and his colleagues found that the largest proportion by far defined themselves as 'Muslim', nearly three times as many as 'Pakistani', with fewer than 10 per cent saying they were Scottish or Asian. However, in terms of bi-cultural identity, the largest numbers identified as 'Scottish Pakistani' or 'Scottish Muslim', with the former being by far the most popular. Saeed's work suggests that hybrid identities (such as Scottish-Italian) have long been in use for and by ethnic minorities in Scotland, and hence 'the deployment of terms such as 'Scottish-Pakistani' and/or 'Scottish-Muslim' would facilitate simultaneously strengthened links to the host culture and to individuals' ethnic group or origin' (ibid.: 840). It is important to stress that these data on identity do not imply anything as regards discrimination and racism in Scotland, for cases are well documented by the Commission for Racial Equality in Scotland. What we can say, however, is that the construction and mobilisation of ethnic identities north of the border is likely to take a different – and at present largely unknown – form, given distinctive cultural and political conditions which pertain in Scotland.

What makes a Scot?

It might seem peculiar that we know relatively little about the criteria for Scottish identity, given its long historical pedigree. Perhaps, however, that is the point. With the exception of immigration from Ireland in the second half of the nineteenth century, and waves of Italians, Lithuanians, Poles, and latterly Asians and English, there has been no large-scale influx of people labelled as 'foreigners' on a scale seen in England. By the 1850s, a quarter of a million Irish people had settled in Scotland, and this continued at a diminishing rate until the 1920s. The impact, however, of the Irish in Scotland (including Protestants from Ulster) was probably twice that in England, given the different sizes of population (Devine, 1999: 487). The largely successful assimilation of this population – reflected in the fact that in identity terms they are now indistinguishable from the rest of the population – has meant that there has been no serious debate about who can and who cannot be Scottish in the past half-century.

There are, of course, significant numbers of people born in Scotland, and still more of Scottish extraction, of whom we know very little in identity terms. As an emigrant society for well over 400 years, the Scottish 'diaspora' has been largely ignored, in contrast, for example, with the Irish in North America whose impact on the 'homeland' has been much greater in economic and cultural terms. There is evidence that, because Scots were better educated, skilled and spoke English, they reacted to economic downturns at home by emigrating to where better prospects existed (ibid.: 484–5). We know even less at the time of writing about the so-called Anglo-Scots, three-quarters of a million – 15 per cent of the population of Scotland – who live in England. The creation of the Scottish Parliament has helped to create a category of Scots by residence who have full voting rights, unlike the 'ethnic' Scots south of the border. It will be interesting to see how these criteria for 'being Scottish' – birth, descent and residence – develop in the cultural and political agendas. We have begun to ask people in surveys how they judge the criteria for being a Scot. They were asked: 'How important or unimportant is each of the following to being truly Scottish?' (Table 7.13).

For most people living in Scotland, birth, ancestry and residence are the main markers of Scottishness, probably in that order, with 82 per cent saying birth is very or fairly important, 73 per cent ancestry, and 65 per cent residence. The relative standing of these different criteria is reflected in answers to a question about putative Scottish citizenship (Table 7.14). It is important to note that over half accept a very liberal criterion for citizenship – residence alone – which would make Scotland one of the most open societies in western Europe in terms of citizenship. Birth, descent and residence are distinct frames of reference. They are not, however, politically 'active' categories at the present time because there is no political or cultural reason for people to have to choose whether birth is more important than residence, for example.

Table 7.13 Criteria for Scottishness

Question: 'How important or unimportant is each of the following to being truly Scottish?'

Response	Birth (%)	Ancestry[1] (%)	Residence (%)
Very important	48	36	30
Fairly important	34	37	35
Not very important	14	22	23
Not at all important	3	4	10
Sample size	*882*	*882*	*882*

Note
1 Defined as having Scottish parents or grandparents.

Source: Scottish Election Study, 1997.

There is for the moment no systematic political agenda of exclusion and inclusion in terms of race and ethnicity in Scotland.

Table 7.14 Criteria for Scottish citizenship

Question: 'Say Scotland did become independent, which of the following kinds of people do you think should be entitled to a Scottish passport?'

Criterion	(%)
Born in Scotland and currently living in Scotland	97
Born in Scotland but not currently living in Scotland	79
Not born in Scotland but currently living in Scotland	52
Not born in Scotland, not living in Scotland, but with at least one parent born in Scotland	34
Not born in Scotland, not living in Scotland, but with at leaast one grandparent born in Scotland	16
Sample size	*1482*

Source: Scottish Parliamentary Election Study, 1999.

Conclusion

Discourses about societies, including Scotland, are frequently locked into a set of comfortable assumptions. In the previous chapter, we argued that cultural representations of Scotland are often at odds with the complex reality of the society. In this chapter, we have sought to correct what are frequently outmoded accounts of what it means to be Scottish.

History matters. As Christopher Smout put it: 'National identities are constructed out of references to history or, more exactly, to received popular ideas about history that achieve mythic status irrespective of what modern academic historians perceive to be their actual truth or importance' (1994: 108). The 'cultural turn' in Scottish historiography (Broun, 1998; Ferguson, 1998) has helped to refocus the debate about national identity in Scotland at a time when it is central to the political project.

The evidence we have reviewed in this chapter indicates that being Scottish has become stronger and more culturally diverse in the past twenty years. To say this is not to imply that we know what people mean when they say they are Scottish, or that it is like a badge pinned to the lapel, there for everyone to read. Willie McIlvanney commented: 'Having a national identity is a bit like having an old insurance policy. You know you've got one somewhere but often you're not entirely sure where it is. And if you're honest, you would have to admit you're pretty vague about what the small print means' (*Herald*, 6 March 1999).

This 'insurance policy' is frequently opaque and implicit. It operates indirectly through the culture and habits in which people are engaged. It would frequently not occur to them that they are operating in a particularly 'Scottish' way. However, out of the myriad actions and attitudes, often imperceptibly, these take on a Scottish tone and meaning. Take the example of social and political attitudes. We have made the point that people in Scotland are, by and large, left-of-centre in their views about state intervention, social welfare, the redistribution of income and wealth, as well as a whole slew of attitudes to civil and moral conduct. The former surprises few, but the latter surprises many, thirled as they are to a view that Scotland is an illiberal, morally conservative and misogynistic society. (It is frequently easier to hold on to one's beliefs even when the world that created them has radically altered.) Social, moral and political attitudes are increasingly taken as evidence that Scotland is more egalitarian, social democratic, liberal and so on (Brown *et al.*, 1999; Paterson *et al.*, in press). In other words, this is what it means to be Scottish. It is a basic expression of Scottish identity. One then finds that very similar attitudes and values are abroad in England, and strong support for Welfare State values help to define people in the Scandinavian countries. Does that mean they are Scottish too? Of course not. What it does mean is that the attitudes and values have been distilled (a useful metaphor, and aptly Scottish) so that they have become 'as if' Scottish, even though such attitudes are fairly widespread throughout most Western capitalist societies. There would, then, be nothing to stop people in England or elsewhere taking on board the same set of attitudes and values, and packaging them as their own, as 'English' if that was their wont. In other words, there is nothing innately distinctive about them, but they become useful markers of how a society wishes to present itself. It is in essence about the presentation of self as a society or nation, and it is to the social construction of nation-ness that we now turn in the final chapter.

8 The sociology of a nation

The events of the decade since the first edition of this book was written could scarcely have been predicted. That edition, published in 1992, ended with the words: 'Czechoslovakia in 1989; Scotland tomorrow?' A number of people commented on the apparent prescience of these words, assuming they referred to the so-called 'velvet divorce' which divided the Czech lands and Slovakia into separate states. In fact, they were meant as a comment on the collapse of communism, and in particular the role of civil society in its downfall. I, at least, had no way of knowing that a mere three years later, in 1995, two new states would be born out of the old socialist one, and in a peaceful, almost absent-minded manner, that it would be a velvet divorce.

To be sure, the social and political conditions leading to that particular break-up do not apply in these islands, although one should never ignore the influence of unintended consequences which might result in the secession of Scotland from the United Kingdom. While nothing is certain in politics, least of all Scottish Independence, there can be little doubt that in 2000 compared with 1990 it has grown more rather than less likely. One should not, of course, jump from the assumption that it will never happen, to another that it is inevitable. Both positions reflect bad social science, just as the view that nationalism was yesterday's ideology has as its other side of the coin the view that ethnic and national disorder is the order of the day.

The rise of nationalism

In this chapter, we will explore the sociology of Scottish nationalism, its nation-ness, but will do so in a manner reflecting the broader trends and processes of the last decade. Even a casual glance will suggest to us that it would be a mistake to focus simply on those happening to and in Scotland. We began this chapter with a reference to the collapse of communism, and while the events of central and eastern Europe would seem to have very little to do with those in these islands, we would do well to take the broader perspective. The fall of the communist regimes like so many dominoes meant that political commentators had to find a new language. In Tom Nairn's words, the cold war Armageddon was replaced by a discourse of the 'ethnic abyss' (1993: 3). The unfreezing of 'normal' social and political relations between and within countries led some to proclaim 'the end of history' (Fukuyama, 1989) whereby the grand narrative of capitalism versus communism had hastily to be replaced by something more complex and messy. Where Fukuyama got it quite wrong was that in fact 'history' was only recommencing, such that territories were busily working out how they had got here, the better to understand the way forward: '*receuler pour mieux sauter*', as the phrase has it. Far from history having ended, it had been forcibly recharged. It cannot be a coincidence that a new politics of nations has emerged out of the wreckage of two-bloc geo-politics. It is no longer feasible to chase some recalcitrant territory or the other back into line, the better to hold the fortress against communism or capitalism.

What, one might ask, has this to do with Scotland? The differences between capitalism and communism are obvious and do not need to be laboured, but the end of communism has meant that nationalism cannot be dismissed either as some partial and inadequate form of political socialisation (Alter, 1989), or as a reaction against processes of modernity (Hobsbawm, 1990). The growth in nationalism studies as a field of academic work during the 1990s reflects the collapse of conventional paradigms more generally, and has opened up the field of comparative studies of nationalism. It is now common to find comparisons between Scotland, Wales, Quebec, Catalunya, Flanders, Bavaria, the Czech Republic, Slovakia, the Baltic and Balkan states, among others, and while the differences are plain, so is interest in the conditions which give rise to nationalism in these territories. In short, compared even with 1990, it is no longer necessary to justify why one should be interested in processes of state de-formation and re-formation.

Further, there is now much greater appreciation of the point which this book has sought to stress, namely that states, nations and societies are not, or at least should not be, synonyms of each other in social science vocabulary. In particular, as Manuel Castells has commented: 'Nationalism, and nations, have a life of their own, independent from statehood, albeit embedded in cultural constructs and political projects' (1997: 29). Rather, we now find a plethora of political and cultural forms: stateless nations, nationless states, multinational states, shared nation-states, as well as a few – possibly only around 10 per cent (Connor, 1990) – genuine nation-states in which the political and cultural realms are reasonably aligned. Castells again: 'In this *fin de siècle*, the explosion of nationalisms, some of them deconstructing multinational states, others constructing pluri-national entities, is not associated with the formation of classical, sovereign, modern states' (1997: 32). We will explore later the particularly relevant social, economic and political conditions of 'neo-nationalism' which seem especially relevant to Scotland, but it is sufficient for the moment to point out that it is considerably easier to make the case in 2000 than it was a decade earlier. The tide is running in the direction of nationalism.

If the global conditions in which nations and states operate are now different, so it has become easier to treat Scotland as a suitable case for sociological treatment. The issue of Scottish 'exceptionalism' *vis-à-vis* nationalism has receded somewhat. It used to be argued that somehow Scotland did not fit the conventional models, because it did not have the distinctive cultural apparatus, such as language, religion and similar cultural markers which other nations had. Thus it was an important part of Benedict Anderson's account that, because Scotland was English-speaking, it did not have sufficient wherewithal to generate a distinctive nationalism. He observed: 'that already in the early seventeenth century large parts of what would one day be imagined as Scotland were English-speaking and had immediate access to print-English, provided a minimal degree of literacy existed' (1996: 90). This allowed the migration of intellectuals to England, as well as politicians and capitalists, so that a pan-British culture developed. There were, he comments, 'no barricades on all these pilgrims' paths towards the centre' (ibid.).

In the past decade or so we have heard far less about the weakness of nationalism in Scotland in comparison with nations with stronger linguistic traditions such as Wales, Quebec and Catalunya. If anything, in fact, the weak language tariff which people have to pay to be 'Scots' has been low to the point of non-existence, and yet the sense of nation-ness is stronger, as we saw in Chapter 7. We now have a much better appreciation that there are no 'objective' cultural markers in accounting for nationalism generally, so much as a complex set of subjective ones which are constructed and mobilised according to the political conditions of the time. In an important new book, called *Self and Nation*, social psychologists Steve Reicher and Nick Hopkins argue that the goal of nationalists is to create an 'essentialised' sense of nation out of cultural fragments. Their point is not that some nations are more 'real' than others, but that political process is all, such that nationalists are successful when they capture the 'nation' for their own political project. In other words, national categories are not so much givens, as the means whereby appeals can be made to the whole population. What the past decade has taught us is that it is futile to try to find what makes a nation, as much as why the sense of being a nation is such a powerful political force.

As far as nationalism in Scotland is concerned, much has been made of the fact that it belongs at the 'civic' rather than the 'ethnic' end of the spectrum. This is in part because its cultural distinctiveness *vis-à-vis* England appears thin, and hence it has been forced to develop a 'political' rather a 'cultural' sense of what it means to be Scottish, which, almost as a by-product, emphasises territorial inclusivity rather ethnic exclusivity. If this, to some, sounds like special Scottish pleading, it also connects with a broader conception of what constitutes nations in general. The civic–ethnic distinction is one which lies at the heart of studies of nationalism, and, following Hans Kohn in his famous 1945 *Encyclopaedia Britannica* entry, has frequently been mapped on to 'Western' and 'Eastern' forms of nationalism. This has helped to justify the alleged superiority of Western – civic – forms over Eastern – ethnic – forms of nationalism. While scholars like Ernest Gellner used the distinction to generate a theoretical model to explain the character and development of nationalism in the modern world, it has been hard to escape the ethnocentricist assumptions to which others have fallen prey that while 'we' are patriotic, 'you' are nationalistic. Western intellectuals – in so far as they thought of nationalism at all – extolled the virtues of inclusivity and openness which purported to pertain to their own cultures, while abhorring the narrowness and exclusivity of others.

This essentially statist view gave comfort to Western political classes. After all, if the state represents, indeed, is, the nation, why not use the terms interchangeably? The problems are, however, well known. Not only do they not correspond in any major way, but the terms are too easily value loaded. As Jonathan Hearn points out, the difference between a useful distinction and a misleading dichotomy is hard to discern when it comes to civic–ethnic, or liberal–illiberal forms of nationalism. He observes; 'we should bear in mind that what these conceptual pairs ultimately define is opposing styles of arguments about what nations are, and how social values are created, rather than actual types of nations, or societies' (2000: 194). Hearn is sceptical of the claim that nationalism in Scotland is indeed purely 'civic'. If, however, it is presented that way, this is because the political pay-off has historically been greater. As we have seen in previous chapters, making an ethnic claim in terms of language, culture, religion and so on was bound to exclude a sizeable group of people. Better in terms of *realpolitik* to draw the boundary around as many as possible; better to have them inside the tent than out of it if one was trying to govern the kingdom.

In recent years, we have seen a redefining of what it means to be Scottish in terms of socio-political values. Thus, being collectivist, social democratic, liberal was conveniently juxtaposed from 1979 until the 1990s against a Thatcherite government which was seen to be none of these things, and – almost by default – somehow spoke for 'the English' because the Conservatives got elected on the back of English votes. The fact that there is relatively little difference in social and political values north and south of the border was neither here nor there when it came to defining identity. This is an ongoing process, nicely captured by Hearn:

> The metaphor of the covenant/contract in modern Scottish politics not only has a rich, concrete history, but it also has an array of current reference points, a set of variations on a theme. Of key importance are these three relationships: labour to capital; citizen to state; and Scotland to England. These dimensions are concretely historically interrelated, and the image of the contract tends to assimilate these tensions to one another in the political imagination.
>
> (Hearn, 2000: 185)

The point of this exercise is that it is in the broadest sense political, for it maps out the Scottish dimension as distinctive. This is not a party political matter per se, although different parties seek to capture the essence of being Scottish, and as we saw in Chapter 5, this marks out the key battleground for Labour and the SNP in particular, although all parties in the Scottish Parliament sign up to this struggle by default. It would be easy to think that we inevitably talk about politics when we talk about nationalism, and in a basic sense that is so. However, it is a 'politics' in the widest sense of the term. In the Scottish case, for example, there is little doubt that nationalism has infused virtually all social and cultural life, even when there was broad political consensus about the virtues of the Union. Thus all political parties accept that Scotland is a nation, even those, like the Conservatives, who are most strongly tied to the Union and who opposed setting up a devolved parliament. This made it easier for Scottish Tories to adjust to constitutional change, unlike, for example, the Liberal Party in Canada which has trouble accepting the national status of Quebec. Accepting Scotland or Quebec as nations, however, does not prevent parties, like the SNP or *Parti Québécois*, from claiming a monopoly of national identity; indeed, it is the very essence of politics that they should seek to naturalise themselves in this way.

Those trying to understand nationalism often try to search out the key political carrier, focusing on the 'nationalist' party, or try to identify what makes the nation distinctive compared with its relevant 'others'. While this is not an unreasonable strategy, it does encourage us to essentialise nationalism by looking for its distinctive features, when we should be focusing on the 'space' it occupies rather than its 'content'. In other words, it is not what is in the box that matters so much as the box itself, at least the space it marks out. Such an approach is close to what the Norwegian social anthropologist Fredrik Barth meant by 'boundaries' in his seminal (1981) paper, which we referred to in Chapter 2. Barth made the point that nationalism is not the mobilisation of objective differences in ethnicity, but the mobilisation of those differences which actors deem salient. It is the social boundary which the group erects around itself rather than the cultural stuff which the boundary contains. Thus, generating national differences between Scotland and England does not depend on there being 'real' and 'objective' differences which stand outside the process of definition and counter-definition, but on the constructing and amplifying of these differences themselves. Barth's perspective has been very influential in ethnic and national studies, but for our purposes we might take his insight one stage further. Barth has been criticised for assuming that ethnicity is generalised to group members almost by default, without relying over-much on their own self definitions (Cohen, 1996). We might extend this point by focusing on how these differences are sustained and routinised. Plainly, people do not sally forth into daily life having to work it all out for themselves, making it up as they go along. Social institutions are the key here, for they help to take the uncertainty out of most decisions. They are the social means whereby 'relevance' is defined, and the boundaries of responsibility marked out.

Let us return to the question: What does this tell us about Scotland? We take it as axiomatic that Scotland has distinctive institutions – legal, educational, religious, financial and so on – but we often move on without letting the implications sink in. These are, in essence, social fields, and the metaphor is important and revealing. They set apart the space within which rules are set and interactions take place. Their success in so doing helps to naturalise social processes, so that we take it for granted that there is a 'Scottish' way of practising law, religion, education, politics and so on. If and when we are confronted with the fact that there is relatively little difference in practice between the 'Scottish' way and the 'English' way, we are not sure what to make of it. Somehow we have assumed a model whereby distinctive social practices are 'fenced off' (space again); first the distinctiveness, then the fencing or separation. In fact, the very act of fencing – creating a boundary – defines what goes on within it in a distinctive way. Thus, for example, Scottish private law does not in and of itself reflect innate differences between, say the Scots and the English. However, as J. M. Thomson, regius professor of law at Glasgow University observed: 'there is little doubt that the fact that Scotland has retained a separate legal *system* from England has played an important role in keeping alive our Scottish national identity' (Thomson, 1995: 31; emphasis in original). Thus, European law will not be a threat to Scottish national identity provided it keeps its independent legal system. Usually much of this boundary creation and maintenance is a 'state' function, and so we have little difficulty in appreciating that they do things differently in France and Germany than in Britain, even though we know that the similarities between Western industrial countries are much greater than the differences. The problem, if that is what it is, comes within states where there are different institutional ways of doing similar things, which in turn generates a sense of essentialised and naturalised difference.

Scotland's institutional distinctiveness within the United Kingdom preceded the formation of the state itself, and was one of the key conditions for its very creation in 1707 in the first place. Staking out the institutional boundaries in this way made it easier to extend it to further pastures, so that the normal way for the British state to react to the many political demands over the past three centuries has been to cede more and more institutional autonomy to the burgeoning apparatus of Scottish government. Governments of both Right and Left have followed this course to the point that the issue of the democratic accountability of this system of governance bubbled almost naturally to the top of the political agenda, and resulted in the creation of a directly elected Scottish parliament and government. Stifling such demand at various points in history would have meant incorporating Scotland further into the institutions of Westminster government, but politically this was not possible without threatening the Union itself. After all, it was a Tory, Walter Scott, who wrote a passionate defence of Scottish banknotes in his tract *Letters of Malachi Malagrowther* (1826), and the British state duly backed off. In truth and in hindsight, only a Union in which Scotland had a high degree of institutional autonomy was possible (Paterson, 1994).

Scotland developed a 'deliberative space' (Schlesinger, 1999) which grew rather than diminished in importance as the British Union burgeoned. The key to understanding this space lay in the way it structured social communication (Deutsch, 1953), and while the convention was to see this as coterminous with the state, in what one might call the Scottish 'semi-state', politico-communicative space was indigenous. The most obvious manifestations of this distinctive space lay in the print and broadcasting media. Benedict Anderson's thesis on the rise of nationalism rested on the role of print capitalism in generating just such a vernacular space (Anderson, 1991). Similarly, Ernest Gellner (1983) made much of the way in which the nation provided the defining cultural frame within which 'every man is a clerk'. Both writers took the defining frame to be the nation as meaning the state, but the same can be said of a sub-state level of sufficient institutional density as Scotland. Thus, the gathering up of administrative powers to the Scottish level grew apace after the Scottish Office was founded in 1885. The apparatus of government was vital as the midwife of economic regeneration in the second half of the twentieth century. In the late 1950s and 1960s the idea of Scotland as the key unit of economic management was transmitted via the political process to the electorate, and charged by the new politics of North Sea oil. As we saw in Chapter 5, the Scottish National Party was in the right place at the right time during the late 1960s and early 1970s to take advantage of, as well as helping to ratchet up, the idea of Scotland as the 'natural' – that is, national – unit of political and economic management. It also helps explain why the agenda of the Scottish Parliament is, in truth, a national one.

It is tempting to conclude that the media has been the prime instrument in manufacturing this new Scottish communicative space. The argument, however, needs careful handling. While the existence and development of a distinctive media has been important in generating this space, it is not a sufficient condition in and of itself. If anything, the print media was even more dominantly Scottish in the nineteenth century in the absence of radio and television, yet it did not generate a Scottish national dimension of an overt political sort. Only when the socio-economic and cultural conditions of the second half of the twentieth century were present could this come to pass. In particular, only when the post-war Welfare State helped to usher in an encompassing sense of social citizenship (Marshall, 1963) were the political conditions present for a Scottish frame of reference recognisably modern.

It is important not to lose sight of the British dimension in Scottish nationalism. By this stage, the reader will hopefully have been disabused of the simplistic notion that Scotland is or was an oppressed colony of England. It had entered the Union of 1707 as, in Tom Nairn's felicitous phrase, a 'junior partner' in British imperialism, an autonomous nation which, whatever the vexatious conditions of entry, had taken advantage of its new-found status in the world. The Union was a marriage of convenience, which, whatever was to become of it in later years, gave Scotland unprecedented access to power and privilege for such a small and peripheral nation. Holding to the marriage metaphor of a political 'marriage' allows us to see how, as the bargain grew less advantageous and British power waned with its empire, so Scotland emerged into the post-imperial twenty-first century with its apparatus of governance not merely intact but more highly developed. Thus one of the keys to the growth of nationalism in Scotland is the changing character of Britishness.

In the previous chapter we saw how for most people in Scotland their national identity – being Scottish – was more important than being British, their state identity. We also saw that a substantial majority, over three-quarters, still said they were British to a degree, so it would be wrong to believe that being Scottish and being British have turned out to be in some sense competing with each other. This, in part, tends to happen because 'English' and 'British' are often used interchangeably, and as a result, as Anthony Barnett observed, for many people south of the border, being asked to distinguish between them 'seems like one of those puzzles that others can undo but you can't: Englishness and Britishness are inseparable' (1997: 293).

We now know that a large part of the difficulty seems to result from the way 'Britain' was made. We have already alluded to Linda Colley's influential book, *Britons: Forging the Nation*, in which she argued that this 'forging' process (a reference to joining elements together rather than counterfeit, although both metaphors might apply) resulted from the long war, virtual and real, with France from 1707 until 1837, as well as Protestantism. Of course, the wars were in large part religious wars, so the two elements were connected. Thus, the overthrow of the Catholic Stewarts in 1689 and their replacement with the Protestant monarch William of Orange reinforced the politico-religious nature of the new British regime, except in Ireland, where the mass of the population could not participate.

The point about this process is that 'Britishness was superimposed over an array of internal differences in response to contact with the Other, and above all in response to conflict with the Other' (Colley, 1992: 6). Being British could be thought of as an overarching state identity, which sat lightly upon the constituent nations of these islands, except in most of Ireland, where it was seen as antithetical to being Irish both by colonisers and colonised. It is important to grasp what this meant. For most people in these islands, being British was not an alien imposition, but a complementary identity to one's nationality, and, above all, one with strong imperial connotations in which people took pride and confidence. The empire, after all, did not have much difficulty persuading them to make the ultimate sacrifice – *dulce et decorum est pro patria mori* – and even in Ireland, where one might have expected it to be otherwise, substantial numbers were killed fighting for, not against, Britain during the Great War. It is also important to grasp that this was not confined to these islands, for Britain existed as an imperial state with colonies and dominions which saw themselves as attached to the 'mother-country' even after formal independence was achieved. Britain, then, was never simply England, nor, in truth, was it simply the United Kingdom, but a wider imperial cache: *civis Britannicus sum*.

The empire, of course, is no more. When, post-1945, former colonies like India and Canada sought to redefine citizenship in national rather than imperial terms for immigration purposes, the UK somewhat reluctantly followed suit (Goulbourne, 1991). The 1948 Nationality Act performed a sleight of hand by defining people as 'citizens of the UK and colonies', with implications for later patterns of migration from the 1950s onwards. Being a subject of the Crown retained a residual sense of Britishness, and by the 1980s laws of 'patriality' gave people from the white Commonwealth particular rights to settle and work in the UK.

The result of this imperial history meant that, in Robin Cohen's useful term, Britishness was 'fuzzy':

> British identity shows a general pattern of fragmentation. Multiple axes of identification have meant that Irish, Scots, Welsh and English people, those from the white, black and brown Commonwealth, Americans, English-speakers, Europeans and even 'aliens' have had their lives intersect one with another in overlapping and complex circles of identity-construction and rejection. The shape and edges of British identity are thus historically changing, often vague and, to a degree, malleable – an aspect of British identity I have called a 'fuzzy frontier'.
>
> (Cohen, 1994: 35)

Let us situate Scotland more centrally in this discussion. After 1945, the creation of the British Welfare State reinforced the unitary nature of the state, and for the next two decades there was little challenge from alternative nationalisms in these islands. The Welfare State had an intimate, a daily, impact on people's lives, and so being 'British' was easily internalised. In other words, nationalism was by no means absent, but it was an implicit, all-British nationalism of the centre rather than the peripheries. The state operated in the 'national interest', frequently in competition with other Western states. The ambiguities of national identities in the United Kingdom were highlighted in the late 1970s with the election of Mrs Thatcher. While for much of the post-war period nationalism, as in other Western countries, had been largely implicit, the relative economic decline of the UK made appeals to the 'national' interest more urgent and explicit. Politics ceased to be simply a matter of elect-ing the best team of economic managers, and became instead a struggle for the 'national soul'. The Thatcherite project set out to revolutionise British society and its economy by deliberately destabilising institutional structures. Large sectors of the economy were opened up to international competition, state industries were privatised, trade unions deregulated, and considerable redistri-bution took place to the advantage of the better-off. Faced with this politico-economic project, appeals to 'the national interest' became more urgent, but which 'national interest'? Thatcherism was usually equated with economic liberalism, but contained within it a powerful strand of neo-Conservatism whose motif was 'authority' rather than 'freedom'. As Thatcherism developed, and particularly after the Falklands War of 1982, the neo-Conservative strand became more prominent.

Such nationalism, however, depended upon a powerful sense of 'Britain' to encapsulate the other national identities in these islands. As Thatcherism mobilised British nationalism, it became increasingly clear – at least to the periphery – that this had become an empty shell, or at least was indistinguishable from English nationalism. It was as if the sleight of hand necessary to maintain the Union began to appear more clumsy. As Conservative nationalism became more explicit and strident, so competing nationalisms asserted themselves, and Thatcher's success in England had its counterpart in electoral unpopularity in Scotland and Wales, both which were, in terms of electoral arithmetic, fairly unimportant.

British nationalism had long been a fragile and complex affair, depending on the empire, the monarchy and institutions like the BBC. Much of 'Britain' depended upon its external reinforcement. As Bill Mackenzie pointed out: 'One might add that commonwealth and colonies were symbols of "Britain", and that "Britain" is rather an empty word now that they have gone' (1978: 172). Such an imperial tradition had successfully incorporated Scottish militarism, for example, which was nested within it such that British national and imperial identity chimed nicely with that older strand of Scottishness reinforced by Protestantism, Unionism and militarism. Institutions like the monarchy were also losing their power to charm, to perform their magic, except as a latter-day soap opera. Tom Nairn (1988) observed that the monarchy had been an invention of the late seventeenth century, constructed to provide ideological cement in a state with inherently fissile tendencies. The monarchy increasingly found itself without a meaningful role as the empire declined, as Britishness eroded, and as counter-nationalisms grew. Could the monarch ever be spoken of as anything other than the Queen of England?

Britishness had largely been a political rather than a cultural construct, a mobilising device almost entirely defined by its external relations. In the late twentieth century, its key political carrier, the Conservative Party, lost its sense of Britishness – in 1997 it had no MPs outside England. It was almost a natural consequence of the political project. Writing in the late 1980s, Andrew Gamble observed:

> What the Conservatives have learned ... and particularly during Thatcher's leadership, is that it is no longer necessary or possible to project themselves as the party of the Union in order to win elections. Unionism has declined with the Empire. Conservatism has had to find a new identity. The Conservative Nation now is no longer the nation of Empire and Union. The appeal is directed much more towards England, and towards certain regions of England, the old metropolitan heartland of Empire.
>
> (Gamble, 1988: 214)

The Englishing of the Conservative Party was both the cause and the consequence of the electoral success of Thatcherism in the 1980s, and helps to explain the disaffection of the electorate in the rest of the kingdom. The demise of empire, the erosion of monarchy, and the diminishing capacity of quintessentially British institutions like the BBC to manufacture and sustain a unified and homogenised British culture have helped to weaken the sense of Britain. In Neal Ascherson's words, 'Britain is not so much a nation as a sort of authority, a manner of speaking rather than a matter of weeping' (1988: 152). Without a strong centralised state, there was probably little to sustain the idea of Britain, for the dominant *mentalité* in England had little comprehension as to its complexity and fragility.

Let us gather together at this stage the key strands of our argument. Nationalism in Scotland, indeed, like nationalism generally, is not simply the outcome of a set of internally generated factors specific to the territory. The thrust of our argument is that the contextual effects are crucial. Thus, Scotland has long existed as a public 'space' defined by its institutional apparatus even when it did not have a government of its own. This communicative space provided the agenda within which political, social and cultural matters were naturalised in such a way that Scotland became the key frame of reference. This framing effect was reinforced as the imperial context declined, and with it an older sense of Britishness underpinned by empire and Protestantism. A social democratic vision replaced this imperial one after 1945, and with it a new sense of secular Britishness was ushered in with the Welfare State. The consequence of this was to tighten up the state's powers such that the old territorial *laisser-passer* could not be maintained.

The long decline in British political and economic power in the second half of the twentieth century ushered in a more radical vision of a privatised and deregulated Britain, but one based upon an English rather than a British national project. The old bargain which had sustained the British state such that national and state identities could coexist was unravelling, and economic liberalism severed the economic and cultural sinews which had kept this 'fuzzy' state together. The marriage of convenience which had been the British state disintegrated under the contradictory tensions of liberalism and conservatism, and Scotland, which had the greatest degree of institutional autonomy of all the territories of the British state, was best able to develop its alternative political agenda of nationalism.

The focus on contextual effects might strike some readers as odd. After all, does nationalism not depend on marking out what is distinctive about a culture and a people? Should an analysis not focus on what is specific and particular rather than on what is general? It is of course important to do this, but the contention here is that such a focus runs the risk of essentialising what should be analytically problematic, namely the nation itself. In other words, we cannot simply take the existence of 'Scotland' for granted as if the reasons for its nationalism only lie within it, and define our task as uncovering them like social archaeologists. We began this chapter by pointing out that nationalism was a vibrant political force in the new millennium wherever we look, and that this suggested that that we should focus on general rather than specific processes to account for it. We also mentioned that Scotland struck some authors as an odd case, because it resembled its larger neighbour, England, in more ways than it differed from it. Others have pointed to the fact that there is something of a contradiction taking place: the rise of nationalism just at the point where the nation-state appears to be losing its capacity to control its destiny. Why, then, should nationalist movements be chasing a goal – the nation-state – which appears to be going out of fashion?

Nationalism: the gravedigger of the nation-state?

> There was this Englishman who worked in the London office of a multi-national corporation based in the United States. He drove home one evening in his Japanese car. His wife, who worked in a firm which imported German kitchen equipment, was already home. Her small Italian car was often quicker through the traffic. After a meal which included New Zealand lamb, Californian carrots, Mexican honey, French cheese and Spanish wine, they settled down to watch a programme on their television set, which had been made in Finland. The programme was a retrospective celebration of the war to recapture the Falkland islands. As they watched it they felt warmly patriotic, and very proud to be British.
>
> (Williams, 1983: 177)

Raymond Williams was poking fun at the confused sentiments of nationalism in the modern age. However, he was careful to argue that nationalism is far from dead and provides the means for people to combat new, alienating and centralising powers in the modern world. As Benedict Anderson commented: 'the end of the era of nationalism, so long prophesied, is not remotely in sight' (1983: 12). Nevertheless, we seem to have entered a post-nationalist age. How, if at all, can these ideas be reconciled?

What is indubitably clear is that the historic creation of classical nationalism, the nation-state, is losing its *raison d'être*. The nation-state is a historical product, not a fact of nature, and emerged as the dominant political formation between the mid-nineteenth and mid-twentieth centuries. The late nineteenth century in particular was a period of intense cultivation of national symbols – flags, anthems, ceremonies, holidays and buildings. The nation-state laid claim to supreme territorial jurisdiction, sovereignty; its source of jurisdiction derived from the people, the nation. The nation-state in its classical form was an adaptation to the economic, military and political circumstances of the nineteenth and early twentieth centuries. Those states were economically successful where a free market was established based on a unified national system of law, taxation and administration (Beetham, 1984). In military terms nation-states succeeded where they asserted their autonomy and mobilised the nation in its defence.

Politically, they incorporated the population as citizens by means of the electoral franchise.

In key respects, the nation-state has been undermined by precisely the forces which gave it strength. The development of global, mobile capital and a more complex international division of labour have reduced the capacity of the national state to determine its economic policy. Multinational capital is able to 'optimise conditions for its operation without reference to the interests of particular national economies' (Beetham, 1984: 212). Transnational organisations like the World Bank and the International Monetary Fund have also acquired substantial powers over national states. The nation-state has also been eroded by its own *raison d'état*, namely its capacity to defend its citizens. The modern state was by and large the outcome of war successfully waged, but in the second half of the twentieth century the state no longer had the power to protect its citizens in anything like the same capacity. Technological developments, and especially the potency of nuclear weapons, together with the wider ramifications of localised conflicts, have made limited warfare much more difficult to wage. The more nation-states try to control their own means of destruction, the more they are vulnerable to others. Partly as a result, international law has developed to circumscribe the claims of nation-states, thereby increasing the tension between national sovereignty and international law. Finally, it is difficult to find a simple correspondence between culture and the state any more. Multiculturalism is embedded in virtually all states, and claims that 'a people' have a single and distinct culture become much harder to maintain and defend.

We have, however, to be careful in arguing that the nation-state is being eroded to the point of extinction by economic, political-military and cultural changes in the modern world. States are still the key actors in modern geopolitics, and supranational bodies like the European Union (*Europe de Patries*, after all) and the United Nations are still beholden to their military and economic power. Internally, too, the state demands and largely gets the obeisance of its citizens. However, while the nation-state remains a key organising feature of modern politics, 'any conception of sovereignty which assumes that it is an indivisible, illimitable, exclusive, and perpetual form of public power – embodied within an individual state – is defunct' (Held, 1988: 15).

The message is stark, and not only for those in possession of nation-states. Thatcherism was an uneasy mix of liberal, free-market economics and conservative nationalism. In the last half-century, not only the UK, but France, Belgium, Spain, Canada and other Western states have been subject to territorial pressures from within. The long view of history would indicate that there is but a loose correspondence between nations and states. Many nations, like Scotland and Catalunya, did not survive as independent states, and many states, most notably the United States of America, were formed out of non-nations. The pressures on existing states will not diminish, and are likely to come from two directions, from below and above. Supranational government such as the European Union will erode states' powers from above. At the same time submerged nations will become more vociferous in asserting their rights to self-determination. Juan Linz has argued that nationalism in the modern age has shifted away from a simple emphasis on what he terms 'primordial ties', to a focus on territoriality. He observes: 'The definition would change from an emphasis on common descent, race, language, distinctive cultural tradition, in some cases religion, to one based on "living and working" in an area, on a willingness to identify with that community, or on both' (1985: 205).

This shift from ethnicity to territoriality embodies changes within national-ism itself. The implication of Linz's remarks is that simple, primordial demands based on exclusivity are not suited to a multicultural, interdependent world. Nationalist movements which take that regressive, primordial route may flourish in the short term, but ultimately are doomed to fail. The assault by nationalists on existing nation-states is a symptom of the decay of these political formations, as well as a search for new forms of self-determination. The irony is that nationalism is probably the gravedigger of the conventional nation-state with its commitment to 'a world of sovereign, self-reliant nation-states claiming the right to assert themselves and pursue their essential national interests by taking recourse to force' (Mommsen, 1990: 226). In its classical form, nation-alism is pursuing precisely those political structures which appear to be falling into disuse. As such, nationalism is likely to consume its own offspring. In that sense, these are post-nationalist times.

Stateless nations in the twenty-first century

The argument so far has been that the political, economic and cultural con-ditions of the new millennium make conventional nationalism which seeks out a sovereign, self-contained nation-state redundant, yet at the same time erode and ultimately destroy conventional states created and shaped by modernity in the past 200 years. How, if at all, does Scotland fit? There has arisen in the second half of the twentieth century one of the most paradoxical forms of nationalism of all: neo-nationalism, a new territorial politics in Wes-tern states. It is this form of nationalism which best approximates to the Scottish case, and we will explore this in the rest of the chapter.

To call such forms 'neo' – new – is to imply that they are unforeseen and not easily accommodated into conventional theories of nationalism. Such theories usually imply that nationalism in the West was well and truly over by the mid-twentieth century in so far as the process of state-building had been completed by then. This led a number of authors to argue that 'regionalism' resulted in peripheral territories being inadequately incorporated into central state struc-tures (Alter, 1989; Hobsbawm, 1990). There is, however, in these sorts of explanation, an unwillingness to take neo-nationalism at face value. John Breuilly acknowledges that the situations in Scotland, Quebec and the Basque country take the form of 'a rather tough-minded, frequently radical nationalism which is very different from the anti-modernist, rather romantic nationalist movements of "peripheral" regions in many 19th century European countries' (1993: 333). Relying on contingent explanations in order to get such cases to fit theories of nationalism will only get us so far. It is important to recognise that we are dealing with a different and quite modern form of nationalism which cannot be accommodated or dismissed. The term 'neo-nationalism' was originally coined by Tom Nairn in *The Break-Up of Britain*, published in 1977. Describing it as a new political movement, he commented: 'it is in a number of ways analogous to historical or mainstream nationalism. But a more careful consideration shows its different place in history and its different character and potential. It deserves to be called "neo-nationalism" rather than nationalism' (1977: 127).

What, then, is new about neo-nationalism? In the first place, it occurs in highly developed states with highly developed economies. It does not, for example, share too many features with nationalism in the Third World, which takes the form of politicised religion, or in the post-communist world, where it resembles a catching-up process of economic and political development. Let us note too how quickly post-communist states have adjusted to a world of shared and limited sovereignty, reflected in their desire to join an enlarged European Union (MacCormick, 1995, 1996). Neo-nationalism tends to occur in relatively advantaged territories rather than underdeveloped ones. Catalunya, for example, has long been the most advanced part of Spain, and Quebec has more recently developed an economy taking advantage of its niche in the North American continent as a whole. In Scotland's case, it is the shift in the relative economic fortunes in these islands which has made the difference. In the post-war period its unemployment rate had been significantly higher than the UK rate as a whole, and as the economy was restructured, so the relative economic disparities diminished. The discovery of oil in the North Sea in the late 1960s helped to transform Scotland's economic prospects, and with it a new political force was brought into play, the Scottish National Party. The political-psychological boost of oil – at least its promise – coupled with wholesale modernisation of the economy as a whole in which the state through the Scottish Office played a major part, helped to bring into focus the historic deal struck in 1707. No longer was Scotland part of the Union simply because it had no economic alternative.

The world of the later twentieth century was increasingly an economically globalised one. The transformation of Scotland's economy had been achieved with substantial amounts of foreign, notably American, capital. By the end of the century, Scotland exported a higher share of its manufacturing output than the rest of the UK, notably in the electronics sector which was marketed as 'Silicon Glen'. The effect was to reposition Scotland in the international economy, and this time outwith imperial markets as in the nineteenth century. That the leader of the Nationalist Party at the time of writing was a bank economist by profession rather than a poet is a revealing feature of modern Scottish nationalism. It owes far more to the pocket-book than the prayer-book. In passing, we might note that the leaders of the nationalist parties in Catalunya and Quebec have plied their trade in this sector also. The Catalan economy is relatively 'overdeveloped' compared with the rest of Spain, and Quebec has moved rapidly from having a predominantly agricultural economy to an advanced manufacturing and financial one. As Michael Keating has observed: 'Deregulation, neo-liberalism and free trade have not destroyed the Quebec model of development but they have transformed it. It is geared now to the interests of large corporations, based in Quebec but increasingly continental or global in their scale of operations' (1996: 6). These shifts in the international division of labour have helped to give neo-nationalism a sense of being of the elect rather than the damned, of the future rather than the past.

This economic transformation has crucially taken place within a new geometry of power. Instead of the territory relating only and directly with the state of which it is part – classical centre–periphery relations – a further dimension of supra-state power has been added. In the case of Scotland (and Catalunya), this is the European Union such that there emerges a complex and variable speed geometry in which the nation in question is engaged in relationships with both the state and the supra-state body. Thus there appears to be a more pro-European stance in the two nations, at least among political and economic elites. In part, this is because a third player can offset the necessity of always having to dealing with only one other, usually the central state. In the case of Quebec, there is the hope that a wider North American market will help to lessen its dependence on Canada in which the economic levers available to central governments may not operate in the interests of the province. Thinking beyond the state can also help in re-imagining the nation as part of a bigger entity, and reconnecting with an older historical identity, in the case of Scotland, as one of Europe's oldest nations with a past beyond its British one. Such a strategy is also helped by the UK's reluctance to embrace Europe for fear of losing control over its own affairs. Pursuing a European strategy highlights the conservatism of the central state which takes on a defensive and reactionary stance usually associated with the negative aspects of nationalism. The more this occurs, the easier it is for peripheral nationalism to present itself as progressive, optimistic and in touch with the mood of the times.

This stance is also reflected in the ability of neo–nationalist movements to move around the political spectrum, notably from Right to Left. Different ideological elements are mixed and mobilised as required: right/left; ethnic/civic; corporatist/neo-liberal/social democratic. The Scottish National Party, for example, has deliberately shifted its position from right to left, in large part to compete for the largest block of left-of-centre votes with the Labour Party. The *Parti Québécois* has positioned itself as a leftist party, but with strong links to the local business elite. The nationalist coalition in Catalunya, *Convergencia i Unio*, is closely tied into local capital, yet has a strong appeal to working-class voters in autonomous elections. All these political formations are of recent vintage, dating from the 1960s in large measure, when they were re-formed out of nationalist fragments, and reactivated by an infusion of new social and political movements, mainly on the Left. It is also significant that the movement for self-government – Home Rule, in Scotland's case – is broader than support for the nationalist party. We have already seen (Chapter 5) that a substantial minority – even at times a majority – of those preferring Independence actually vote for another political party. In other words, there is no easy alignment of constitutional preference with party vote.

The ambiguity of ideological position is related to an ambiguity of aims. While the nationalist bloc in Catalunya currently supports 'autonomy' rather than full Independence, for reasons, it seems, of contingency rather than principle, the Scottish National Party is a separatist party in that it wishes Scotland to be independent – in Europe – which is in itself an 'autonomous' position. The *Parti Québécois* also adopts a 'sovereignist' goal, but one which is also contingent in maintaining close links with (the rest of) Canada. Thus, these are nationalist movements whose goals turn out to be less than clear-cut. Home Rule, autonomism, sovereignty association do not sound like full-blown traditional Independence. The issue is once more how to adapt in order to maximise political Independence in an increasingly interdependent world.

The focus on finding the appropriate political niche (neo-nationalism can also be thought of as niche-nationalism) highlights the changing relationship between cultural and political issues. We have already commented on John Breuilly's observation that these late twentieth-century movements appear to have a much more tough-minded, political orientation than their nineteenth-century counterparts, which seem more concerned with defending or maximising cultural identity. It would of course be a mistake to think that neo-nationalism has very little concern with the cultural and the ethnic, for there is a complex interplay between cultural and political development. In Chapter 6 we observed that while there is no shortage of cultural iconography in Scotland, the political movement appears to travel light and carry little cultural baggage. In Quebec and Catalunya, cultural affairs, notably in language issues, seem to be more salient, even to the point that language and culture are synonymous. While there is a close relationship between them, we cannot lose sight of the fact that pursuing cultural identity through the medium of language does create that impression, although they are analytically distinct. In Quebec and Catalunya, for example, language laws have been important ways of crystallising and mobilising cultural matters, as well as being rallying points for the political movement as a whole. Once these battles are won, however, the movement does not fade away, any more than in Scotland where such issues are absent.

The important point to make is that nationalism does not derive from a distinctive culture. Rather, it seeks to manufacture and make distinctive such a culture for political ends. In other words, the 'politics' in the widest sense comes first, and cultural issues are then mobilised for political ends. This argument is reinforced by the fact that quite different political agendas use very similar cultural materials, but to draw different political conclusions. For example, Unionists in Scotland often make the point that being a Scot does not imply being in favour of Independence, nor does being a nationalist (lower-case n) mean that one cannot be British also.

The complex relationship between national identity and constitutional preference was examined in the previous chapter, where being Scottish and being British is the norm in Scotland. This is not the result of a fundamental socio-psychological inability to resolve the puzzle, the result of a 'deformed' culture. Rather, it reflects the phenomenon of multiple political identities in the modern world. Just as political sovereignty in the modern world is both layered and shared such that powers and responsibilities operate at different levels for different purposes – Scottish for some, British and European for others – so people appear quite content to attach identity to these levels as and when it suits them. The issue is not which one you are, but which one you choose in different contexts and for different purposes. This will not be to the satisfaction of those who like these matters to be clear-cut. The Scottish nationalist Jim Sillars complained of too many Scots being, in his words, 'ninety minute nationalists', happy to be passionately Scottish in supporting their national team, but operating according to different rules when confronted with the ballot-box. Life, particularly Scottish life, has never operated that way. One might even surmise that if and when Scotland was formally independent from England, being 'British' might linger for some time after. Indeed, we would expect that to happen, because of a strong political-cultural legacy in these islands, much as being 'Scandinavian' has cultural meaning for the independent states of that region. If the citizens of the Republic of Ireland are not likely to consider themselves 'British', that is because of long-standing political, cultural struggles between the two islands such that Irish and British became antinomies, as they are to this day in Northern Ireland.

A key aspect in neo-nationalism is the existence and development of reasonably coherent and cohesive civil societies. This takes us back to the point made earlier in the chapter that the institutional space marked out in these societies is the driving force behind their distinctiveness. To reiterate, it is as much cultural distinctiveness which generates nationalism, as nationalism which shapes cultural distinctiveness. In other words, staking out institutional autonomy has the effect of generating difference even though comparatively these are relatively minor. The example we have already given bears repeating. Being attached to social and political values of collectivism is deemed to be 'Scottish' even though precisely the same set of values is important in England, where such values are seen as 'British'. North of the border, these are identified and packaged as evidence of being Scottish, though not of being English (as opposed to 'British'), at least not as yet. Having a reasonably dense institutional framework has undoubtedly worked to the advantage of the national movement in Scotland compared with Wales, where we might have expected cultural markers such as language to carry more cultural and political power.

Nationalism in Scotland belongs to that sub-set which we have labelled 'neo-nationalism', but it has much in common with other variants such as state-building nationalism of the nineteenth century, Third World nationalism of the twentieth century, and post-communist nationalism in the final decades of the twentieth century. This is not to deny that all these variants have something in common, but neo-nationalism does seem to have its own dynamic. It seems to stress civic rather than ethnic features – *demos* rather than *ethnos*; it has an adaptable political ideology, appealing to Right and Left as circumstances require, and building in features of neo-liberalism as well as social democracy. While Scotland has a quite different social and political history from Catalunya and Quebec, for example, they all seem to confront opportunities and constraints of 'niche' nationalism at the beginning of the twenty-first century. In that sense, they take on the character of progressive rather than reactionary movements.

Conclusion

Nationalism as a form of identity politics shows no sign of dying. On the contrary, an elegy is premature as it takes on new forms and meets new needs in modern times. What, however, of the paradox that nationalism waxes as the power of the nation-state wanes? One possibility is that the sovereignty of the nation-state was always a trick of the eye. Yael Tamir has observed: 'The era of the homogeneous and viable nation-states is over (or rather the era of the illusion that homogeneous and viable nation-states are possible is over, since such states never existed) and the national vision must be redefined' (1993: 3). In other words, before we write the obituary, we have to recognise that the nation-state when strictly defined was always more of a political aspiration than a sociological reality. It was a powerful legitimating device to claim that the cultural sphere (nation) and political realm (state) coincided.

The general economic, cultural and political trends to which we give the catch-all term 'globalisation' show no sign of ridding the world of nationalism. The assumption that such forces sweep across the world producing cultural homogenisation and common identities is simply not borne out by the very rise of nationalism. Nor can it be treated as some kind of reactionary movement to globalisation, as people draw so many lines in the sand to little avail. This does not ring true, at least in the cases of neo-nationalism we have discussed. The fall of communism, for example, has allowed many territories to rediscover their identities in a process we can call the re-charging, not the ending, of history. Neither does globalisation erode nationalism, because nationalism is 100 per cent global in the sense that it is an integral part of the new world order. Benedict Anderson has observed that nationality is a universal sociocultural notion, while being irremediably particular in its manifestations (1996: 5). He is also surely correct in saying that there is a crisis of the hyphen for nation-states, for the neat alignment of nation and state is not, and probably never was, a feature of the modern world. Its problem is that, in Daniel Bell's phrase, the nation-state 'is too small for the big problems of life, and too big for the small problems of life' (quoted in McGrew, 1992: 87). Various processes in the modern world do not come naturally to rest on the platform offered by the national state. Thus we are forced to adopt a new way of looking at sovereignty, of treating it as a layered and shared concept. As David Held has put it: 'any conception of sovereignty which assumes that it is an indivisible, illimitable, exclusive and perpetual form of public power – embodied within an individual state – is defunct' (Held, 1988).

As perhaps the most obvious expression of identity politics in the modern world, nationalism is not simply one of the most pervasive but also one of the most flexible forces in the twenty-first century. It is pressed into the service of central states as well as peripheries which seek to build up their political autonomy; it lends itself to ideologies of right as well as left; it provides a sense of historical continuity coupled with strategies for addressing the future. The Italian sociologist Alberto Melucci commented:

> The ethno-national question must be seen . . . as containing a plurality of meanings that cannot be reduced to a single core. It contains ethnic identity, which is a weapon of revenge against centuries of discrimination and new forms of exploitation; it serves as an instrument for applying pressure in the political market; and it is a response to needs for personal and collective identity in highly complex societies.
>
> (1989: 90)

Thus we can see that nationalism combines three key aspects: the sociological ('a weapon of revenge'); the political ('an instrument . . . in the political market-place'), and the psychological ('needs for personal and collective identity'). That is why nationalism is such a potent force in the twenty-first century, at a time when conventional state structures struggle to maintain their claim to absolute sovereignty in the modern world. Nationalist movements can encapsulate cultural defence, the pursuit of political resources, as well as being vehicles for social identity in periods of rapid social change. We should therefore not be surprised that nationalism is a catch-all movement, lending itself to versions of ecological or green politics, as well as seeking out new forms of self-determination and self-management. Such plans are based on accepting limited and shared sovereignty in an interdependent world.

To argue that we are living through a period in which political structures are being dismantled as well as rebuilt is not to imply that, for example, the demise of the United Kingdom and the political independence of Scotland is inevitable. As people seek out new ways of running their affairs, so we cannot predict what the end-product will look like. On the one hand, a British state which recognises its multinationality and multiculturalism is well placed to adapt to the emerging power centres above and below it. The fundamental contradiction which has lain at the heart of the British state – that it is multinational, but until 1999 it was formally a unitary state – seems slowly to be tackled. However, whether or not it is tackled in time to prevent breakup is as much an issue of *mentalité* at the centre as it is of the willingness of the non-English people of these islands to stay within its boundaries. The fact that it is Scotland which has been pushing at the frontiers of self-government is a manifestation of its status as a founding partner with a highly developed structure of social institutions. The key to understanding Scotland lies in recognising that nationalism derives from this institutional autonomy, and is not some vague set of historic emotions which politicians can manipulate. Nationalism is endemic to Scotland, just as it is to all societies. What we cannot read off, however, is precisely what set of constitutional arrangements follow from this, because that is a matter of contingency and adaptability to the conditions of a rapidly changing world. What we can say, however, is that the future, above all Scotland's future, is very unlikely to resemble the past.

Bibliography

Adler, A., Petch, A. and Tweedie, J. (1989) *Parental Choice and Educational Policy*, Edinburgh: Edinburgh University Press.

Allan, C. (1965) 'The genesis of British urban redevelopment: the Glasgow case', *Economic History Review*, 18: 598–613.

Alter, P. (1989) *Nationalism*, London: Edward Arnold.

Anderson, B. (1983) *Imagined Communities: Reflections on the Origin and Spread of Nationalism*, London: Verso.

Anderson, B. (1996) *Imagined Communities: Reflections on the Origin and Spread of Nationalism*, London: Verso, revised edition.

Anderson, E. (1979) 'The Kailyard revisited', in Campbell, I. (ed.), *Nineteenth Century Scottish Fiction*, Manchester: Carcanet Press, pp. 130–47.

Anderson, M. (1992) 'Population and family life', in Dickson, T. and Treble, J. H. (eds), *People and Society in Scotland, Volume 3*, Edinburgh: John Donald, pp. 12–47.

Anderson, M. and Morse, D. (1990) 'The people', in Fraser, W. H. and Morris, R. J. (eds), *People and Society in Scotland, Volume 2, 1830–1914*, Edinburgh: John Donald, pp. 8–45.

Anderson, R. D. (1983) *Educational Opportunity in Victorian Scotland*, Oxford: Clarendon Press.

Anderson, R. D. (1985) 'In search of the "lad of parts": the mythical history of Scottish education', *History Workshop Journal*, 19: 82–104.

Anderson, R. D. (1991) 'Universities and elites in modern Britain', *The History of the Universities*, 10: 225–50.

Anderson, R. D. (1999) 'The history of Scottish education, pre-1980', in Bryce, T. G. K. and Humes, W. M. (eds), *Scottish Education*, Edinburgh: Edinburgh University Press, pp. 215–24.

Arrighi, G., Hopkins, T. K. and Wallerstein, I. (1983) 'Rethinking the concepts of class and status group in a world-systems perspective', *Review*, 6: 283–304.

Ascherson, N. (1988) *Games with Shadows*, London: Hutchinson Radius.

Ash, M. (1980) *The Strange Death of Scottish History*, Edinburgh: The Ramsay Head Press.

Ash, M. (1990) 'William Wallace and Robert the Bruce: the life and death of a national myth', in Samuel, R. and Thompson, P. (eds), *The Myths We Live By*, London: Routledge, pp. 83–94.

Ash, M. (n.d.) *The St Andrews Myth* (mimeo).

Bain, R. (1968) *The Clans and Tartans of Scotland*, Glasgow: Collins.

Banton, M. (1983) *Racial and Ethnic Competition*, Cambridge: Cambridge University Press.

Barnett, A. (1997). *This Time: Our Constitutional Revolution*, London: Vintage Books.

Barth, F. (1981) 'Ethnic groups and boundaries', in *Process and Form in Social Life: Selected Essays of Fredrik Barth: Volume 1*, London: Routledge & Kegan Paul, pp. 198–227.

Bauman, Z. (1992) 'Soil, blood and identity', *Sociological Review*, 40: 675–701.

Bauman, Z. (1996) 'From pilgrim to tourist: – or a short history of identity', in Hall, S. and DuGay, P. (eds), *Questions of Cultural Identity*, London: Sage, pp. 18–36.

Bealey, F. and Sewel, J. (1981) *The Politics of Independence: A Study of a Scottish Town*, Aberdeen: Aberdeen University Press.

Bechhofer, F., McCrone, D., Kiely, R. and Stewart, R. (1999) 'Constructing national identity: arts and landed elites in Scotland', *Sociology*, 33: 515–34.

Beetham, D. (1984) 'The future of the nation state?', in McLennan, G., Held, D. and Hall, S. (eds.), *The Idea of the Modern State*, Milton Keynes: Open University Press, pp. 208–22.

Beetham, D. (1985) *Max Weber and the Theory of Modern Politics*, Cambridge: Polity Press.

Beveridge, C. and Turnbull, R. (1989) *The Eclipse of Scottish Culture: Inferiorism and the Intellectuals*, Edinburgh: Polygon.

Beveridge, C. and Turnbull, R. (1997) *Scotland After Enlightenment: Image and Tradition in Modern Scottish Culture*, Edinburgh: Polygon.

Billig, M. (1995) *Banal Nationalism*, London: Sage.

Bjørn, C., Grant, A. and Stringer, K. (eds) (1994) *Social and Political Identities in Western History*, Copenhagen: Academic Press.

Bochel, J. and Denver, D. (1970) 'Religion and voting: a critical review and a new analysis', *Political Studies*, 18: 205–19.

Boden, H. (2000) 'Kathleen Jamie's semiotic of Scotlands', in Christianson, A. and Lumsden, A. (eds), *Contemporary Scottish Women Writers*, Edinburgh: Edinburgh University Press, pp. 27–40.

Bond, R. (2000) 'Squaring the circles: demonstrating and explaining the political "non-alignment" of Scottish national identity', *Scottish Affairs*, 32: 15–35.

Bourdieu, P. (1984) *Distinction: A Social Critique of the Judgement of Taste*, London: Routledge & Kegan Paul.

Breuilly, J. (1993) *Nationalism and the State*, Manchester: Manchester University Press.

Broun, D. (1994) 'The origins of Scottish identity', in Bjørn, C., Grant, A. and Stringer, K. J. (eds), *Nations, Nationalism and Patriotism in the European Past*, Copenhagen: Academic Press, pp. 35–55.

Broun, D. (1998) 'Defining Scotland and the Scots before the Wars of Independence', in Broun, D., Finlay, R. J. and Lynch, M. (eds), *Image and Identity: The Making and Remaking of Scotland Through the Ages*, Edinburgh: John Donald, pp. 4–17.

Brown, A., McCrone, D. and Paterson, L. (1998) *Politics and Society in Scotland*, London: Macmillan (2nd edn).

Brown, A., McCrone, D., Paterson, L. and Surridge, P. (1999) *The Scottish Electorate*, London: Macmillan.

Brown, C. (1987) *Religion and Society in Scotland Since 1730*, London: Methuen.

Brown, C. (1988) 'Religion and social change', in Devine, T. and Mitchison, R. (eds), *People and Society in Scotland, Volume 1, 1760–1830*, Edinburgh: John Donald, pp. 143–62.

Brown, C. (1990) 'Each take of their several way? The Protestant churches and the working classes in Scotland', in Walker, G. and Gallagher, T. (eds), *Sermons and Battle Hymns: Protestant Popular Culture in Modern Scotland*, Edinburgh: Edinburgh University Press, pp.69–85.

Brown, G. D. (1967) *The House with the Green Shutters*, London: Cassell. First published 1901.

Brubaker, R. (1996) *Nationalism Reframed: Nationhood and the National Question in the New Europe*, Cambridge: Cambridge University Press.

Bruce, S. (1985) *No Pope of Rome: Militant Protestantism in Modern Scotland*, Edinburgh: Mainstream Press.

Bruce, S. (1993) 'A failure of the imagination: ethnicity and nationalism in Scotland's history', *Scotia*, XVII: 1–16.

Bruce, S. and Yearley, S. (1989) 'The social construction of tradition: the restoration portraits and the kings of Scotland', in McCrone, D., Kendrick, S. and Straw, P. (eds), *The Making of Scotland: Nation, Culture and Social Change*, Edinburgh: Edinburgh University Press, pp.175–88.

Budge, I. and Urwin, D. (1966) *Scottish Political Behaviour*, London: Longman.

Bulletin of Scottish Politics, 2 (1981) Special Issue on 'The politics of tartanry'.

Burnhill, P., Garner, C. and McPherson, A. (1990) 'Parental education, social class and entry of higher education, 1976–1986', *Journal of the Royal Statistical Society*, Series A, 153: 233–48.

Burns, T. (1966) 'Sociological explanation', inaugural lecture, Edinburgh University, 8 February. Reprinted in Emmet, D. and MacIntyre, A. (eds) (1970), *Sociological Theory and Philosophical Analysis*, London: Macmillan, pp. 55–74.

Callander, R. F. (1998) *How Scotland is Owned*, Edinburgh: Canongate Books.

Campbell, I. (1981) *Kailyard*, Edinburgh: Ramsay Head Press.

Campbell, R. H. (1980) *The Rise and Fall of Scottish Industry*, Edinburgh: John Donald (2nd edn, 1988).

Carter, I. (1971) 'Economic models and the history of the Highlands', *Scottish Studies*, 15: 99–120.

Carter, I. (1974) 'The Highlands of Scotland as an underdeveloped region', in DeKadt, E. and Williams, G. (eds), *Sociology and Underdevelopment*, London: Tavistock, pp. 278–311.

Carter, I. (1979) *Farm Life in Northeast Scotland, 1840–1914*, Edinburgh: John Donald.

Castells, M. (1997) *The Power of Identity*, Oxford: Basil Blackwell.

Caughie, J. (1982) 'Scottish television: what would it look like?', in McArthur, C. (ed.), *Scotch Reels: Scotland in Cinema and Television*, London: BFI Publishing, pp. 112–22.

Chapman, M. (1978) *The Gaelic Vision of Scottish Culture*, London: Croom Helm.

Chapman, M. (1992) *The Celts: The Construction of a Myth*, London: Macmillan.

Cheape, H. (1995) *Tartan: The Highland Habit*, Edinburgh: National Museums of Scotland.

Checkland, S. and Checkland, O. (1984) *Industry & Ethos: Scotland 1832–1914*, London: Edward Arnold.

A Claim of Right for Scotland (1988) A Report of the Constitutional Steering Committee presented to the Campaign for a Scottish Assembly, Edinburgh.

Cohen, A. P. (ed.) (1982) *Belonging: Identity and Social Organisation in British Rural Cultures*, Manchester: Manchester University Press.

Cohen, A. P. (1985) *The Symbolic Construction of Community*, London: Routledge.

Cohen, A. P. (1994) *Self Consciousness: An Alternative Anthropology of Identity*, London: Routledge.

Cohen, A. P. (1996) 'Personal nationalism: a Scottish view of some rites, rights and wrongs', *American Ethnologist*, 23: 1–14.

Cohen, A. P. (2000) 'Peripheral vision: nationalism, national identity and the objective correlative in Scotland', in A. Cohen (ed.), *Signifying Identities*, London: Routledge, pp. 145–61.

Cohen, R. (1994) *Frontiers of Identity: The British and Others*, London: Longman.

Colley, L. (1992) *Britons: Forging the Nation, 1707–1837*, New Haven, CT: Yale University Press.

Connor, W. (1990) 'When is a nation?', *Ethnic and Racial Studies*, 13: 92–103.

Connor, W. (1994) *Ethnonationalism: The Quest for Understanding*, Princeton, NJ: Princeton University Press.

Corr, H. (1990) 'An exploration into Scottish education', in Fraser, W. H. and Morris, R. J. (eds), *People and Society in Scotland, Volume II, 1830–1914*, Edinburgh: John Donald, pp. 290–309.

Cosgrove, D. (1994) 'Terrains of power', *Times Higher Education Supplement*, 11 March, p. 18.

Craig, C. (1983) 'Visitors from the stars: Scottish film culture', *Cencrastus*, 11: 6–11.

Craig, C. (1990) 'Twentieth century Scottish literature: an introduction', in Craig, C. (ed.), *The History of Scottish Literature, Volume 4, The Twentieth Century*, Aberdeen: Aberdeen University Press, pp. 1–9.

Craig, C. (1996) *Out of History: Narrative Paradigms in Scottish and British Culture*, Edinburgh: Polygon.

Craig, D. (1961) *Scottish Literature and the Scottish People, 1680–1830*, London: Chatto & Windus.

Craig, F. W. S. (1981) *British Electoral Facts, 1832–1980*, Chichester: Parliamentary Research Services.

Craig, F. W. S. (1984) *Britain Votes 3*, Chichester: Parliamentary Research Services.

Craig, F. W. S. (1989) *British Electoral Facts, 1983–1987*, Dartmouth: Parliamentary Research Services and Gower.

Damer, S. (1974) 'Wine Alley: the sociology of a dreadful enclosure', *The Sociological Review*, 22: 221–48.

Davie, G. (1961) *The Democratic Intellect: Scotland and Her Universities in the Nineteenth Century*, Edinburgh: Edinburgh University Press.

Davis, H. (1969) *Beyond Class Images: Explorations in the Structure of Social Consciousness*, London: Croom Helm.

Devine, T. M. (1999) *The Scottish Nation, 1700–2000*, London: The Penguin Press.

Devine, T. M. and Finlay, R. J. (eds) (1996) *Scotland in the Twentieth Century*, Edinburgh: Edinburgh University Press.

Deutsch, K. (1953) *Nationalism and Social Communication*, London: Chapman and Hall.

Dickson, A. and Treble, J. H. (eds), (1992) *People and Society in Scotland, Volume III, 1914–1990*, Edinburgh: John Donald.

Dickson, M. (1994) 'Should Auld Acquaintance be Forgot? A comparison of the Scots and English in Scotland', *Scottish Affairs*, 7: 112–34.

Dickson, T. (ed.) (1980) *Scottish Capitalism: Class, State and Nation from Before the Union to the Present*, London: Lawrence & Wishart.

Donaldson, G. (1974) *Scotland: The Shaping of a Nation*, London: David & Charles.

Donaldson, W. (1986) *Popular Literature in Victorian Scotland*, Aberdeen: Aberdeen University Press.

Dunlop, A. (1993) 'A united front? Anti-racist mobilisation in Scotland', *Scottish Affairs*, 3: 89–101.

Eley, G. and Suny, R. G. (eds) (1996) *Becoming National*, Oxford: Oxford University Press.

Elias, N. (1978) *The Civilising Process*, Oxford: Basil Blackwell.

Eriksen, T. H. (1993) 'Formal and informal nationalism', *Ethnic and Racial Studies*, 16: 1–25.

Fanon, F. (1967) *The Wretched of the Earth*, Harmondsworth: Penguin.

Ferguson, A. (1966) *An Essay on the History of Civil Society 1767*, Edinburgh: Edinburgh University Press.

Ferguson, W. (1998) *The Identity of the Scottish Nation: An Historic Quest*, Edinburgh: Edinburgh University Press.

Fewell, J. and Paterson, F. (eds) (1990) *Girls in Their Prime: Scottish Education Revisited*, Edinburgh: Scottish Academic Press.

Finlay, R. J. (1994) 'Controlling the past: Scottish historiography and Scottish identity in the 19th and 20th centuries', *Scottish Affairs*, 9: 127–42.

Firn, J. (1975) 'External control and regional policy', in Brown, G. (ed.), *The Red Paper on Scotland*, Edinburgh: Edinburgh University Students' Publications Board, pp. 153–69.

Flinn, M. (ed.) (1977) *Scottish Population History from the 17th Century to the 1930s*, Cambridge: Cambridge University Press.

Foucault, M. (1980) *Power/Knowledge*, Brighton: Harvester Press.

Frank, A. G. (1971) *Capitalism and Underdevelopment in Latin America*, Harmondsworth: Penguin.

Fry, M. (1987) *Patronage & Principle: A Political History of Modern Scotland*, Aberdeen: Aberdeen University Press.

Fukuyama, F. (1989) 'The end of history?', *The National Interest*, summer, pp. 3–18.

Gallagher, T. (1987a) *Edinburgh Divided: John Cormack and No Popery in the 1930s*, Edinburgh: Polygon.

Gallagher, T. (1987b) *Glasgow: The Uneasy Peace*, Manchester: Manchester University Press.

Gamble, A. (1988) *The Free Economy and the Strong State*, London: Macmillan.

Gellner, E. (1964) 'Nationalism', in *Thought and Change*, London: Weidenfeld and Nicolson, pp. 147–78.

Gellner, E. (1978) 'Nationalism, or the confessions of a justified Edinburgh sinner', *Political Quarterly*, 49: 103–11.

Gellner, E. (1983) *Nations and Nationalism*, Oxford: Basil Blackwell.

Giddens, A. (1991) *Modernity and Self-Identity*, London: Polity Press.

Gifford, D. (ed.) (1988) *The History of Scottish Literature, Volume 3, The Nineteenth Century*, Aberdeen: Aberdeen University Press.

Goffman, E. (1973) *The Presentation of Self in Everyday Life*, New York: Overview Press.

Goldthorpe, J. (1980) *Social Mobility and Class Structure in Modern Britain*, Oxford: Oxford University Press.

Goldthorpe, J. (1987) *Social Mobility and Class Structure in Modern Britain*, Oxford: Oxford University Press (2nd edn).

Gordon, E. and Breitenbach, E. (eds) (1990) *The World is Ill-Divided: Women's Work in Scotland in the Nineteenth and Early Twentieth Centuries*, Edinburgh: Edinburgh University Press.

Goulbourne, H. (1991) *Ethnicity and Nationalism in Post-Imperial Britain*, Cambridge: Polity Press.

Grant, A. (1994) 'Aspects of national consciousness in medieval Scotland', in Bjørn, C., Grant, A. and Stringer, K. (eds), *Social and Political Identities in Western History*, Copenhagen: Academic Press, pp. 68–95.

Grant, W. and Murison, D. (1974) *Scottish National Dictionary*, Edinburgh: The Scottish National Dictionary Association.

Greenfeld, L. (1993) *Nationalism: Five Roads to Modernity*, Harvard, MA: Harvard University Press.

Hall, J. (1986) *Powers and Liberties: The Causes and Consequences of the Rise of the West*, Harmondsworth: Penguin.

Hall, S. (1983) *The Politics of Thatcherism*, London: Lawrence & Wishart.

Hall, S. (1984) 'The state in question', in McLennan, G. Held, D. and Hall, S. (eds), *The Idea of the Modern State*, Milton Keynes: Open University Press, pp. 1–28.

Hall, S. (1990) 'Cultural identity and diaspora', in Rutherford, J. (ed.), *Identity: Community, Culture and Difference*, London: Lawrence & Wishart, pp. 222–37.

Hall, S. (1992) 'The question of cultural identity', in Hall, S., Held, D. and McGrew, T. (eds), *Modernity and Its Futures*, London: Polity Press, pp. 273–316.

Hall, S. (1996) 'Introduction: Who needs identity?', in Hall, S. and DuGay, P. (eds), *Questions of Cultural Identity*, London: Sage, pp. 1–17.

Hardy, F. (1990) *Scotland in Film*, Edinburgh: Edinburgh University Press.

Harvie, C. (1975) 'The devolution of the intellectuals', *New Statesman*, 90: 65–6.

Harvie, C. (1981) *No Gods and Precious Few Heroes*, London: Edward Arnold.

Harvie, C. (1988) 'Industry, religion and the state of Scotland', in Gifford, D. (ed.), *The History of Scottish Literature, Volume 3, The Nineteenth Century*, Aberdeen: Aberdeen University Press, pp. 23–42.

Harvie, C. (1990) 'The covenanting tradition', in Walker, G. and Gallagher, T. (eds), *Sermons and Battle Hymns: Protestant Popular Culture in Modern Scotland*, Edinburgh: Edinburgh University Press, pp. 8–23.

Hastings, A. (1997) *The Construction of Nationhood: Ethnicity, Religion and Nationalism*, Cambridge: Cambridge University Press.

Hay, J. McDougall (1970) *Gillespie*, Edinburgh: Canongate. First published 1914.

Hearn, J. (2000) *Claiming Scotland: National Identity and Liberal Culture*, Edinburgh: Polygon.

Hechter, M. (1975) *Internal Colonialism: The Celtic Fringe in British National Development, 1536–1966*, London: Routledge & Kegan Paul.

Hechter, M. (1982) 'Internal colonialism revisited', *Cencrastus*, 10: 8–11.

Held, D. (1988) 'Farewell to the nation state', *Marxism Today*, December, pp. 12–17.

Hesketh, C. (1972) *Tartans*, London: Octopus Books.

Hobsbawm, E. J. (1969) *Industry and Empire*, Harmondsworth: Penguin.

Hobsbawm, E. J. (1986) 'Mass-producing traditions: Europe, 1870–1914', in Hobsbawm, E. J. and Ranger, T. (eds), *The Invention of Tradition*, Cambridge: Cambridge University Press, pp. 263–308.

Hobsbawm, E. J. (1990) *Nations and Nationalism since 1780: Programme, Myth and Reality*, Cambridge: Cambridge University Press.

Hood, N. (1999) 'Scotland in the world', in Peat, J. and Boyle, S. (eds), *An Illustrated Guide to the Scottish Economy*, London: Duckworth, pp. 38–53.

Hood, N. and Young, S. (eds) (1984) *Industry, Policy and the Scottish Economy*, Edinburgh: Edinburgh University Press.

Hope, K. (1984) *As Others See Us: Schooling and Social Mobility in Scotland and the United States*, Cambridge: Cambridge University Press.

Houston, R. (1985) *Scottish Literacy and the Scottish Identity: Literacy and Society in Scotland and Northern Ireland, 1600–1800*, Cambridge: Cambridge University Press.

Howson, A. (1993) 'No gods and precious few women', *Scottish Affairs*, 2: 37–49.

Hunter, J. (1976) *The Making of the Crofting Community*, Edinburgh: John Donald.

Hunter, J. (1999) *Last of the Free: A Millennial History of the Highlands and Islands*, Edinburgh: Mainstream.

Hutchison, I. (1986) *A Political History of Scotland 1832–1924: Parties, Elections, & Issues*, Edinburgh: John Donald.

Inglehart, R. (1977) *The Silent Revolution: Changing Values and Political Styles among Western Publics*, Princeton, NJ: Princeton University Press.

Jamieson, L. (1990) 'We all left at 14: boys' and girls' schooling, 1900–30', in Fewell, J. and Paterson, F. (eds), *Girls in their Prime: Scottish Education Revisited*, Edinburgh: Scottish Academic Press, pp. 16–37.

Jarvie, G. (1991) *Highland Games: The Making of the Myth*, Edinburgh Education & Society Series, Edinburgh University Press.

Jedrej, M. C. and Nuttall, M. (1996) *White Settlers: The Impact of Rural Repopulation in Scotland*, Luxemburg: Harwood Academic.

Keating, M. (1996) *Nations against the State: The New Politics of Nationalism in Quebec, Catalonia and Scotland*, London: Macmillan.

Keating, M. and Bleiman, D. (1979) *Labour and Scottish Nationalism*, London: Macmillan.

Kellas, J. (1980) *Modern Scotland*, London: Allen & Unwin.

Kellas, J. (1989) *The Scottish Political System*, Cambridge: Cambridge University Press (4th edn).

Kidd, C. (1993) *Subverting Scotland's Past: Scottish Whig Historians and the Creation of an Anglo-Scottish Identity, 1689–c.1830*, Cambridge: Cambridge University Press.

King, A. (1976) *Why is Britain Becoming Harder to Govern?* London: BBC Publications.

Kirby, M. W. (1981) *The Decline of British Economic Power since 1870*, London: Allen & Unwin.

Kluegel, J. R. and Smith, E. R. (1986) *Beliefs about Inequality*, New York: Aldine de Gruyter.

Knowles, T. D. (1983) *Ideology, Art, and Commerce: Aspects of Literary Sociology in the Late Victorian Scottish Kailyard*, Gothenborg: Acta Universitatis Gothoburgensis.

Kohn, H. (1945) *The Idea of Nationalism: A Study of its Origins and Background*, London: Macmillan; extract reprinted as 'Western and eastern nationalisms', in Hutchinson, J. and Smith, A. D. (eds) (1994), *Nationalism*, Oxford: Oxford University Press, pp. 162–5.

Kumar, K. (1978) *Prophecy and Progress*, Harmondsworth: Penguin.

Lee, C. H. (1979) *British Regional Employment Statistics, 1841–1971*, Cambridge: Cambridge University Press.

Lee, C. H. (1995) *Scotland and the United Kingdom: The Economy and the Union in the Twentieth Century*, Manchester: Manchester University Press.

Lenman, B. (1977) *An Economic History of Modern Scotland*, London: Batsford.

Lindsay, I. (1991) 'Scottish migration: prospects for the nineties', in Brown, A. and McCrone, D. (eds), *Scottish Government Yearbook 1991*, Edinburgh: Unit for the Study of Government in Scotland, pp. 87–103.

Linz, J. (1985) 'From primordialism to nationalism', in Tiryakian, E. and Rogowski, R. (eds), *New Nationalisms of the Developed West*, London: Allen & Unwin, pp. 203–53.

Lythe, S. G. E. (1960) *The Economy of Scotland in its European Setting, 1550–1625*, Edinburgh: Oliver & Boyd.

McArthur, C. (1981) 'Breaking the signs: "Scotch myths as cultural struggle', *Cencrastus*, 7: 21–5.

McArthur, C. (1982) *Scotch Reels: Scotland in Cinema and Television*, London: BFI Publishing.

McArthur, C. (1983) 'Scotch reels and after', *Cencrastus*, 11: 2–3.

McArthur, C. (1993) 'Scottish culture: a reply to David McCrone', *Scottish Affairs*, 4: 95–106.

McArthur, C. (1994) Culloden: a pre-emptive strike', *Scottish Affairs*, 9: 97–126.

MacArthur, M. (1993) 'Blasted heaths and hills of mist', *Scottish Affairs*, 3: 23–31.

McClure, D. (1988) *Why Scots Matters*, Edinburgh: The Saltire Society.

MacCormick, N. (1995) 'Sovereignty: myth and reality', *Scottish Affairs*, 11: 1–13.

MacCormick, N. (1996) 'Liberalism, nationalism and the post-sovereign state', *Political Studies*, XLIV: 553–67.

McCrone, D. (1999) 'Culture, nationalism and Scottish education: homogeneity and diversity', in Bryce, T. G. K. and Humes, W. M. (eds), *Scottish Education*, Edinburgh: Edinburgh University Press, pp. 235–43.

McCrone, D. and Elliott, B. (1989) *Property and Power in a City: The Sociological Significance of Landlordism*, London: Macmillan.

McCrone, D. and Kiely, R. (2000) 'Nationalism and citizenship', *Sociology* 34: 19–34.

McCrone, D., Bechhofer, F. and Kendrick, S. (1982) 'Egalitarianism and social inequality in Scotland', in Robbins, D. (ed.), *Rethinking Social Inequality*, Farnborough: Gower Publications, pp. 127–48.

McCrone, D., Morris, A. and Kiely, R. (1995) *Scotland – the Brand: The Making of Scottish Heritage*, Edinburgh: Edinburgh University Press.

McCrone, D., Stewart, R., Kiely, R. and Bechhofer, F. (1998) 'Who are we? Problematising national identity', *The Sociological Review* 46: 629–52.

Macdonald, S. (1999) 'The Gaelic Renaissance and Scotland's identities', *Scottish Affairs*, 26: 100–18.

MacDougall, H. (1982) *Racial Myth in English History: Trojans, Teutons and Anglo-Saxons*, Montreal: Harvest House.

McGrew, A. (1992) 'A global society?', in Hall, S. *et al.* (eds), *Modernity and its Futures*, Cambridge: Polity Press, pp. 61–116.

McIlvanney, W. (1985) *Strange Loyalties*, London: Sceptre.

MacInnes, J. (1998) 'The myth of the macho Scotsman: attitudes to gender, work and the family in the UK, Ireland and Europe', *Scottish Affairs*, 23: 108–124.

Mackenzie, W. J. M. (1978) *Political Identity*, Harmondsworth: Penguin.

Mackintosh, J. P. (1982) *John P. Mackintosh on Scotland*, ed. H. Drucker, Harlow: Longman.

MacLaren, A. A. (1974) *Religion and Social Class*, London: Routledge & Kegan Paul.

MacLaren, A. A. (ed.) (1976) *Social Class in Scotland*, Edinburgh: John Donald.

MacLaren, I. (1940) *Beside the Bonnie Briar Bush*, New York: Dodd, Mead & Co. First published 1894.

McPherson, A. (1992) 'Schooling', in Dickson, A. F. and Treble, J. H. (eds), *People and Society in Scotland, Volume III, 1914–1990*, Edinburgh: John Donald, pp. 80–107.

McPherson, A. F. (1983) 'An angle on the Geist: persistence and change in Scottish educational tradition', in Humes, W. M. and Paterson, H. M. (eds), *Scottish Culture and Scottish Education, 1800–1980*, Edinburgh: John Donald, pp. 216–43.

McPherson, A. F. and Raab, C. (1988) *Governing Education: A Sociology of Policy since 1945*, Edinburgh: Edinburgh University Press.

Mann, M. (1986) *The Sources of Social Power, Volume 1, A History of Power from the Beginning to A.D. 1760*, Cambridge: Cambridge University Press.

Marquand, D. (1988) *The Unprincipled Society*, London: Fontana.

Marquand, D. (1995) 'How united is the modern United Kingdom?', in Grant, A. and Stringer, K. J. (eds), *Uniting the Kingdom? The Making of British History*, London: Routledge, pp. 277–91.

Marr, A. (2000) *The Day Britain Died*, Harmondsworth: Penguin.

Marsh, C. (1986) 'Social class and occupation', in Burgess, R. (ed.), *Key Variables in Sociological Investigation*, London: Routledge & Kegan Paul, pp. 123–52.

Marshall, G. (1980) *Presbyteries and Profits: Calvinism and the Development of Capitalism in Scotland, 1560–1707*, Oxford: Clarendon Press.

Marshall, G. (1982) *In Search of the Spirit of Capitalism*, London: Hutchinson.

Marshall, T. H. (1963) 'Citizenship and social class', in Marshall, T. H. (ed.), *Sociology at the Crossroads*, London: Heinemann, pp. 67–127.

Marwick, A. (1986) *British Society Since 1945*, Harmondsworth: Penguin.

Marx, K. (1959) 'The Eighteenth Brumaire of Louis Bonaparte', in Feuer, L. (ed.), *Marx and Engels: Basic Writings in Politics and Philosophy*, New York: Doubleday, pp. 318–48.

Maxwell, S. (1976) 'Can Scotland's political myths be broken?', Q, 19 November, p. 5.

Meehan, E. (1993) 'Citizenship and the European Community', *Political Quarterly*, 64: 172–86.

Melucci, A. (1989) *Nomads of the Present: Social Movements and Individual Needs in Contemporary Society*, London: Hutchinson Radius.

Mercer, K. (1990) 'Welcome to the jungle: identity and diversity in post-modern politics', in Rutherford, J. (ed.), *Identity: Community, Culture and Difference*, London: Lawrence & Wishart, pp. 43–71.

Middlemas, K. (1979) *Politics in Industrial Society: The Experience of the British System Since 1911*, London: Deutsch.

Middlemas, K. (1986) *Power, Competition and the State, Volume 1*, London: Macmillan.

Miller, D. (1995) *On Nationality*, Oxford: Clarendon Press.

Miller, W. (1981) *The End of British Politics? Scots and English Political Behaviour in the Seventies*, Oxford: Clarendon Press.

Mitchell, C. (1968) *A Dictionary of Sociology*, London: Routledge & Kegan Paul.

Modood, T. (1997) *Ethnic Minorities: Diversity and Disadvantages*, London: Policy Studies Institute.

Mommsen, W. (1990) 'The varieties of the nation-state in modern history: liberal, imperialist, fascist and contemporary notions of nations and nationality', in Mann, M. (ed.), *The Rise and Decline of the Nation-State*, Oxford: Basil Blackwell, pp. 210–26.

Moore, C. and Booth, S. (1989) *Managing Competition: Meso-corporatism, Pluralism and the Negotiated Order in Scotland*, Oxford: Clarendon Press.

Moreno, L. (1988) 'Scotland and Catalonia: the path to home rule', in McCrone, D. (ed.), *Scottish Government Yearbook 1988*, Edinburgh: Unit for the Study of Government in Scotland, pp.166–81.

Morris, R. J. (1990) 'Scotland, 1830–1914: the making of a nation within a nation', in Fraser, W. H. and Morris, R. J. (eds), *People and Society in Scotland, Volume II, 1830–1914*, Edinburgh: John Donald, pp. 1–7.

Morton, G. (1999) *Unionist-Nationalism: Governing Urban Scotland, 1830–1860*, East Linton: John Tuckwell Press.

Mueller, W. and Karle, W. (1990) 'Social selection in educational systems in Europe', International Sociological Association, Twelfth World Congress of Sociology, Madrid, July.

Muir, E. (1980) *Scottish Journey*, Edinburgh: Mainstream. First published 1935.

Munro, A. (1996) *The Democratic Muse: Folk Music Revival in Scotland*, Aberdeen: Scottish Cultural Press.

Murison, D. (ed.) (1986) *Scottish National Dictionary*, Aberdeen: Aberdeen University Press.

Nairn, T. (1977) *The Break-Up of Britain*, London: New Left Books.

Nairn, T. (1988) *The Enchanted Glass: Britain and its Monarchy*, London: Radius.

Nairn, T. (1993) 'Demonising nationalism', *London Review of Books*, 25 February, p. 3.

Nairn, T. (1997) *Faces of Nationalism: Janus Revisited*, London: Verso.

Nairn, T. (2000) *After Britain*, London: Granta Books.

Paterson, L. (1991) 'Ane end of ane auld sang: sovereignty and the renegotiation of the Union', in Brown, A. and McCrone, D. (eds), *Scottish Government Yearbook*, Edinburgh: Edinburgh University Press, pp.104–22.

Paterson, L. (1994) *The Autonomy of Modern Scotland*, Edinburgh: Edinburgh University Press.

Paterson, L. (1996) 'Liberation or control? What are the Scottish educational traditions of the 20th century?', in Devine, T. M. and Finlay, R. J. (eds), *Scotland in the Twentieth Century*, Edinburgh: Edinburgh University Press, pp. 230–49.

Paterson, L. (1997a) 'Student achievement and educational change in Scotland, 1980–1995', *Scottish Educational Review*, 29: 10–19.

Paterson, L. (1997b) 'Trends in higher education participation in Scotland', *Higher Education Quarterly*, 51: 29–48.

Paterson, L. (1998a) 'Education, local government and the Scottish Parliament', *Scottish Educational Review*, 30: 52–60.

Paterson, L. (ed.) (1998b) *A Diverse Assembly: The Debate on a Scottish Parliament*, Edinburgh: Edinburgh University Press.

Paterson, L. (2000) 'Civil society and democratic renewal', in Baron, S., Field, J. and Schuller, T. (eds), *Social Capital: Social Theory and the Third Way*, Oxford: Oxford University Press, pp. 39–55.

Paterson, L. and Wyn Jones, R. (1999) 'Does civil society drive constitutional change?', in Taylor, B. and Thomson, K. (eds), *Scotland and Wales: Nations Again?*, Cardiff: University of Wales Press, pp. 169–98.

Paterson, L., Brown, A., Curtice, J., Hinds, K., McCrone, D., Park, A. and Surridge, P. (in press) *New Scotland, New Politics?*, Edinburgh: Edinburgh University Press.

Payne, G. (1987) *Employment and Opportunity*, London: Macmillan.

Penrose, J. (1993) 'Reification in the name of change: the impact of nationalism on social constructions of nation, people and place in Scotland and the United Kingdom', in Jackson, P. and Penrose, J. (eds), *Constructions of Race, Place and Nation*, London: University College London Press, pp. 27–49.

Pi-Sunyer, O. (1985) 'Catalan nationalism: some theoretical and historical considerations', in Tiryakian, E. and Rogowski, R. (eds), *New Nationalisms of the Developed West*, London: Allen & Unwin, pp. 254–76.

Pittock, M. (1991) *The Invention of Scotland: The Stuart Myth and the Scottish Identity, 1638 to the Present*, London: Routledge.

Pocock, P. (1975) 'British history: a plea for a new subject', *Journal of Modern History*, 47: 601–28.

Poggi, G. (1978) *The Development of the Modern State*, London: Hutchinson.

Poggi, G. (1983) *Calvinism and the Capitalist Spirit: Max Weber's Protestant Ethic*, London: Macmillan.

Poggi, G. (1990), *The State: its Nature, Development and Prospects*, Cambridge: Polity Press.

Punnett, M. (1985) 'Two nations? Regional partisanship, 1868–1983', in McCrone, D. (ed.), *Scottish Government Yearbook 1985*, Edinburgh: Unit for the Study of Government in Scotland, pp. 30–52.

Reicher, S. and Hopkins, N. (forthcoming) *Self and Nation: Categorisation, Contestation and Mobilisation*, London: Sage.

Renan, E. (1882) 'What is a nation?, reprinted in Bhabha, H. K. (ed.) (1990), *Nation and Narration*, London: Routledge, pp. 8–22.

Rojek, C. (1993) *Ways of Escape*, London: Macmillan.

Rosie, M. and McCrone, D. (2000) 'The past is history: Catholics in modern Scotland', in Devine, T. M. (ed.), *Scotland's Shame? Bigotry and Sectarianism in Modern Scotland*, Edinburgh: Mainstream Press, pp. 199–217.

Runciman, W. G. (1990) 'How many classes are there in contemporary British society?', *Sociology*, 24: 377–98.

Russell, J. B. (1905) 'Life in one room', a public lecture delivered on 27 February 1888, in Chalmers, A. K. (ed.), *Public Health Administration in Glasgow*, Glasgow: Maclehose and Sons, n.p.

Saeed, A., Blain, N. and Forbes, D. (1999) 'New ethnic and national questions in Scotland: post-British identities among Glasgow Pakistani teenagers', *Ethnic and Racial Studies*, 22: 821–44.

Samuel, R. (ed.) (1992) *Patriotism: The Making and Unmaking of British National Identity*, London: Routledge.

Schama, S. (1996) *Landscape and Memory*, London: Fontana Press.

Schlesinger. P. (1999) 'Changing spaces of political communication', *Political Communication*, 16: 263–79.

Scott, J. and Hughes, M. (1980) *The Anatomy of Scottish Capital*, London: Croom Helm.

Scott, P. H. (1979) *1707: the Union of Scotland and England in contemporary documents*, Edinburgh: Chambers [for] the Saltire Society.

Scottish Council for Voluntary Organisations (1999) *Access and Influence: The Role of Voluntary Organisations in the New Scottish Politics*, discussion paper, Edinburgh: SCVO.

Seligman, A. (1995) 'Animadversions upon civil society and civic virtue in the last decade of the 20th century', in Hall, J. (ed.), *Civil Society*, London: Polity Press, pp. 200–23.

Sennett, R. and Cobb, J. (1977) *The Hidden Injuries of Class*, Cambridge: Cambridge University Press.

Shepherd, G. (1988) 'The Kailyard', in Gifford, D., *The History of Scottish Literature, Volume 3, The Nineteenth Century*, Aberdeen: Aberdeen University Press, pp. 309–20.

Skocpol, T. (1977) 'Wallerstein's world capitalist system: a theoretical and historical critique', *American Journal of Sociology*, 82: 1075–90.

Smith, A. (1986) *The Ethnic Origins of Nations*, Oxford: Basil Blackwell.

Smout, T. C. (1970) *A History of the Scottish People, 1560–1830*, Glasgow: Collins.

Smout, T. C. (1980a) 'Scotland and England: is dependency a symptom or a cause of underdevelopment?', *Review*, 3: 601–30.

Smout, T. C. (1980b) 'Centre and periphery in history', *Journal of Common Market Studies*, 18: 256–71.

Smout, T. C. (1987) *A Century of the Scottish People, 1830–1950*, Glasgow: Collins.

Smout, T. C. (1994) 'Perspectives on the Scottish identity', *Scottish Affairs*, 6: 101–13.

Stevenson, J. (1984) *British Society: 1914–45*, Harmondsworth: Penguin.

Stewart, D. C. and Thompson, J. C. (1980) *Scotland's Forged Tartans: An Analytical Study of Vestiarium Scoticum*, Edinburgh: Paul Harris.

Storrar, W. (1990) *Scottish Identity: A Christian Vision*, Edinburgh: The Handsel Press.

STUC (Scottish Trades Union Congress) (1989) *Claiming the Future: Scotland's Economy: Ownership, Control and Development*, London: Verso.

Stringer, G. and Grant, A. (1995) 'Scottish foundations', in Grant, A. and Stringer, G. (eds), *Uniting the Kingdom? The Making of British History*, London: Routledge, pp. 85–108.

Surridge, P. and McCrone, D. (1999) 'The 1997 Scottish Referendum vote', in Taylor, B. and Thomson, K. (eds), *Scotland and Wales: Nations Again?*, Cardiff: University of Wales Press, pp. 41–64.

Surridge, P., Brown, A., McCrone, D. and Paterson. L. (1999) 'Scotland: constitutional preferences and voting behaviour', in Evans, G. and Norris, P. (eds), *Critical Elections: British Parties and Voters in Long-term Perspective*, London: Sage, pp. 223–39.

Tamir, Y. (1993) *Liberal Nationalism*, Princeton, NJ: Princeton University Press.

Taylor, A. (1986) 'Overseas ownership in Scottish manufacturing industry from 1950 to 1985', *Scottish Economic Bulletin*, 33 (June): 20–8.

Telfer-Dunbar, J. (1962) *History of Highland Dress*, London: Batsford.

Telfer-Dunbar, J. (1981) *Costume of Scotland*, London: Batsford.

Therborn, G. (1983) 'Why some classes are more successful than others', *New Left Review*, 138: 37–56.

Thompson, E. P. (1968) *The Making of the English Working Class*, Harmondsworth: Penguin.

Thomson, J. M. (1995) 'Scots law, national identity and the European Union', *Scottish Affairs*, 10: 25–34.

Tilly, C. (1975) *The Formation of National States in Western Europe*, Princeton, NJ: Princeton University Press.

Touraine, A. (1981) 'Une Sociologie sans Société', *Revue Française de Sociologie*, 22: 3–13.

Trevor-Roper, H. (1984) 'Invention of tradition: the Highland tradition of Scotland', in Hobsbawm, E. and Ranger, T. (eds), *The Invention of Tradition*, Cambridge: Cambridge University Press, pp. 15–42.

Turner, R. (1960) 'Sponsored and contest mobility and the school system', *American Sociological Review*, 25: 855–67.

Walker, G. and Gallagher, T. (eds) (1990) *Sermons and Battle Hymns: Protestant Popular Culture in Modern Scotland*, Edinburgh: Edinburgh University Press.

Wallerstein, I. (1974) *The Modern World-System: Capitalist Agriculture and the Origins of the European World-economy in the 16th Century*, New York: Academic Press.

Wallerstein, I. (1979) *The Capitalist World-Economy*, Cambridge: Cambridge University Press.

Wallerstein, I. (1980) 'One man's meat: the Scottish Great Leap Forward', *Review*, 3: 631–40.

Watson, T. J. (1980) *Sociology, Work and Industry*, London: Routledge & Kegan Paul.

Watt, I. (1982) 'Occupational stratification and the sexual division of labour', in Dickson, T. (ed.), *Capital and Class in Scotland*, Edinburgh: John Donald, pp. 212–50.

Weber, E. (1977) *Peasants into Frenchmen: The Modernisation of Rural France, 1870–1914*, London: Chatto & Windus.

Weber, M. (1966) *General Economic History*, New York: Collier Books.

Weber, M. (1978) *Economy and Society: An Outline of Interpretive Sociology*, Berkeley: University of California Press. First published 1922.

Williams, G. (1980) *When was Wales?*, BBC Radio Wales, annual lecture.

Williams, R. (1973) *The Country and the City*, London: Chatto & Windus.

Williams, R. (1977) *Marxism and Literature*, Oxford: Oxford University Press.

Williams, R. (1983) *Towards 2000*, Harmondsworth: Penguin.

Willms, J. D. (1992) 'Pride or prejudice? Opportunity structures and the effects of Catholic schools in Scotland', *International Perspectives on Education and Society*, 2: 189–213.

Willms, J. D. (1995) 'School choice and community segregation: findings from Scotland', paper given to 1994 annual meeting of the American Educational Research Association, and available from the Centre for Educational Sociology, University of Edinburgh.

Winckler, J. (1976) 'Corporatism', *Archives Européennes de Sociologie*, 17: 100–36.

Wittig, K. (1958) *Scottish Tradition in Literature*, Westport, CT: Greenwood Press.

Wood, S. (1987) *The Scottish Soldier*, London: Archive Publications.

Womack, P. (1989) *Improvement and Romance: Constructing the Myth of the Highlands*, London: Macmillan.

Wright, P. (1985) *On Living in an Old Country: The National Past in Contemporary Britain*, London: Verso.

Young, S. (1984) 'The foreign-owned manufacturing sector', in Hood, N. and Young, S. (eds), *Industry, Policy and the Scottish Economy*, Edinburgh: Edinburgh University Press, pp. 93–127.

Youngson, A. J. (1973) *After the Forty Five: The Economic Impact on the Scottish Highlands*, Edinburgh: Edinburgh University Press.

Index